THE BUSINESS WRITING PROBLEM SOLVER

Instant Solutions For Every Business

THE BUSINESS WRITING PROBLEM SOLVER

Instant Solutions for Every Business

Herman R. Holtz

DOW JONES-IRWIN

Homewood, Illinois 60430

We recognize that certain terms in this book are trademarks, and we have made every effort to print these throughout the text with the capitalization and punctuation used by the holder of the trademark.

ISBN 0-87094-901-2

Library of Congress Catalog Card No. 86-72270

Printed in the United States of America

1 2 3 4 5 6 7 8 9 0 BC 4 3 2 1 0 9 8 7

Preface

WHAT CAN YOU EXPECT THIS BOOK TO BE AND DO FOR YOU?

There are a great many "business writing" books, manuals, tape cassettes, programs, and training courses already in existence. Why another one? What has this book to say on the subject that has not already been said elsewhere? How is this book different?

This book is based on two premises: The first is that the problem of most people who find writing difficult and do not "write well" is not how to write; it is what to write. The second is that writing well does not really come easily even to those professional writers who achieve the highest acclaim, but is always hard work. (And there is a definite relationship between how hard the writer works and the quality of the product that results.)

Of course, the logical inference or corollary to be drawn from these premises is that with enough hard work anyone can learn to write well—reasonably well, at least. I certainly have no quarrel with anyone who draws those conclusions from these premises. I think such conclusions are justified and reflect truth.

Ergo, the focus of this book is not as much on how to write as it is on what to write—how to solve the many problems that arise, planning the solution before attempting to write instead of floundering about aimlessly trying to find a thread of logic with which to approach the subject and hoping that somehow a coherent product will result.

It is my belief that most of us with even a high school education know how to write, at least in the basic sense of stating what is on our minds. Certainly, except perhaps for some who are foreign born and have not yet become completely fluent in the language, we know how to use our English (or is it our American?) language well enough. We know how to express ourselves and we know how to construct a sentence. We can use a dictionary to verify spellings, although today word processors and electronic dictionaries—dictionaries on floppy disks—are so commonplace that we can even have the desktop computer verify the spellings automatically.

Several decades of experience as an engineer, writer, editor, manager, and consultant, working with professionals assigned to writing chores (technical manuals, proposals, reports, training courses, and others), have had their effect on and been responsible for these convictions about writing, especially writing in the typical technical, professional, and/or business environment. I have become convinced, as a result of these many experiences, that the problems of writing commonly encountered by so many who are not professional writers lie far more in that domain of what to write. I believe that it is in the struggle to come to grips with the subject and establish the main point that so many sink into the morass of purple prose, that meaningless flood of verbiage that the late U.S. Congressman Maury Maverick characterized as "gobbledegook," the chatter of turkeys. And that is not because the writer lacks the ability to state the point as much as it is that the writer often does not know at the outset what the point is to be, and so struggles desperately seeking it. Unfortunately, the writer often never finds it at all, or manages to bury it so deeply in the meandering prose that the reader never finds it. And even when the poor reader does manage to stumble across it, he or she is not sure that it was the point, after all.

Consider this prize statement from a federal government brochure and try to figure out what the writer thought he was trying to say:

> The ratio (or amplification factor) of private sector activity to federal activity can be characterized by the ratio of the number of privately financed to federally financed solar heating and cooling systems installed annually.

Give up? Of course there is much wrong with this statement as to clarity of expression, but even the meaning is obscured because what it really says is nonsense. Ratios are not "characterized." They are absolute quantities. The intention was to point out that the ratio of private to federal activity is reflected by (or is a measure of) the numbers of heating and cooling systems installed by each. A bit of clear thinking about what the real message is would have prevented this particular bit of bureaucratese. The writer may have failed to think this out or, perhaps, was unsure of the facts and obscured the statement, consciously or unconsciously, as a defensive measure. This is a rather common occurrence, too.

There are several root causes for this kind of difficulty. The principal one appears to be, however, that many begin writing too soon, before they have gathered all the information they need, verified their facts, and/or before they have thought the matter out and decided what their *presentation strategy* is to be—before planning, that is, before deciding on an objective and a way to achieve it. They are trying to think the problem out while writing, instead of before writing.

Even that would be all right if they operated on the established premise of professional writers that the first writing is only a rough draft that must be revised at least once, and probably several times, perhaps even completely reorganized or discarded to be totally rewritten as a fresh start. (I have discarded as many as 50 pages of a manuscript when I became convinced that I was on the wrong track and that it would be more efficient to start over than to try to repair the draft through revision.) Only the nonprofessional writer has the naive belief that it is possible for an ordinary mortal to write truly well in a first draft. (There are perhaps occasional exceptions, but one cannot plan on the unlikely event of being that rare exception.)

All of this is as true in principle for a brief letter as it is for a lengthy report or other thick manuscript, although obviously the methodology is going to be quite different, in proportion to the scale of the total effort. One does not normally prepare formal outlines or do detailed formal planning for a brief letter, but it is still necessary to decide *in advance* what you are going to say and how you will make the point—to set a chief objective and *presentation strategy*.

One more point: *Writing* does not refer entirely to the use of words, nor should the writing activity be so confined. *Writing* is the conveyance of meaning via the written or printed page, and often illustrations, such as simple diagrams, are far more effective and far more definitive than words are. (And using such aids relieves the writer of a great deal of the work, itself an excellent reason for using illustrations wherever and whenever possible.)

Today's office tools—desktop computers with their word processors and even sophisticated electronic typewriters—make it easy to produce many kinds of simple diagrams and other illustrations once only available from professional illustrators. You should learn to prepare and use such aids.

You may reasonably expect from all of this that you are not confronted here with a text on grammar and "composition," nor are you being asked to master those subjects, although I reserve the right to make a very brief run through a few basics of usage later, strictly as a refresher for anyone who feels a need for it.

Nor is this a training program in any sense of the word, although it does include frequent tutorials. However, learning that results from use of this book, however desirable, is not a major purpose of this work.

And, finally, this book is not represented as a complete set of models for each and every occasion, despite the large number of models offered for a great number of situations and applications. (In today's complex society it would be futile to attempt anything approaching a complete set of models for all occasions.)

Those are some things this book is not. But here are some things it is:

It is a reference, not to be read as a book or program, but to be referred to as circumstances make such recourse necessary. The models are representative and not total and complete for all possible needs, although I have made an effort to provide models for most kinds of situations.

It includes a number of illustrations that you may emulate or adapt as models for your own use. Many of the originals were drafted by computer, using the WordStar word processor. (It includes, also, some guidance in when and how to use illustrations most effectively.)

But it is something more, reflecting a somewhat more sophisticated goal: This book is, in its entirety, a model and set of patterns from which you can construct a complete system of your own, tailored to your own needs. (I urge you to do so!)

The many tutorials were written with this in mind: to *explain* the models and their uses and so enable you to develop and create your own models, custom designed to suit your own needs, whatever they may be. Study the models and tutorials with that in mind, to get the greatest utility from this book.

Further, I hope that you will install this system of your own in your own desktop computer (with its word processing system) as a complete set of files from which you can readily summon the models you need to create whatever you need at the moment—correspondence, reports, proposals, brochures, sales letters, catalog sheets, or other. (Some suggestions for doing this are made later.)

Overall, the purpose of this system is to ease the burden and save the time of all who have to write any of these things. Even further, it is to enable office organizations to turn over many of the writing chores to secretaries, assistants, and aides of various kinds, thus reducing the burden on executives and conserving their much more costly time.

Herman Holtz

Contents

Expressions to Shun. How to Make Writing (and Reading) an Easier Task: *How to Judge the Quality of an Illustration.* Research: *The Research Plan. When Is Research Complete?* Report Formats. Word Processing: Important Writing Aid: *Revision/Rewriting Methodology. Swipe Files. Online Research. General Communication. PD Software. Helpful Commercial Software.*

11 An Administrative Guide   216

Today's Business Office. The Need for a Utilization Plan: *Establishing the Priorities of Your Needs. Selecting Most Appropriate Models. Alternatives.* The Trouble With Form Letters: *Adapting and (Adopting) the System.* Paper System or Computer System? The System Library. Word Processing: *Free and Nearly-Free Software. Desktop Publishing.* Telecommunications Research and Online Databases. A Few Final Words.

LIST OF FIGURES

Chapter 1

Introduction

Literature is not an abstract science. . . . It is an art, the success of which depends on personal persuasiveness, on the author's skill to give as on ours to receive.

Sir Arthur Thomas Quiller-Couch

A MODERN TOWER OF BABEL

Communication among humans has never been easy. One major reason for the difficulty is the fact that virtually none of us is entirely logical and objective. Quite the contrary, we permit our biases—our emotional drives—to establish the screens and filters through which we strain and color all information to suit our prejudices—what we prefer to believe. When effective communication takes place it is in spite of this problem, and usually the result of careful presentation that is designed to either skirt the barrier of emotional bias or employ it to advantage.

This is not a condemnation of our human nature, however, but only a recognition of it so that we may attack one communication problem intelligently. For that is not the only problem. Communication today also suffers from what appears to be the diminishing returns of an enormous creation and proliferation of new terms, new concepts, and new technology in a shrinking world. Consciously or unconsciously, many of us speak today in a tongue laced heavily with the specialized jargon of our era, with mutual understanding—communication—a casualty of the trend.

Add to that the all too typical distaste many people have for writing even a *brief* note and we have a problem that grows more serious as business life and personal life become more complex: We are becoming less and less effective at communicating with each other, while the need to communicate with each other grows ever greater!

TECHNOLOGY TAKES A HAND

In light of this, it is not surprising that word processing is by far the most common use for modern desktop computers. In fact, it is the word processing capability of these new microcomputers that is one of the major reasons for their swift acceptance. It was soon clear that while not everyone felt a pressing need to automate accounting or inventory functions, many offices, large and small, sensed the need to improve their capabilities for creating correspondence and other literature required to do business effectively today.

An analogous development is underway today, as attention is currently being focused on what is referred to generally as "desktop publishing." It is an evolutionary result of recent technological strides, such as laser printers and greater computer memories. But like word processing it is inspired by need—modern business needs for turning out more and more words on paper—correspondence, reports, bids, proposals, catalogs, direct mail packages, collection letters, brochures, manuals, specification sheets, press releases, contracts, and a great many other documents to be written and printed. The engineers and software developers have sensed and are following a true need.

Many popular magazines devote a great deal of their coverage to this subject. In fact, the entire content of the current issue of *Business Software,* which appeared on my desk only this morning, is slanted to the subject, with the cover headline "Managing Your Manuscripts," illustrated by an artist's representation of a book titled *Desktop Publishing* by U.R. Publisher.

These marvelous machines can do a great deal to make the mechanical production process easier and to help you turn out a more polished and professional-looking physical product. Wisely employed, word processing can help you in the actual writing process. But not even the most elaborate and sophisticated word processing can do the writing for you; it is still you who must create the basic ideas and organize their presentation and expression.

There's the rub, as the Bard observed. Many people dislike writing without even taking the time to become familiar with the most basic writing principles, not to mention the many formats of writing required in modern business and the professions. The documents mentioned earlier do not by any means represent an exhaustive list. They are only general classes of documents within which there are usually many subclasses. For example, one class mentioned was the manual. But there are employee manuals, procedural manuals, technical manuals, policy manuals, and instructor manuals, to name just a few. Even within these subclasses there are subordinate groups. A technical manual for a piece of equipment, for example, involves discussions of theory, installation, preventive maintenance, corrective maintenance, and overhaul and repair. But a large and complex equipment or equipment system today often requires a separate manual for each of these topics.

The same is true for the other documents mentioned. There are many kinds of reports, many kinds of letters, many kinds of brochures, and so forth. In fact, if you were to create a set of models for each and every class of documentation and situation, as many people have done for business letters, you would need the traditional five-foot shelf to contain the resulting library.

WHAT IS TO COME

Fortunately a five-foot shelf is not necessary. It is possible to cover a representative range of needs in each class without creating a complete set of models. What you will encounter in the pages to come is a grouping of needs in a logical hierarchy organized on three levels: a broad class, related groupings within that class, and specific subgroupings and samples within each grouping. Principles and methods will be presented, with a few representative models and guidelines for selecting the model that is closest to your need and adapting it appropriately.

There are three parts: Business Correspondence, Reports, and Miscellaneous Documents and Data. Business correspondence includes a variety of letters pertaining to sales, marketing, collections, and other matters. Reports includes various types, such as annual reports, progress reports, and technical reports. And the miscellaneous class covers materials written for all other matters—press releases, brochures, policy statements, and administrative matters.

In each case you will read rationales for the class, including guidelines for selecting the most appropriate model and adapting it to your immediate need. You will find also suggestions for creating new models designed to meet your own special needs and applications and for preserving the new models for future use. These suggestions will also cover the most effective use of your own word processor in these processes.

ALL WRITING HAS A BASIC PURPOSE

Essentially, all writing is directed to one or more of three objectives:

1. To persuade.
2. To inform.
3. To "document."

Sales and marketing materials are all of the *persuasive writing* category, of course. All persuasive writing is intended to persuade a reader to buy, to sell, to join, to vote, or to do something else the writer wants the reader to do.

Manuals and many other kinds of materials—brochures, letters, reports, and training programs, for example—are ostensibly meant to inform the reader.

Some materials are written merely to document or create a record for future use. Many reports also fall into this category.

A COMPLETE SYSTEM

These basic objectives are among the keys to the system—for it is a complete *system*—offered here. A system, to be a system at all, must have both a clearly defined methodology and a unity of some kind, a common thread that characterizes everything within it. Here, that unity is the logic of a clear objective and a plan for achieving it. Shortly we will discuss some of that in general terms, for which the various parts will be exemplifications. Thus the basics you will learn in these pages can be applied to an infinite number of situations and needs for written expression if you know your basic goal or main objective and the basic principles for achieving that goal or main objective. The plans will be based on and include specific methodologies.

A FEW WRITING BASICS

Belief, Understanding, and Persuasiveness

In a sense, all writing is or is intended to be persuasive, despite the fact that it may have a main goal or objective not focused on persuasion. Even informing or reporting to someone in writing requires persuasion, for it always requires effort to persuade someone to believe. In the conventional thinking of our society most of us tend to assume that belief follows understanding, that we must understand first, and then we will believe. In fact, that is by no means an immutable truth. (We do not even really know what "understand" means.) In most—perhaps all— cases the reverse is true: We "understand" that which we believe. That usually is true even in the most objective of areas, such as in studying the nature of matter. An individual's "understanding" of the nature of matter in particular and physics in general depends on his or her acceptance—belief in—many basic theories of atomic structure and other *never-seen* particles, particles that probably will never be seen by the human eye. There is no way we can verify such theories through our direct physical senses; therefore we can verify them only indirectly through chains of observation and logic or through the acceptance of (*belief* or *faith* in) reasonable theories put forth by those we respect as expert authorities.

But we can find more familiar examples to demonstrate this process. For some people all the explanations and logical rationales in the world will not convince them that man has actually walked on the moon; there are those who are convinced that this is a gigantic fraud perpetrated by the government for reasons unknown. There are also still those who believe that the earth is flat. And it is quite well accepted that it is futile to argue politics and religion, for no logic prevails against the emotional biases that characterize such arguments: It is virtually impossible to persuade most people to believe what they have long disbelieved or to reject what they have long embraced as truth.

Even further, when we have a disagreement we often tend to call this "a failure to communicate." It is usually nothing of the sort; it is most often a failure to persuade. It is a failure to overcome or to somehow avoid the immovable object of emotion-based bias. (And, more often than not, it is the failure to recognize that bias and a failure to even *try* to avoid it that results.)

This is not to say that minds cannot be changed or that your writing cannot "reach" readers intellectually, but the difficulty of doing so is in proportion to the reader's emotional biases. Those without reason to be biased to any great degree can be said to have open minds and are willing to consider your arguments. The reverse is also true, to the point that it is all but impossible to change people's minds when they are heavily biased—at least, to change them by frontal attacks. Oblique approaches, however, are often effective.

There Is Need for Persuasiveness in All Cases

We have been considering the extremes, readers with almost completely closed minds and those with almost completely open minds. Most people are reasonably open-minded on most subjects. Nonetheless, it is necessary, or at least wise, to prove your case. Some readers will accept your representations either on your apparent authority or because of an automatic tendency to believe—to have faith in—whatever appears in print or on-screen. But it is risky to depend on this. More and more in modern society it appears that our well-educated and increasingly sophisticated general public has lost much of yesterday's naivete. Today the public tends more and more to question flat claims and wants evidence of their validity. Even when you are writing something that is not intended especially to be persuasive—not making a great effort to induce the reader to do a specific thing—your writing needs always to have two qualities or characteristics to achieve *acceptance* by the reader:

It needs to be properly oriented emotionally, and it needs to have a logical basis.

This statement is stressed because it sums up in two brief phrases the most basic essence of marketing and sales appeals: the promise (emotional appeal) and the proof (logical argument). As we proceed you will perceive the rationale underlying this in all matters and in all areas. For example, once when an engineering magazine rejected my article on technical writing, I resubmitted the article, after brief pondering, with only a minor change. I added the opening sentences: "Mr. Engineer, much as you dislike writing—many of us do—our profession requires it of us. Here are a few tips on how to make the job of writing less painful."

The editor who had rejected the article only a few days earlier now bought it immediately. Think about why this happened! But for now let us go on to some other matters that are basic to writing.

Preparation for Writing

There is probably no single cause for bad writing more prevalent than the failure to *prepare* to write—to plan properly. And that entails certain steps, some of which you will find familiar, having read earlier pages:

1. Decide what your main purpose is—persuading, informing, reporting, recording, or other.

2. Decide on your goal or main objective and the strategy of your presentation—the general rationale for achieving the goal.
3. Draw up a preliminary outline of projected content and general organization to achieve the goal, implementing the strategy you decided on.
4. Decide on what raw input information is needed.
5. Devise a research plan—where and how to gain the input information.

Until you have done this you are not really ready to write. If you sit before your typewriter or word processor—or, horrors of reactionary tendencies, at your desk with ball-point pen poised over a long, yellow, lined pad—without any such preparation, ready to "wing it" or "play it by ear," the odds for success are against you. Even experienced and highly skilled professional writers find this a profitless way to write. It results at best in many wasted hours seeking a useful beginning and discarding one or more false starts, and at worst in an aborted project or a final product that is unusable.

Obviously you should first decide on your overall purpose. Later you will find that this is not as obvious as it appears, and the decision affects other considerations and plans.

Setting a goal or a main objective is simply deciding where you want to go, and if you do not decide in advance what your destination is you should not be greatly surprised to discover that you have not finally arrived there, but have reached a totally strange and unwanted destination.

The term *strategy* is a rather subtle one in many ways, but it is at the heart of every presentation. It may be the order of presentation (chronological versus order of importance), the mode of argument (inductive versus deductive), or something else, but it cannot be left to chance; it should be planned in advance. It is at the heart of your plan to make your presentation and to persuade your reader to accept what you say. It must at least have a rationale.

Some experienced writers can work from "leads," and that is an entirely legitimate approach to writing, but it does not work for everyone. It particularly does not usually work for nonprofessionals at writing. It does not even work for professionals, as a rule, when writing a lengthy piece, such as a book or formal, large report. Working without at least a rough, preliminary outline is likely to mean floundering around and wasting a great deal of time and effort.

For all of this to make sense you must have already decided what information you need, at least in general terms, and where you are most likely to find it. Regardless of the subject there are three basic sources for information:

1. Library research—books, reports, logs, diaries, and other documentation.
2. Interviews of those who have information recorded mentally and/or who are authorities on the subject.

3. Personal observation—field trips to use your own eyes and ears in gathering information.

The Opposite Extreme

There are many people who are either not aware of the need for organized and planned effort or who by nature tend to engage in interminable pondering and rather aimless—random—research and note-taking they fondly believe represents organized planning and preparation. Unfortunately, that does not work either. Experience in a number of major technical writing programs has demonstrated this rather clearly. Two cases involve the preparation of maintenance manuals for the billion-dollar Ballistic Missile Early Warning System (BMEWS) prepared at the RCA Service Company center in Riverton, New Jersey, and the ill-fated Navy TYPHON missile system at the Vitro Laboratories in Silver Spring, Maryland. In both cases technicians who had no writing experience were recruited to write portions of the extensive manual series required for these systems. In both systems I observed writers doing what they thought was proper research, making mountains of notes for many months, filling thick three-ring binders with their notations. But they failed to draft preliminary outlines or set specific objectives either in advance or at any early time in the projects, although they had been given general—but relatively vague—objectives by management. And they failed, despite many urgings, to prepare an outline and begin to assemble their notes into some sort of corresponding rough draft. (It is the nature of the profession that technical writers are generally left to their own resources for detailed planning and preparation, and are armed by management with only the most general "book plans.") Ultimately, both writers found themselves in difficulty eventually because they did not know what to do with their notes, as deadlines for the submittal of their draft manuals arrived. One, in fact, could not decipher his own notes! Months had passed, and he did not remember the significance of his earlier observations—in fact, he actually could not even read most of his earlier notes. Thus he did not know how to organize and assemble the information. In another case a writer engaged in extensive but random research and note-taking for a full 18 months and then resigned abruptly when deadlines approached and he realized that his mass of notes were of little use in producing the manual he had supposedly been writing.

These are not abnormal cases. In fact, they are the rather typical results of undertaking a writing project without planning or, at least, without an established modus operandi, such as professional writers employ. The problem of "poor writing," it most often turns out, has little or nothing to do with the author's command of the language or with his or her ability to structure sentences. Quite the contrary, many of those who do not write well are quite loquacious and even eloquent in speech; they demonstrate no inherent inability to use language well. This is true despite their apparent difficulty in organizing and presenting information in writing, which appears to soft-boil their brains.

Planning and Organization

My experience as an editor, manager, and consultant in the publications field generally and in the specialized field of proposals and other "sell copy" demonstrated in more than one way that quite often this problem has nothing to do with one's command of the language. In a strikingly large number of cases I found the answer was to send the writer "back to the drawing board" and require him or her to do more research and develop a detailed outline of the written product to be. This is not an outline of what he or she would write *about* but what he or she would write *specifically*, that is, not the vague outline already provided by management:

> Maintenance
> > Preventive
> > Corrective
> > Overhaul and repair

but the detailed outline such as this:

> Maintenance
> > Preventive
> > > Lubrication
> > > > Schedules and frequency
> > > > Points to lubricate
> > > > Lubricants to use
> > > Inspection
> > > > Schedules and frequency
> > > > Points to inspect
> > > > What to inspect for
> > Corrective
> > > Troubleshooting
> > > > Symptom analysis
> > > > (Etc.)

The difference is rather obvious. The second outline must produce a reasonably acceptable result if it is implemented accurately. Although this is not as detailed as it could and should be, it is a vast improvement over the first one. There is more than an *advantage* to using such an outline; there is an absolute *necessity* for it. The detailed outline has the following indispensable attributes:

1. It is a planning tool. It is the writer's blueprint, and writing should be confined to the outline development until the outline has been developed to everyone's satisfaction—until it becomes definitive and describes the final document comprehensively. Attempts to begin developing a manuscript before the planning stage of detailed outline development are almost always wasteful. Even research cannot be carried out intelligently without such planning, for how can you know what information to gather unless you know what information you are going to present? And, for that matter, how can you judge and *make preparations for* supporting work to find or develop needed drawings, photographs, charts, or other such items. (How many writing projects reach

the panic stage at deadline time because advance preparations for such items were not made!)

2. It is a management tool. How can a manager know whether to approve or disapprove even the effort before it is launched without this kind of preview? Or judge how well the end product satisfies the need?

3. It is a production tool, and in more ways than one: It is necessary to enable the editor to judge organization and general presentation effectiveness, and it is useful to all who must support the effort—illustrators or drafters, for example.

Grammar and Punctuation

Through all of this discussion the emphasis has been on planning and organization, rather than on grammar and punctuation. That stress was not by chance; it was by design. It was done to deliver the message that not only are faulty planning and organization most often responsible for what is termed "poor writing," but they are actually of far greater importance to the art of writing than are grammar and punctuation. (Of course, I use the phrase "grammar and punctuation" rhetorically to make the point *planning and organization, not grammar and punctuation,* for the phrase actually refers to all the other factors of English language usage necessary to achieve what is usually termed an ability to "write well.") That rationale needs some explanation, and it is important to our purpose here. It is based on these points:

1. Writing is not mastery of language usage per se, nor does mastery of language usage represent writing. The rules of usage are the tools of writing, as a hammer and saw are the tools of carpentry, but the ability to use the tools is not the ability to plan and build a house. The writer must be able to plan and design, as well as execute through use of the tools.

2. Many capable, even excellent, writers have weaknesses in spelling, punctuation, grammar, and so forth, but these can be and are usually shored up by able editors. (Certainly the writer *ought* to be a master of usage, but the reality is that many writers simply are not.)

3. On the other hand, although an able editor can usually correct problems of usage, the most competent editor cannot supply missing information or reorganize badly organized and badly planned writing. At best, that's a job of rewriting, and at worst, it's a project for the trash can. We must discriminate between what is proper editing and what is revision and rewriting. And writers must never be allowed to lapse into the philosophy that they can afford to be careless because they have editors to support them.

Ergo the philosophy that the manuscript must be *worth* editing.

Who Does the Editing?

Every writer should do some self-editing. It's inherent in the very idea of writing as a profession, with its conventional wisdom, that all good writing results from rewriting. Only tyros even expect to produce good writing in a first draft, let alone actually attempt to make their first rough drafts "fly." The normal writing sequence is, at the minimum, develop a proper outline, conduct research, prepare a rough draft, self-edit the draft, and rewrite it before submitting the draft to an editor. That's an absolute minimum. Few writers, even professionals, produce a really good second draft. The best writers are almost always those who are never quite satisfied, but continue to revise, rewrite, and polish almost endlessly.

A true professional is ashamed to have an editor catch basic errors in usage, errors that a high school sophomore should not commit. The professional turns over to an editor only work he or she believes is *ready* for editing.

Style

Style is an evasive thing. Every writer develops his or her own style in time, and although we are all influenced by the style of those writers whose work we admire and like to read, it's a mistake to deliberately and consciously attempt to emulate the style of others. Developing our own style is a spontaneous and unconscious process, so that most of us can recognize others' styles, but we could not describe our own style! Ernest Hemingway, for example, constantly protested that he did not have a particular style at all, despite all the things he said in describing his own style (e.g., the influences of editors on his early work) and undoubtedly truly believed that. (I can't imagine how he explained the legions of young writers trying consciously to emulate his style.)

At any rate, in business writing the best style is almost always a straightforward one that minimizes the use of unfamiliar or "big" words, gets to the point immediately, and eliminates all unnecessary discussion. However, in that connection, it is useful to stress the term *unfamiliar* and point out that *big* is not used in a literal sense here. Consider the following short sentence that has only six short words, two of which have two syllables and the other four only one syllable each.

The earth is an oblate spheroid.

By some standards that sentence qualifies as simple and straight-forward writing. And it is—if you are writing to an audience of scientists who are likely to be familiar with the words *oblate* and *spheroid*. The lay audience is far less likely to know what those two words mean. They are far more likely to have an easier time with a considerably longer sentence, with several considerably longer—but familiar—words:

The earth is shaped like an orange, round but flattened slightly at the ends.

Our artificial satellites have shown us that the earth is actually shaped more like a pear than like an orange, but the point is the same: A "big" word is an unfamiliar one, no matter how many letters and/or syllables it has.

Style Guides

There are books called style guides that establish or recommend certain style standards. These recommendations extend to methods for organizing tabular data, hyphenating words that must be divided and eliminating hyphens from some compound words, spelling preferences, grammatical guidelines, proper forms of address for various uses, and numerous other useful data. Three of the most popular ones are the *United States Government Printing Office Style Manual,* published by the Government Printing Office (GPO), of course; *A Manual of Style,* University of Chicago Press; and the *New York Times Manual of Style and Usage,* Lewis Jordan, Quadrangle Books, 1976. At least the first two of these are republished periodically in new editions. My own copy of the GPO style manual is dated January 1967, and my Chicago University style manual is the 12th edition, of 1969. (There are later editions extant.)

Some of the Most Basic of Basics about Usage

I make no claims to authority as a grammarian. In fact, I am probably one of those I referred to earlier who is very much in need of the expert assistance of an able editor when I produce a manuscript. Moreover, I am compelled to admit that I was educated at a time when most public schools taught "close" punctuation and were otherwise quite conservative in all matters of usage and style. Moreover, my earliest reading was of Horatio Alger books and, especially, O. Henry, very much a stylist. (He even addressed his audience directly as "Gentle reader!") So it has been only with great difficulty that I have managed to cast off to some degree the tendency to pepper my writing freely with commas, use somewhat convoluted sentence structure, and compel myself to write "I," not "we," when I truly mean I.

It was Mark Twain—Samuel Clemens—who reportedly said that only newspaper editors, royalty, and people with tapeworm have the right to say "we" when they mean "I." I was much happier to learn that he stubbornly refused to permit his editors to modify his punctuation, asserting that no editor knew as well as he did what he was trying to say, and therefore had no right to tamper with his punctuation. I confess that I don't have the courage to be quite that defiant with my publishers and editors, but fortunately Clemens' philosophy is fairly well accepted in general today. It is generally acknowledged that there are few absolute rules per se for how to use the language, but there are the guidelines—opinions—of how those deemed to be authoritative who *recommend* how we should spell, punctuate, define, and so forth. The various dictionaries and style guides are sometimes in conflict with each other in many of these matters, in fact, because opinions even of experts vary. The GPO style manual, for example, insists on the spelling *programer,* rather than *programmer.*

WRITING: WHAT IS IT?

On one occasion I acquired an interesting little writing test I put to good use in examining the writing abilities of applicants. The main element of the test was a requirement to describe in 100 words or less the procedure for writing a personal check.

Few could do so, and only once in a great while did an applicant finesse the test by sketching a check and labeling the key items, thus making it easy to describe the procedure in less than 50 words!

Writing is communication, of course, and there is absolutely no law, recommendation, or standard that suggests, much less mandates, that a writer must confine his or her efforts to the use of words alone. Quite the contrary, the best business writers are those who have learned how to use other methods to support the communication process most efficiently, especially through the judicious use of illustrations: photographs and drawings of all kinds—plots, graphs, charts, and pictorials, to name a few.

In the technical publications world I found many unimaginative—and presumably uninformed—managers complaining about what they deemed to be the excessive use of graphic illustrations. Their complaint was that every use of an illustration, especially that of costly line drawings, was an assault on their budgets because, they alleged, one page of illustration cost (typically) 10 times that of a page of text.

In an absolute sense the statement is true, and yet the argument has no validity because it presumes that the page of illustration is an addition to all the text that would be required whether the illustration were used or not. That's a false premise. An illustration that is really adequate *replaces* text, reducing the amount of text that is required to deliver the information. It should, in fact, as an absolute minimum, "displace its own weight" (cost equivalent) of text, as in the case of the editorial test calling for an efficient description of how to write a check. An illustration that does not displace "its weight" of text should not be used. It is almost surely a poor illustration for that reason alone.

Consider the problem of presenting a schedule in a written presentation, perhaps in supporting and explaining a bid, making a sales presentation, or—more serious than either of those—making a contract commitment. (In the business world there are few areas where absolute clarity and specificity are more important than in the wording of a contract.) And for a complex schedule of interrelated and interdependent events words alone are almost surely inadequate. Not only is it difficult to explain such a schedule in text alone, but the explanation is almost surely going to be subject to interpretation, a made-to-order seed-bed for later problems, such as contract disputes and possible litigation.

Schedules, for example, can be shown in several ways other than straight narrative description. One popular way to present a schedule is by a tabular listing. A hypothetical schedule for a relatively simple project, but one with concurrent and linked activities, is shown as Figure 1–1.

FIGURE 1-1 Tabular Schedule

Schedule of Events		
Event	*Start Date*	*Completion Date*
1. Prepare designs	4/1/87	5/1/87
2. Conduct research	4/12/87	5/15/87
3. Prepare draft	5/1/87	6/21/87
4. Client review	6/22/87	7/22/87
5. Revise per review comments	7/23/87	7/30/87

You will note that tasks overlap each other—most tasks begin before the previous task is finished—and the schedule shown in this manner probably needs the support of text to explain or point that fact out to the reader.

Compare that with the schedule shown as a milestone drawing in Figure 1-2.

Obviously the milestone chart makes it easier for the reader to grasp the phase (time) relationships of the various events. Little text is required to make these relationships clear. (There are other factors, too, in this case, which we will discuss later, in another context.)

Later we will also discuss the factors that make an illustration a good one or a bad one (in the sense of its contribution to meaning and communication, not to its technical quality) but these factors will still be based on that criterion of how well an illustration reduces dependency on words—how well, that is, graphic illustrations convey their own messages, with little or no dependency on text to deliver the entire meaning.

It should be obvious by now that the dollar cost factor is not the only consideration. There are other costs, some of them more important than dollars. Aside from the need to have as clear and unequivocal a contractual agreement as possible, there is the cost in reader's time: Anything that makes the reader's job easier and reduces the time necessary to master the information is a consideration all its own, sometimes far more important than the absolute cost.

FIGURE 1-2 Schedule Shown as Milestone Chart

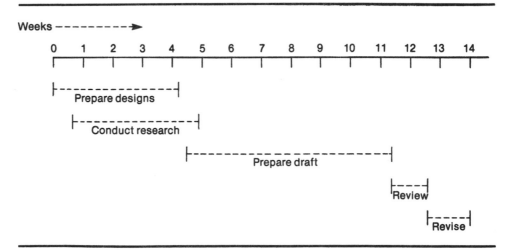

This is no small matter; it goes far beyond efficiency and convenience. Anything that makes a written presentation easier to grasp or shortens the time required to grasp it makes it a far more powerful presentation. That alone can mean the difference between success and failure in attracting new buyers, closing a major sale, consummating a merger successfully, or otherwise bringing some important transaction to a successful close.

There is also a general effect upon persuasiveness. It is certainly going to be more difficult to persuade a prospect to a cause or commitment that is not clearly presented than to one that is easy to grasp. An annual report or a stock prospectus, for example, will certainly be more effective if the reader grasps the major points quickly and easily. In fact, it is a rare written presentation that does not have persuasiveness as a goal.

PART I

BUSINESS CORRESPONDENCE: WHAT DOES THE TERM MEAN?

Business writing today is enormously varied in many ways. Less than a century ago the term referred almost invariably to correspondence in business—letters exchanged among people in business and between businesspeople and their customers or prospective customers. In that era of a century ago or thereabouts business correspondence was rather stiff-necked and almost unbearably formal. The current month was referred to as the "instant" (often abbreviated to "inst," as in "In response to yours of the 12th inst"), and the general tone was one of ultrapolite self-deprecation à la the Chinese custom of super humility.

Fortunately, that era has passed on into a well-deserved obscurity, despite the reluctance of a few to relinquish their grasp on obfuscating formality. The trend today is to state the case as clearly and as briefly as possible, while exercising reasonable tact and diplomacy. Moreover, no longer does "business writing" refer entirely to business correspondence literally—letters exchanged between businesses and their customers—but includes a number of other types of written documentation and presentations. The element of business writing that does consist primarily of correspondence has evolved and become increasingly diverse in modern times, so that it makes sense to treat it as a separate section of this book. In fact, so extensive is the range of just this field of business writing that many complete books and even sets of audio tapes on the market deal with nothing but business letters.

The very term *business correspondence* refers to letters by definition. However, the basic term *letters* has itself acquired a somewhat flexible meaning in today's business world, stretched somewhat in many applications. For example, while a formal proposal is often quite a ponderous document—those for major programs have often run to thousands of pages—an informal proposal is often referred to as a *letter proposal* because it is essentially a letter of several pages in which the proposal is embodied. Similarly, a simple and informal contract is often called a *Letter of Agreement* because it is such a simple, often single-page, document. Hence, such closely related sales presentations are also covered in this first part, treated under the general heading of *business correspondence*. And to give you a little idea in advance of the diversity of such presentations, in this part we will offer ideas, information, and models falling into the following categories:

General correspondence.
Other sales/marketing documents.
Letters of Agreement.
Sales correspondence.
Collection letters.

The diversity is not only in the general classes, purposes, and functions of correspondence, however. A diversity is also introduced by the great variety of the business enterprises that have evolved over the years, especially over the decades following World War II, when postwar circumstances set so many new factors into motion, leading to the mushroom growth of the many new high-tech industries, their satellite (supporting) industries, the spin-off industries, and many other new industries: the fast-food chains, overnight express services, airlines, trucking, and other new or relatively new kinds of ventures. But there are also the classical and conventional professionals—medical and legal practitioners, consultants, architects, and millions of small business-people, as well as people in several thousand supercorporations. So it is not a simple proposition, and there will be no effort in these pages to offer a model for each and every possible need; it would be an entirely impracticable goal. Rather, principles and exemplifying models will be offered to point the way, with guidance to help you adapt these principles and models to meet your own special needs.

There are, as noted, far too many classes and categories of users and far too many applications to furnish a model for each, but applications for the following at least will be offered:

Professionals.
Wholesalers.
Service organizations.
Retailers.
Manufacturers.

There are a few basics of writing letters that are, in fact, basic to all writing:

1. Simplicity. Even the expert writer has trouble when he or she gets into complex writing structures, and some of our most successful writers—Ernest Hemingway, for example—used the simplest writing

styles they could. The following are the measures that help you keep your writing style simple and easy to understand.

a. One idea per sentence. You should have some specific purpose or idea to convey for each sentence, and that sentence should not go beyond that idea. Save the next idea for the next sentence. Use simple sentence structure: a noun or pronoun (subject of the sentence), a verb, and, when necessary, an object. Then stop and go on to the next sentence.

b. Stick to the point. Do not introduce any information or ideas that are not entirely relevant to the point you want to make.

c. Use words that are familiar to most people and used in everyday conversation. (Never mind whether they are "long" or "short" words.) Use *undertaker* when you mean undertaker, for example; not everyone knows what the modern euphemism *mortician* means.

d. Use active and direct voice. Not "Company policy dictates that a 5 percent service charge must be made on all accounts over 30 days old," but "We make a 5 percent service charge on all accounts more than 30 days old." Not "Customers are advised that in event of difficulty the unit should be sent to one of our authorized service dealers for repair," but "If the unit malfunctions, bring or send it to any of our authorized service dealers for repair."

e. Keep paragraphs short. Like sentences, paragraphs should have only one central idea, the one that was introduced by the first sentence. When you have finished with that idea, start a new paragraph if you have another idea to discuss. *But only if you have a new idea to discuss.*

2.   Other considerations. You should keep a good dictionary at hand and verify all spellings if you are not absolutely sure of their correctness. Of course, if you are using a word processor, it is wise to have a spelling checker review your draft before you print it. (I am quite a good speller, but my own spelling checker turns up enough spelling errors—and typos—to cause me chagrin almost constantly.)

Edit your own copy. Read what you have drafted, change all the $5 words to 50 cent ones, eliminate all the extraneous stuff that really has nothing to do with what you are trying to say, and rewrite it into a simple and straightforward—hopefully *brief*—message. Be sure that you don't run on. When you have delivered your message, *stop.*

3.   Decide what you want to say—the *point* of your letter. If there are three rules for writing well, this is all three of them, for this identifies the most common problem: Far too many people write letters (and other things) without knowing what they want to say—doodling verbally, in fact, as though they were engaged in idle conversation over tea, in the hope that eventually they will stumble across the right thoughts and right words. It rarely works, and even when it does the outcome is that much of the result is rambling and pointless and not at all businesslike. In short, if you don't know—*clearly* and in advance—what you want to say, how can you ever be sure that you have said it clearly enough to give the reader a fair chance of understanding your exact meaning?

4.   Remember to sell. In all things generally, but in all business writing especially, you must always *sell.* That means writing persuasively, no matter what the subject of the letter is. Even a response to an inquiry can benefit or hurt your organization by presenting a favorable or unfavorable view of it. (Do not those cold and stilted form letters of government agencies and many corporations create that adverse image so many of us have of government agencies and major corporations?)

Do not be any more formal than circumstances and good taste dictate. Obviously you must address strangers and those you know only slightly by such titles as Mr., Ms., Colonel, and so forth. But in the real business world, executives often address business letters to "Dear Bill" and sign them "Harry," when they happen to be friends or business associates of long standing.

Figure I–1 is offered as a general illustration of some of these principles. It is a copy of my response to a request from another writer to use a portion of an article I wrote for the *Writer's Digest.* The other writer had sent his request to the magazine, a proper action, and the magazine

FIGURE I–1 General Sample of a Business Letter

March 3, 1986

Dear Mr. Bourne:

Writer's Digest sent on your request for permission to use my model proposal in your book. I don't know whether they responded directly to you in any way; I suspect not, from my own experience in asking them for releases.

You certainly have my permission to use this, with attribution. I think the attribution ought to mention where and when the original article appeared,and I would like it to make mention of my name and the fact that this is a model of the proposal format and content I have used successfully in winning 30 book contracts. (I use a condensed form of this for getting magazine article assignments.) There is no cost; the attribution is my only requirement. However, for your information I am enclosing some other information about myself and my work.

I wish you success with your book. Please let me know when it is in print, as I would like to have a copy.

Cordially,

Herman Holtz

passed it on to me for my approval. (In other cases, the magazine might have given approval, depending on the rights agreement between the periodical and the writer.)

Note that each paragraph begins with a sentence that identifies the subject of the paragraph, and that when a new subject is to be discussed, a new paragraph with its own topic sentence begins. Each subject is addressed directly; my requirements are stated as clearly as I know how to state them; and when I am finished I stop.

Chapter 2

General Correspondence

THE NATURE OF THE COVERAGE IN THIS CHAPTER

This chapter offers ideas and models for general business correspondence between individuals and organizations in situations and for reasons that are common to most businesses and organizations. But these ideas and models will extend beyond to those that are not businesses per se; that is, they are not always commercial or for-profit organizations and enterprises, although they do conduct their own "business" activities every day, whatever those activities are. However, where the correspondence includes at least one business enterprise as one of the correspondents, the relationship between the corresponding parties is usually that of seller and buyer or seller and prospective buyer—customer. Either or both correspondents may be individuals or organizations.

The need for most of these kinds of letters is not peculiar to any single type of organization, industry, or profession, but arises regularly in the course of routine business affairs conducted by individual practitioners, government agencies, nonprofit corporations, and virtually every other kind of daily activity.

The chapter is divided into eight sections, each representing a broad class of situations or needs and relevant correspondence, including a section for a general or miscellaneous class. Each section has its own discussion and model letters. The eight sections are as follows:

Responses to inquiries.
Acknowledgment of orders.
Confirmation of appointments.
Requests for bids/quotations.
Responses to complaints.
Notices of delays in shipping.
Acknowledgment of bids/quotations.
Other (general formats).

RESPONSES TO INQUIRIES

There are many situations that affect the way you respond to inquiries. Some of the situations create or reflect problems that must be solved before you can respond properly, and some affect how you must respond. However, there are some general rules that are appropriate for anyone responding to inquiries, including some guidelines for coping with typical problems.

Be Sure You Understand the Inquiry

Take the time to thoroughly read and understand the inquiry. If it is a telephone inquiry, ask the right questions, and if it is an illegible or incoherent scrawled message from someone who took the inquiry by telephone, call the inquirer and find out what the inquiry is before attempting to compose an answer. Be absolutely sure you know precisely what the inquirer wants. So often the response one gets to an inquiry is totally and irritatingly irrelevant. Few things create a worse impression than a response that indicates complete failure to understand the inquiry—perhaps even a complete failure to read the letter of inquiry—such as getting a fancy, colored brochure extolling the company or its products when you asked for a simple quotation or asked why your order has not been shipped.

Be Sure You Understand the Problem

If a problem is involved, such as getting the wrong merchandise, not getting the shipment at all, finding items missing, or other such all too typical business problems, it is essential that you understand the problem exactly.

Give a Direct and Honest Answer

Do not temporize. If you cannot give a final or definitive answer for some reason, state so clearly and frankly, but tactfully, with reasons for your inability to do exactly what the inquirer wants. (For example, if you need more information, ask for it or suggest whatever is necessary as a preliminary to supplying whatever the inquirer asked for.) If you must say no, say no nicely and in a thoughtful and friendly way. Amazingly often responses to inquiries appear hostile and antagonistic.

Be Brief (But Not Brusque)

Come to the point as quickly as possible and don't stray unnecessarily. The other person's time is likely to be as valuable as yours is. Business-like brevity is itself a display of courtesy, as wasting another's time is strongly suggestive of discourtesy.

Answer Promptly

Unfortunately, many businesses today take weeks to respond to inquiries with even a brief letter, resulting in many sales and much good will lost. (However, even if a sale or possible sale is not at stake, common courtesy and, especially, PR—public relations—considerations dictate prompt and courteous response.) Moreover, delay in answering always increases the possibility that the inquiry will never get answered at all, resulting almost certainly in ill will and/or lost sales. I recently ceased, sadly and regretfully, doing business with a software developer principally because they failed to respond to my repeated inquiries regarding delays in shipment. I would have waited patiently for the late shipments had they answered my letters or returned my telephone calls promptly, but their failure to respond at all caused me to lose faith in the firm and to cancel my orders outstanding with them.

Prepare the Groundwork for Follow-Up

Make notes to plan the sales follow-up if the inquiry appears to be a sales lead, as so many are, laying the groundwork in your letter for that follow-up. Inquirers are generally good prospects and inquiries thus become virtual invitations to pursue sales. But follow-up must be prompt and direct, and the inquirer must be prepared to expect follow-up where that is an appropriate action.

Use a Friendly (But Not Familiar) Tone

Use the less formal and friendlier "I" instead of "we," unless the situation mandates the use of the plural pronoun. The use of "we" when you mean "I" is outdated (by about a century, in fact) and more impersonal than it has to be or ought to be. Be informal generally, although not familiar.

Use Proper Salutations

Proper salutations are generally Dear Mr., Mrs., Ms., and so forth rather than Sir or Madam, whenever possible. Try to avoid using the latter salutations; they suggest that you are sending a cold and impersonal form letter. However, you may use first names when you know the other party well enough.

Many problems arise in finding the right salutation. Sometimes a writer uses only initials, such as B. K. Jones, so that you have no way of knowing whether the inquiry is from a man or a woman. And often enough women write and give no clue as to whether they are Miss, Mrs., or prefer to be addressed as Ms.

One way to solve this is to address the letter to Dear B. K. Jones or Dear Lilian Smith. That is perfectly proper, although it has become commonplace to use the form Dear Ms. Smith.

In many cases protocol or standard practices of courtesy in our society dictates that the individual you are addressing is entitled to be addressed by his or her title. Retired military officers, for example, usually are addressed by their rank at the time of retirement—major, colonel, general. Officers on duty or retired are addressed by the higher or more general of their ranks when it is a compound noun: Both second and first lieutenants are addressed as Lieutenant, lieutenant colonels and full colonels as Colonel, all ranks of general as General. Of course the same thing holds for naval ranks—lieutenant and lieutenant junior grade, admirals, and so forth.

Government has its protocol generally, with respect to correspondence and forms of address. By now probably everyone knows that the president is always addressed as Dear Mr. President, even by intimate friends, and the proper complimentary close is Sincerely, as it is with other government officials, elected and appointed. In most cases—cabinet members, under secretaries, assistant secretaries, heads of other agencies, special assistants to the president, senators, representatives, judges, ambassadors, and most other government dignitaries—the proper address is The Honorable (full name), followed by the title if the individual has another title, such as Secretary of State, Special Assistant to the President, Speaker of the House, Committee Chairman, or other. Foreign ambassadors are addressed as His Excellency, followed by the ambassador's full name. Then, with that protocol observed and courtesy accorded, the direct address may be made to Dear Senator Willoughby, Dear Madam Secretary, or whatever is appropriate.

There are occasions when you must address a company and do not know of any individual in the company. "To whom it may concern" is outdated and smacks of a preprinted form letter. It is far better to address the letter to whatever functional title you think most appropriate, such as Dear Marketing Manager. Someone at the other end will see to it that it gets into the right hands.

Complimentary Closes

The same philosophy applies generally to complimentary closings: They should be friendly and informal, without becoming overly familiar, but should be suitable for the occasion. One friendly closing that can be used in a great many cases is *Cordially,* but you may also use such closings as *Thank you, With best wishes, Warmest regards, In sincerest appreciation,* or another such friendly and informal closing if it fits the situation and the relationship. Still in widespread use are several slightly more formal closings: *Sincerely, Yours truly, Very truly yours,* or others of a similar nature, all perfectly proper. (*Sincerely* is generally considered proper in writing to government dignitaries and for other formal or semiformal uses.) But do not use such ancient closings as *Your Obedient Servant.* The time for that is past. When you are well acquainted with the addressee, you may sign off with *Regards, As always,* or another informal close.

Models

The model letters that follow illustrate several of the typical situations and problems mentioned and some suggested approaches and methods for coping successfully with problems.

Dear Mr. Franklin:

I am most pleased to send you our Spring catalog, as you requested. It is loaded with special sale items again this year, all on our usual easy terms.

You are most welcome to take advantage of our liberal credit policy by opening an account with us. Forms for doing so are included in the catalog. But you don't have to wait for credit approval to order. Just send your credit application along with your first order for our prompt action.

I welcome you to our family of happy customers and look forward to the opportunity to satisfy your needs.

Cordially,

Dear Miss Wilson:

Thank you for your inquiry concerning a new sun room addition to your house. It gives us great pleasure to be of service to you.

I can tell you that we have added beautiful new sun rooms to houses in your neighborhood for as little as $2,500. However, each case is individual, and it is difficult to give you even a rough idea of the cost for adding a sun room to your own house without first getting more information as to exactly what your requirements are and what work will be

continued
necessary. To be entirely fair to you by making a realistic and firm estimate it is necessary to examine the premises, make some measurements, and have you look at sample books and make choices.

I will be most pleased to visit you, at your convenience and absolutely without obligation on your part, to show you samples and discuss your new sun room, after which I will prepare an estimate which will constitute a firm price. I stress that this is a free estimate; you will not be obligated in any way.

I will call you in a day or two to arrange an appointment to visit you and discuss your needs for a beautiful new addition to your home.

Most cordially,

Dear Colonel Henry:

I truly regret our inability to ship your order more promptly, due to a local strike that has affected our shipping department. I expect your order to go out to you the day after tomorrow, and I will advise you immediately if anything arises to interfere with this schedule.

Please feel free to write or call me personally if I can be of further service to you.

Sincerely,

Dear Mrs. Jobseeker:

Thank you for thinking of us in connection with your services as a possible employee of this organization.

Although such openings as those you inquire about do occur here from time to time, I regret that we have none at the moment. However, with your permission, I would like to retain your resume for possible future action, should a suitable position become available.

With best wishes for your success,

Dear J. D. Rocker:

Unfortunately we have discontinued the Azerbaijanian line of food processors. I regret that we are therefore unable to fill your order. Enclosed, however, is literature describing the Electromagic food processors we do carry, along with full information for ordering them. I believe that you would find these equally satisfactory, while also slightly less expensive.

Please feel free to call or write again if you require more information. I hope that we can be of service to you in this matter.

Sincerely,

Dear Mr. Jonas:

I am pleased to enclose a sample copy of our newsletter, per your request. I hope that you will find it appropriate to your needs and expectations.

Also enclosed are forms for subscribing. I look forward to being of service to you.

Cordially,

Dear Senator Willoughby:

I regret that the demand for our Report No. G–764–AT–34 was so great that we have completely exhausted our stock, so I am unable to comply immediately with your request for three copies of this report. Since the size of this report is such that duplicating three copies by office copier would be impractical I have ordered additional copies printed on an emergency rush basis, and have been promised delivery within a few days.

I will, of course, send you three copies by special messenger as soon as they arrive.

I hope that this will satisfy your need. In the meanwhile you are welcome to visit and examine our file copy, if you wish.

Sincerely,

ACKNOWLEDGMENT OF ORDERS

Not every order must be acknowledged formally by return mail. Most firms filling routine orders, such as the mail order firm from whom I order many of my office supplies, do not normally send out formal acknowledgments. Filling and shipping the order promptly is usually all the acknowledgment that the customer expects, and is generally satisfactory. (Nevertheless, a written acknowledgment, even a postcard, is a pleasant surprise to most customers, and is usually appreciated enough to make the expense worthwhile. This is especially true when you receive the first order from a new customer.)

On the other hand any order that cannot be filled promptly for any reason, even a small order, should be acknowledged formally in writing to maintain good customer relationships.

A Need for Tact and Diplomacy

Of course all large orders and especially those that will require some time to fulfill and ship or consummate (e.g., an order from Mrs. Wilson to go ahead and build her sun room addition) definitely merit a written acknowledgment, including an expression of appreciation for the order. However, it is important in acknowledging orders to be careful that you do not unsell the order, as people occasionally do when they do not think carefully about what they are saying. One hazard that might lead to unselling an order is the problem of being unable to fill the order promptly for some reason.

Tact is called for here. You must be careful to avoid suggesting that your salesperson may have misled the customer with regard to availability of the merchandise ordered, for example. If the delay is to be rather short—a few days, at most—it is probably best to treat that as a matter of course, a normal condition, and not as a delay or anything unusual. That means either say nothing at all about the expected shipping date or mention it casually as a routine observation.

Turn Liabilities into Assets

If the delay will be a fairly lengthy one, it cannot be ignored or brushed over without ultimately causing problems. You must at least make it clear that any delay, other than a very slight one, concerns you deeply. However, you can often turn the liability of even a lengthy delay into an asset by pointing out that the customer has selected the most popular item of its kind.

Several ways of handling such problems tactfully are suggested in the following models:

Dear Mrs. Huston:

Thank you for your order of our HardWear pot and pan set. Your order was processed immediately, and your set should be on its way to you by the time you read this.

Please feel free to call me directly if there is any other way in which I can be of service to you.

It has been a pleasure serving you, and I look forward to the opportunity to do so again in the near future.

Cordially,

Dear Mrs. Wilson:

I want to thank you for your order of a sun room addition to your home. The installation crew is scheduled to begin work on Monday, and you and your family should be enjoying this new room 30 days from now. I know that you will be thoroughly delighted with this beautiful addition to your home.

Please feel free to call me at any time if there is anything you wish to ask me or to discuss.

In appreciation,

Ref: Contract No. 276-A-569
Confirmation of receipt

Dear Mr. Hankins:

Your signed contract arrived this morning, and work on your order was begun promptly in our fabricating plant, as promised. Shipments will be on a monthly basis, as agreed, the first shipment to be made within 30 days from date and remaining shipments every 30 days thereafter.

continued
    I want to thank you personally for your patronage and assure you of our complete cooperation and diligence in completing your order in strict accordance with our agreement. I will see to it personally that all goes exactly as pledged. Please call on me personally if you need anything.

In appreciation,

Dear Mrs. Hanratty:

    This is to confirm receipt of your order for a LongLife stereo system Model 312–ZZAB–1, and to thank you sincerely for your patronage.
    This our most popular model, and we have ordered a factory-fresh system shipped directly to you from our central warehouse in Louisville. It should arrive within a few days.
    Please feel free to call me directly if I can be of further service to you.

Cordially,

                                                    Ref: Your Purchase Order 17A34

Dear Hank:

    Thank you for your order, cited above.
    As you know Burntwood Furniture, Inc. has only recently settled their strike and gotten their plant back into operation after being shut down for several weeks. This means a slight delay in filling orders: The Burntwood factory advises that your order would be shipped directly to you approximately three weeks from this date.
    If this causes you a problem we can ship you virtually identical items immediately from our Southern Forests line of furniture. Should you wish to take advantage of this alternative we would bill you at the prices listed in your purchase order, despite the fact that the Southern Forests products are slightly higher than those of Burntwood Furniture.

Regards,

CONFIRMATION OF APPOINTMENTS

What Appointments Should Be Confirmed?

As in the case of acknowledging orders, not all appointments need be confirmed by mail. This is especially the case when the appointment is informal and for the near future—a day or two away, since the purpose of confirmation is primarily to remind the other party of the appointment. Typical examples are appointments with a tailor or seamstress for fittings and appointments to have your hair done.

Theoretically it is also not usually necessary to confirm appointments for medical checkups, dental care, and other such occasions. However, many medical practitioners do choose to confirm appointments by mail, usually with postcards, although many others confirm appointments by telephone calls.

On the other hand and at the opposite extreme many appointments are made months in advance and involve substantial commitments by both parties. When I am retained to present a seminar, for example, it is usually a number of weeks or even months in advance, and usually at some distant city. I must make my arrangements for travel and lodging, as well as for materials for the seminar, while the client must arrange the meeting room and all the other details attendant on that end of the event.

Confirmations May Be More Than Confirmations

In many cases the confirmation is more than a reminder. It is, in fact, often used to confirm a verbal agreement and actually acts as a contract between the parties, confirming not only the general agreement, but specifying the terms of the agreement. Even so, the client usually reminds me a few days before the event that we have the appointment.

Between the two extremes are many cases where the appointment does not involve special commitments, other than perhaps travel, but is still set for some time in the future. It is a usual practice to verify the appointment in writing to ensure that the two parties do understand each other and have agreed to the appointment: Verbal agreements are not always true understandings (hence the need for absolute specificity and clarity in written confirmations), and it is always a good idea to remind each other of the appointment. It is not unheard of for someone to travel many miles only to find the other party not there, having apparently completely forgotten the appointment. (I can recall being forced to waste an entire day idling in a small town in Wisconsin because of just such a lapse of memory on the part of the executive I had traveled to see.)

Important although it is to remind each other of the appointment, frequently the confirming letter has at least one other purpose, such as furnishing each other information relevant to the matter with which the appointment is confirmed.

Who Writes the Letter of Confirmation?

Either party may write a letter of confirmation, and in many cases the appointment is made with a telephone call and then followed up by an exchange of letters, as some of the models will demonstrate. However, it is customary for the letter of confirmation to be written by the party who sought or asked for the appointment.

Note that the divisions made among the classes of correspondence are somewhat arbitrary, for the lines are never that sharp. The example of writing to confirm and document an agreement to conduct a seminar or workshop, for example, is a confirmation of an appointment, written by the client. At the same time, when the seller writes it is to acknowledge the order to present the workshop, as well as to confirm the appointment.

Very much the same situation would prevail in the case of a consultant retained by a client. The client might write to confirm the agreement, but the consultant would normally write to acknowledge the order for his or her services, and would confirm the dates and understanding at the same time.

The model letters that follow will illustrate the points made in these preceding paragraphs.

Dear Ms. Radcliff:

This will confirm our telephone conversation and agreement of yesterday concerning the two-day workshop you have agreed to conduct for our staff on 25–26 March 1987. The terms include payment to you of a fee of $750 plus expenses for travel, meals, and lodging. (A copy of our travel regulations is enclosed.)

The workshop will be conducted at the Footsore Rest Motel in Daly City, Missouri, and the sessions will run from 9 A.M. to 4 P.M. each day, with two coffee breaks and an hour for lunch.

If you have handout materials you wish duplicated please send us a master set not less than three weeks before the session is to be held. Please advise, also, whether you require an overhead projector, blackboard, or other presentation devices.

I have enclosed literature describing our organization, as I promised.

Please sign and return one copy of this letter to confirm your agreement with its terms, and retain the copy I have signed for your own files.

Cordially,

Dear Dr. Wharton:

Thank you for the confidence you have expressed in me in retaining me to aid you in designing an organizational development plan. I am returning a signed copy of the Letter of Agreement and will be in your offices at 8:30 A.M. on Monday the 22nd of this month for the kickoff meeting and initial discussion session.

As you requested, I will bring along those resource materials I have from earlier projects, which we discussed in our earlier conversation at the Training '86 Conference.

I look forward to working with you in this interesting project and making a contribution to the Forward Corporation.

Sincerely,

Dear Mrs. Mortimer:

This is to confirm our agreement to meet on September 14 in our offices at 2 P.M. to discuss our concerns regarding the schedule slippage in the ANDES project you are conducting for us and to plan a recovery program.

Please feel free to bring along any materials or other personnel you feel necessary to make this meeting productive. To help discuss technical aspects of our requirements Dr. William McHenry and Mrs. Madeline Corson, both of our own staff, will be present.

I appreciate your cooperation in this matter, and I look forward to renewing our acquaintanceship.

Best wishes,

Dear Miss Hunsaker:

This letter is to confirm your registration for the April Conference on Health Care Concerns. The Conference will be held in the Gold Room of the Metropole Hotel in Dryport, Virginia, starting at 9 A.M. and will last until 5 P.M., with one hour for lunch. (Lunch will be served at the Conference.)

The Conference will be followed by a cocktail party and awards dinner. I hope that you will be able to remain with us for this event also.

Please feel free to call if there are any questions I have left unanswered.

Sincerely,

REQUESTS FOR QUOTATIONS, BIDS, AND PROPOSALS

Although requests for quotations, bids, and proposals are all solicitations for vendor or contractor support and all are used for competitive procurement, each has a slightly different purpose and is suitable for slightly different situations and applications than are the others. Following are brief discussions to make these differences clear and guide you in deciding which type of solicitation you need for your own circumstances.

Requests for Quotations

A request for quotation (often referred to as RFQ) is the simplest possible form of solicitation. It describes what the requestor wants quotations on, with any relevant terms and conditions, such as delivery schedules and warranties. So physically the RFQ includes a letter from the requestor and an item description (specification) or work statement. (In some cases, where the requestor does a great deal of buying and asks for quotations frequently, the RFQ may be a standard form.)

The item description or work statement (the latter if the request is for services rather than some product) is important, of course. The vendor must know precisely what he or she is asked to quote. For this reason RFQs are normally confined to standard commodities or, at least, to that which can be specified precisely.

An RFQ is normally not binding on either party. Although normally the idea behind an RFQ is to find the least expensive source, the requestor does not guarantee to make the purchase from the lowest bidder (or to make the purchase at all), and the quoter does not guarantee that the prices quoted will be firm for any period of time—that is, each party leaves his or her options completely open.

Normally, a requestor issues an RFQ under either of two circumstances: (1) when he or she is completely uncertain of what something is likely to cost and is simply seeking information without having yet made a firm decision to buy or (2) when the firm decision to buy is made, and the only question remaining is to whom to issue the purchase order. Generally, an RFQ is used when the purchase is not large enough to merit a formal contract. The requestor often confirms by telephone the quotation and availability of what has been quoted, and then sends out the purchase order.

Requests for Bids

Bids are requested under somewhat the same conditions as quotations in that the request must include an item description/specification or work statement of what is to be bid on, but requests for bids are usually issued with the firm intention of buying, usually from the lowest bidder. As in the case of the RFQ, a bid solicitation may include a standard form designed for that purpose.

Bids are usually sealed, to be opened at a specific time and place, especially when a public agency of some sort issues them, to ensure that no bid is opened—that is, no bid amounts are revealed—before the closing date and time. As in the case of quotations, the award may be made by purchase order or by formal contract. In some cases the form on which the bid is made must be signed by the bidder and is, in fact, a contract or becomes one when the requestor signs the form. That is, bids are usually firm and binding offers, within whatever terms are established, and bidders are usually reminded that such is the case and therefore cautioned to verify all prices, terms, and conditions before submitting their bids.

Requests for Proposals

Requests for proposals (RFPs) are made under circumstances where costs are not the only nor necessarily the most important concern, and the requestor wishes to keep his or her options open in selecting an awardee or selecting candidates with whom to conduct negotiations in quest of an agreement. Nevertheless, proposals are used in competitive situations, for the principal competition is a technical or quality competition, and price is a competitive factor, second to the technical or quality factor.

This is a condition most often found where what is sought is not a standard commodity and it is not possible—or, at least, not practicable—to describe or specify the item (service) with any great degree of accuracy or precision. Probably the most common case is that in which the requestor wants to buy custom services and/or custom-designed products. And usually those are cases where the customer is not at all expert or knowledgeable in relevant matters, but must rely on the expert knowledge and skills of the supplier. Typical cases would involve soliciting the services and/or custom-designed products of an architect, interior designer, professional engineer, consultant, training specialist, or other specialist. (Of course, the term *specialist* is not confined to individuals but includes organizations offering individual and specialized services or custom-designed products.)

Typically, in issuing an RFP, the requestor includes a detailed statement of work or specification, describing the problems, needs, symptoms, and requirements, as appropriate, and invites the proposer to describe his or her plan of attack, qualifications, and terms. The requestor then analyzes the proposals and selects an awardee or conducts negotiations in quest of an agreement and final award. Usually a formal contract results if the project is a large one and a great deal of money is involved, but it is possible also to use purchase orders to make the purchase from the successful proposer.

Letters of Request

For major procurements and especially where the purchaser is a frequent issuer of solicitations there is usually a well-organized procurement system, replete with standard forms and practices. However, where the issuance of a request for quotation, bid, or proposal is an occasional event, rather than a frequent one, the requestor generally relies on a simple letter to make the request, rather than a large and formal document and standard forms. It is for this case that model letters are offered here. However, there are some problems that should be discussed briefly, problems that will be recognized in some of the model letters.

One common problem is that of deciding who is the low bidder when the circumstances of the quotation, bid, or proposal do not permit direct translation of the prices into the lowest-bid determination. That is frequently the case when the request calls for a number of items or services, but is of the indefinite-quantity type (i.e., the requestor cannot predict with any certainty how many of each item will be purchased).

In such cases the customer generally hypothesizes the total purchase or a typical purchase and prices it according to the figures supplied by each bidder or proposer. In this way a lowest bidder is established, at least hypothetically.

Another problem is that of giving proposers some guidance in preparing their proposals so that it is possible to determine which are most favorable, all factors considered—that is, which factors are considered most important. Many requestors therefore suggest criteria by which proposals will be evaluated.

The following letters are suggested as models to be adapted to your occasional needs for quotations, bids, and/or proposals.

Ref: Request for Quotation

Dear Dr. Morrison:

You are invited to quote your best prices on the following items:

One (1) Leading Edge Model D desktop computer sans software.
One (1) Silver Reed EXP–550 printer with tractor feed.
One (1) Hayes Smartmodem model 1200 modem.

Quotation is wanted on all items. However, you may quote on any and/or you may quote on equivalent items. In the latter case, please furnish complete descriptions of equivalent items demonstrating that equivalency completely.
Response to this request is needed by August 15th.

Sincerely,

Ref: Request for Quotation

Dear Mr. Wooster:

We are in need of quotations on 25,000 each DS/DD 5–1/4-inch floppy disks, soft sectored and unformatted, with Tyvek sleeves, labels, and write-protect tabs. They may be packaged in bulk or in standard packages of 10 each, and they may be a recognized "brand name" or they may be generic, but they must have a standard lifetime guarantee and packaging details must be specified clearly.

Your quotation is invited, but must reach us by the 22nd of this month. This quotation is not binding on either party, but we anticipate issuing a purchase order for this item before the end of this month.

I thank you for your assistance and cooperation.

Very truly yours,

Ref: Invitation for Bids

Dear Ms. Marvin:

We invite your bid for the following items, a contract for which will be awarded to the lowest qualified bidder.

Consecutive number stamp machine, per enclosed sketch and specifications, in quantity:	150 each
Spare parts:	
Springs	50 each
Ink pads	50 each
Handles	25 each
Supplies:	
Ink, black	10 quarts
Ink, red	20 quarts

Bids are to be sealed, and will be opened at the closing date and time of February 25, 1987, 2:30 P.M. in our own purchasing office.

Prices furnished are to include prompt-payment discounts for payment in not less than 20 days from date invoice is received. Discounts for lesser periods will not be considered in evaluations.

Only bids for all items listed will be accepted. Exceptions to the qualifications and terms, stated elsewhere in attachments, will not be accepted or considered.

> continued
> Award is to be made to the lowest qualified bidder. The lowest quali-
> fied bidder is defined as the bidder who meets all terms and require-
> ments of this procurement and offers the lowest total price.
> Your response to this solicitation is appreciated.
>
> Sincerely,

Ref: Invitation for Bid

Dear Mr. Blacker:

You are invited to submit your best prices for the following items:

Consecutive number stamp, per enclosed sketch
and specifications, in quantity: 150 each

Please bid also your prices for each of the following items on a quan-
tity indefinite basis:
Spare parts:
    Springs, each
    Ink pads, each
    Handles, each
Supplies:
    Ink, black, per quart
    Ink, red, per quart

Bids are to be sealed, and will be opened at the closing date and time
of February 25, 1987, 2:30 P.M.
Prices furnished are to include prompt-payment discounts for payment in not less than 20 days from date invoice is received. Discounts
for lesser periods will not be considered in evaluations.
Only bids for all items listed will be accepted. Exceptions to the
qualifications and terms, stated elsewhere in attachments, will not be
accepted or considered.
Award is to be made to the lowest qualified bidder, which is defined
as the bidder who meets all terms and requirements of this procurement and offers the lowest price for our hypothetical (estimated) procurement quantities.
Your response to this solicitation is appreciated.

Sincerely,

Ref: Request for Proposal

Dear Mr. Carter:

Cement Casting Corporation produces casting molds and forming dies using a new and inexpensive process. These new forms and dies are the equal of hardened steel physically, but are far less costly because they can be cast or pressed, using our special hardened cement and cement with metal aggregate compound.

We wish to have a contractor to make a survey of the potential U.S. market over the next decade for (1) forms and casting dies manufactured by us, using our patented materials and methods and (2) the potential market for licensing others to use our system. The system, materials, methodology, and other pertinent facts are summarized in the accompanying specification sheet.

We invite proposals for carrying out a national survey, as described and specified. Proposals must describe survey plans and methods in sufficient detail to enable Cement Casting Corporation to evaluate practicality of approach and probability of accuracy in results obtained. Proposals must also describe the proposer's resources and experience in market research and estimate costs, with relevant rationale.

Offers must be firm for at least 60 days from date of proposal, and proposals must reach this office not later than 4 P.M., September 17, 1987, to be considered. Award will be made within 60 days following.

Please address any questions to the undersigned.

Sincerely,

Ref: Request for Proposal

Dear Mrs. Harmon:

The National Development Corporation is seeking a consultant to automate our existing office system. To be included in the automation are our complete payroll and accounting system, inventory control, and purchasing activities. These are all described in the accompanying description, listing such items as number of employees, average number of payables and receivables processed each month, size and number of items carried in inventory, along with typical inventory traffic and average number of purchase orders and contracts issued each month. The description lists also all existing related equipment, such

> continued
> as computers and their peripheral items, and the current use made of these.
>
> Please include in your proposal a detailed description of your plan, experience, resources, and estimated costs, including your projection of capital items (e.g., computers) required for the project and to provide a capability for ready expansion in the future, contemplating an average 5 percent annual growth.
>
> Offers are to be firm for not less than 90 days, and proposals must be received by close of business October 15, 1987.
>
> All questions are to be addressed to this office.
>
> Sincerely,

RESPONSES TO COMPLAINTS

Unfortunately, complaints, written and oral, are a fact of life for all organizations, and they must be responded to, even when they appear to be the complaints of cranks. Failure to respond to complaints or, even worse, responding to complaints improperly and injudiciously can have disastrous consequences for the organization and especially for the individual responsible for an unwise response.

There are a few basic ideas that should be applied to all or nearly all responses to complaints:

Thank the writer for bringing the problem to your attention, stating your regret (i.e., apologizing) that the complaint was made necessary.

Explain why (if you know) the problem occurred, and what you plan to do about it. If you do not know, state that you are investigating the matter and will report back as soon as you have uncovered all the facts. Then, in your follow-up letter, explain what you plan to do to adjust the matter, if an adjustment is necessary, and/or what you plan to do to prevent a recurrence.

If you do not have enough information, explain that and ask the writer to furnish the additional information required.

It is important that you respond promptly, even if it means that you will have to respond a second time, after you have done whatever you have to do. Simply responding promptly and courteously, with an apology, is often itself enough to pacify the other party. (Sometimes the other party merely wishes you to be made aware of the complaint and does not expect any direct action.)

There are occasions when you cannot do what the writer wishes. However, if you have to reject the complaint as unjustified, do so diplomatically and without counterattacking.

Illustrations of these points are made in the following models.

Dear Mr. Colodny:

I sincerely regret our failure to ship all the necessary hardware with the knockdown bookcase you ordered from us two weeks ago. We of course do not manufacture the item ourselves, but we did fail to inspect the kit before we shipped it, as we should have. We have taken steps to ensure that this does not happen again.

A full hardware package was shipped to you by express service yesterday, and will probably arrive before this letter.

Thank you for bringing this to our attention and please accept our apologies for this oversight on our part.

Sincerely,

Dear Mrs. Gulden:

Thank you for writing to let us know about your problem in connection with purchasing a TV in one of our dealer outlets. If the TV was defective we certainly will repair it or make other suitable arrangements to adjust the matter to your satisfaction.

Unfortunately, we have not received a warranty card on this set, and I cannot do much until I know who the dealer was from whom you purchased the receiver. It would help also to know the model number and, if possible, the name of the salesperson from whom you bought the set.

As soon as I get that information I will be in touch with that dealer and get back to you promptly. I am sure that we can resolve this matter satisfactorily.

Please accept our apologies for any inconvenience this causes you.

Very truly yours,

Dear Mr. Warden:

After receiving your letter objecting to our bill of $41.95 for the slacks you purchased in our men's wear department I went over the bill with our billing department. It is true enough, as you stated, that the slacks were on sale for $39.95, but there was a $2.00 sales tax added.

continued

Unfortunately, the laws of this state forbid our including sales tax in the advertised price. We are required by law to collect sales tax separately and on the advertised price.

I regret the misunderstanding and hope that we shall continue to be favored with your patronage. Thank you for giving us the opportunity to explain this matter.

Sincerely,

Dear Miss Hanford:

You are entirely correct in pointing out that our carpet cleaners did not get all the stains out of your carpet, and I quite understand your unhappiness over this. I checked with our service department immediately after receiving your letter and talked to the technicians who cleaned your carpet.

They told me that the stains they could not remove appeared to have been made by an indelible substance, such as ink, and that they informed you of that. They told me, also, that they had managed to get all other stains out of the carpet and were able to make the ink stains much lighter. It is their belief, as I understand they told you, that there is a good chance that with successive cleanings the stains will get lighter and lighter.

I quite agree with you that they should have made a closer inspection of your carpet and determined whether all the stains could be removed before beginning work. Because of that I have had your account credited with $45, one half the original $90 price for which you were billed, and a new invoice will be sent out for $45, voiding the original invoice.

I apologize for any inconvenience we have caused you, and trust that you will find this a satisfactory settlement.

Very truly yours,

ACKNOWLEDGMENT OF QUOTATIONS, BIDS, AND PROPOSAL REQUESTS

It is both a courtesy and a good marketing practice to respond to all invitations or requests to compete for orders, even those to which you will not respond with a quotation, bid, or proposal. Ordinarily, when you will be submitting a quotation, bid, or proposal in the near future, that submittal is itself response enough. However, if the requested date is several months away, the customer may very well want to have some idea of how many of those invited will respond so that he or she may seek other sources, if it is necessary to do so to have adequate competition. But in all cases customers appreciate your affirming your interest and intention to compete for the order.

On the other hand, if you fail to make any response at all, ignoring the invitation, the customer may very well assume that you are not interested in remaining on the bidders list and simply drop your name from the list of prospective suppliers, so that you will not be invited again to participate.

Ergo, it is wise in both these cases to respond. Following are models suggesting responses to suit both situations.

Dear Mr. Margate:

Thank you for your invitation to submit our proposal and compete for the "California Project" you have described in your RFP. No. ADP-33-87. We have studied your RFP briefly and believe that we have a great deal to offer you in satisfying the needs you have described. It is therefore our intention to respond to your request with a formal proposal.

We hope to be of service to you in this project, and we look forward most enthusiastically to presenting our plans for providing the support you seek.

Sincerely,

Dear Mr. Whiteside:

With reference to your Request for Quotation No. H-11A-2-1, please be advised that we are currently running behind schedule in producing cadmium plated screw fasteners and consequently would be unable to meet your stipulated delivery schedule. We therefore regretfully advise you that we are unable to submit an earnest quotation for this item.

This of course does not mean that we are not most desirous of doing further business with your firm. We regard you as a valued customer, and I am sincerely sorry that circumstances prevent us from responding more positively to your present need. However, we do wish to remain on your bidders list for future procurements, in which we expect to participate.

Thank you for your attention to this.

Most sincerely,

LETTERS OF COMPLAINT

The guidelines for writing letters of complaint are rather similar to those suggested for responding to letters making complaints. You must be quite clear and specific about what your complaint is and what you seek. Provide as much detail as possible. The more information you provide the easier it is for the other party to make a proper response. And remember that by far the most effective approach, usually, is a most civilized and courteous one, written on the assumption that the other party is honorable and courteous, and will respond promptly and properly. Most of the time the other party will respond in a manner that reflects the tone of your own letter. Only if and when the other party disappoints you and gives you reason to believe that you will not get this kind of treatment should you consider sending an "angry letter" or "getting tough" about the matter.

If you do happen to be friendly with or be an old acquaintance of the party you are addressing you may be informal, even in these circumstances. In fact, that is likely to be an advantage in most cases. Still, you must be clear about your purpose and desires, no matter how friendly the terms of your relationship. It is necessary to be businesslike in all cases, if you wish your letter to be taken seriously.

As in all writing, you need to think out your problem and wants first, before you begin to actually write. If you are to be clear and specific about what your complaint is and what you want done about it, you must first decide in advance, before you compose the letter, precisely what it is that you want to accomplish: Do you simply want to vent anger? Be compensated? Negotiate a settlement? Get a refund? Have your account credited? Clear up a chronic problem?

Consider then the practicality of what you ask. If you have a computer in your office that has malfunctioned now, after a year's usage, is it reasonable to expect the dealer or manufacturer to take it back and give you a new computer? Obviously, this is not going to happen. On the other hand, even though the computer may now be out of warranty, you may be able to persuade the dealer to service it and correct the trouble without charge to you, or at least a charge only for the parts needed. That would be a reasonable request, and even if the dealer did not agree with you, you might very well be able to negotiate repair service at some reduced price.

This is quite important, for an unreasonable demand easily escalates into anger and polarizes positions so that any settlement becomes difficult to achieve.

Here are a few models to illustrate these points:

Dear George:

I don't know what has happened to your quality control, but we have had a sharp increase in our incoming-inspection rejections of your

continued

circuit boards. From less than the usual 1 percent or less it has gone up to nearly 10 percent.

I know that you will make good on these and ship replacement boards without charge, George, but this is rapidly becoming a problem for you, as well as for us. Our engineering people are beginning to question whether or not we should consider seeking another supplier to fabricate our boards.

To overcome this, George, you need to do two things: First and foremost, take immediate steps to get the rejection rate down to where it was; second, send me a formal letter assuring me that you will get the problem under control immediately and explaining what immediate measures you are taking (greater production-line sampling, improved final inspection, or whatever) to show that you really mean business.

I know that you will get hold of this immediately, and we will continue to do business, as we always have.

All the best,

Dear Mr. Wharton:

The recent shipment of Mr. FormFit jeans you sent was less than one half the quantity we ordered, so that we ran out of stock long before the end of the special sale we held. We managed to persuade only a few of our customers to accept a rain check and wait for a fresh shipment to come in, so we lost many sales. Unfortunately the rest of our original order never arrived, even after I called about it and was promised it would be sent out promptly, so the entire sale was considerably less than the success it would have been if we had had ample stock on hand.

We still want the rest of our original order but, frankly, we are reluctant now to announce another special sale with success depending on your faithfulness in shipping. Yet, it is a problem of another kind to wait until we have the stock on hand before planning the sale.

Therefore, I would like to have definite word about the rest of this shipment and some explanation of what went wrong, in the hope that we can prevent such problems in the future. I want you also to advise me of what assurance we have that we shall not have a repetition of this.

Sincerely,

Dear Mrs. Stone:

Although we have paid your invoices for the three office temporaries you supplied last week, I must advise you that the services of two of them were not truly satisfactory, and we kept them working for the entire week, even on overtime, because our workload was so great and our schedule so tight that we could not afford even a brief interruption.

More specifically, Mrs. Smythe and Miss Washington were very slow typists and showed no understanding of filing systems at all, although they had been represented to be experienced office workers and skilled typists.

Nothing can be done about this now, but I do want you to know that if there is another such occurrence on the next occasion we call on you for assistance, we will be forced to turn elsewhere for these services.

Very truly yours,

Dear Mr. Miller:

Unfortunately the typewriter repairs you performed for us recently have proved unsatisfactory. And when your technician returned, after we called to report that the problems were not resolved, the additional work also failed to correct the problem. We then were forced to call on another typewriter repair service, who then managed to get our machines working properly again.

I have therefore held up payment of your bills for the original service calls and the subsequent one, and want them adjusted. You have billed us $178.90 for your work, and we have had to pay $46.35 to the second repair service to get our typewriters working again. I will not challenge the amount of your bill or question whether it is a just one, but I do want an adjustment in your bill to compensate us for that extra cost, which we should not have experienced. That is, I want your bill reduced by $46.35.

I request that you send us either a credit memorandum for $46.35 or an amended invoice in the amount $132.55, either of which will adjust this.

Sincerely,

OTHER, MISCELLANEOUS CORRESPONDENCE

Most busy offices conduct a great deal of correspondence, falling into all the classes enumerated here, but also in many others. There are truly an almost infinite number of cases, far too numerous to even list, much less typify with individual models. However, here are some of the miscellaneous and assorted kinds of letters (other than those to be covered in succeeding chapters of this book) that you may receive or have occasion to write:

Internal letters (memoranda).
Letters of reference.
Requests for contributions.
Letters of condolence.
Confirmation of understanding.
Letters of introduction.
General thank you letters.
Congratulatory letters.

Chapter 3

Sales Correspondence

WHAT IS SALES CORRESPONDENCE?

Both this and the next chapter are devoted to the writing of sales materials of various kinds. This is, of course, one of the main writing activities in many organizations, even in those which are nonprofit organizations: A great many nonprofit organizations engage in activities that can be characterized only as marketing and sales efforts. They include, for example, such efforts as recruitment of new members, fund raising, soliciting votes, and recruiting volunteer workers.

The subject is enormous—many large books have been written on the subject without exhausting it—and it would therefore be unwieldy to attempt to handle in a single chapter here, on even a somewhat summary basis. Therefore I have divided it into two chapters, of which this is the first, dealing with what I choose to refer to as sales correspondence. But that requires some definition:

Sales correspondence, as defined here, is correspondence sent out in quest of sales. Both words used to identify this category are significant, for the reference is confined to that which may be considered correspondence, but only to correspondence connected directly with a sales effort.

The distinctions as to what is identified as sales correspondence and therefore included here and what is properly classified in one of the other categories are admittedly arbitrary. They reflect my own opinions and prejudices so that some letters that relate more or less directly to sales may be found elsewhere in these pages. These arbitrary standards account, for example, for the fact that *packages* of sales material that include sales letters (i.e., direct-mail packages) are covered in the next chapter, rather than in this one. They account also for having informal (letter) proposals being covered here, whereas the subject of formal proposals is covered in the next chapter.

Thus this chapter includes sales letters, bids and quotations, letter proposals, and sundry related items. And it includes such materials for all those purposes noted earlier—sales, recruitment of members, recruitment of volunteer workers, solicitation of votes, fund raising, and related purposes.

As in the earlier chapters, this one will be divided into sections for each of these classes, and each section will have some introductory text to serve as a tutorial, usually a brief one, however, not intended to be nor represented as being exhaustive or comprehensive.

SALES LETTERS

Some of the model letters illustrating suggested modes of response to inquiries might fairly be called sales letters, since they are intended to solicit or at least encourage sales, while responding to inquiries. However, here we are going to be concerned with letters that are sent out in some quantity—to many prospects, who may or may not already be established customers—as preprinted form letters, a further example of the arbitrary nature of the classifications used. (In the case of computer-supported efforts, however, such letters may be individually addressed and individually typed, so that they do not appear to be printed form letters.)

All letters, including sales letters, must be easy to read, have specific objectives, and state specific facts in the clearest terms possible, as well as following a number of other considerations expressed elsewhere in these pages. But aside from that sales letters must be based on and comply with certain sales principles if they are to have even a faint chance of succeeding in their purpose. Ergo, the necessity to digress here into a brief discussion of those principles.

A Few Sales Principles

The first and foremost principle of all selling efforts is that of showing the customer why it is in his or her interest to listen to and consider your offer—sales presentations are or should be *offers*—and, finally, to accept your offer (buy). (Actually, the addressee is, at this point, still a prospect and not yet a customer, but for convenience I will refer to the prospect as the "customer.")

This focus on the customer's self-interest is often referred to as "selling benefits." It is, in fact, an explanation of what you *offer* to *do* for the cutomer. Some typical benefits customers seek are saving money, making money, being more attractive, being more secure, getting a better job, losing weight, having more prestige and status, having life easier, being admired by others, being loved, having someone to love, belonging (feeling part of something and/or being accepted), avoiding disasters, and many similar *emotional* desires.

Note that term *emotional*, for it is important in this context. You may be sure that without exception, or with only the rarest exceptions, people are motivated to buy by emotional drives, not rational ones. Reason does enter the picture to support the buying decision, but only as a support of the decision already made emotionally. The customer needs to be able to rationalize the decision; hence the necessity for rationale.

The principle is illustrated every day in successful advertising. For minor purchases, where the risk of monetary loss is insignificant because the money involved is insignificant, the advertiser rarely bothers to introduce much of a rationale, but relies entirely on the emotional motivation. Beer commercials are a good example. They don't really sell beer, of course, and they certainly waste little or no time discussing quality. Instead they focus entirely on selling good times—fun—which allegedly results from buying and drinking their product. It is that which is the (alleged) benefit.

On the other hand, the commercial that sells homes or automobiles introduces the selling argument with eye and prestige appeal, and perhaps other emotional arguments, but then goes to discussions of value, quality, and other rational arguments. It is an obvious recognition of the fact that emotional appeal is not enough to sell items of such magnitude. In fact, it also recognizes that the commercial or sales letter is—can be—only the opening gun in the campaign to win the sale.

For that latter reason, in such big-tag items as these the commercial does not really attempt to make the sale per se, for it cannot do so. The commerical or sales letter cannot directly produce an order or sales contract to buy a home or automobile, of course. What commercials and sales letters can and do attempt to do is to create *leads*—persuade viewers to visit model homes and sales offices or showrooms, where more serious and directed personal sales efforts can be made by salespeople. It is, in fact, selling only the value and desirability of a visit to the model or showroom, nothing more.

It is important that you know which goal (objective of your sales letter) you are in pursuit of—which goal you *should be* in pursuit of. In general, recognizing that you can't sell big-tag items with a sales letter, your sales letter should pursue the goal of generating sales leads in such cases. But the reverse is also true.

There is no convenient rule for discriminating the big-tag item from the small-tag one, except in a gross measure. It is fairly obvious that few customers are going to call and order an item costing many hundreds of dollars as the direct result of a simple sales letter. It is also obvious that you can't afford to waste time and postage generating leads for a $10 item. But where the line falls between these extremes you must judge for yourself.

One word of caution here: Don't go overboard in being too conservative about what can or cannot be sold directly via a sales letter, especially one accompanied by a suitable brochure: Many sales running to hundreds of dollars each *are* consummated as the result of a single sales letter under certain circumstances. And one of these circumstances is the status of the addressee. What is a big-tag item to an average householder may be a small purchase to a business executive. The term "big tag" is obviously a subjective one and one that can be defined in only relative terms.

Summation of Sales Principles

It is beyond the scope of this work to probe all the parameters of sales and marketing principles, despite the need to cover them at least in basic terms. But before going on to the presentation of models that will illustrate the principles covered here, it is useful to summarize the principles in terms of the two basic elements of sales, the promise and the proof.

The promise is the benefit per se—the *offer*. It is the promise to make the customer wealthier, more secure, more beautiful, thinner, and so forth.

The proof (or evidence, if you prefer that term) is the rationale that demonstrates the logic of the promise—*proves*. However, it is not subject to law court "rules of evidence" or even scientific standards for evidence, but is *whatever the reader will accept as evidence.*

That latter is important, for nothing is really important in sales presentations except the *customer's perception*. Only the customer's perception of fact—*truth*—matters materially in the sales equation.

So we must concern ourselves, finally, with those two factors: promise and proof. Offer the properly motivating *promise*—what your offer will *do* for the customer—and the *proof,* the rationale (evidence) that you can and will keep the promise. Remember that "proof" or "evidence" is whatever the customer will *accept* as proof or evidence.

Be careful you don't dilute the impact of your letter by promising the moon. The sales appeal ought to be built around one central feature, one major benefit that you believe will have wide appeal and that you believe you can back up—prove—effectively. Then concentrate on proving that promise a valid one: Far better a modest promise that you can back up than a blue sky promise that you can't substantiate.

These are the principal points to remember about the content of a sales letter. But there is also the matter of style, which itself has a great deal to do with how effective a sales letter will be.

Style in a Sales Letter

Persuasion is the principal objective of a sales letter, and the effort to be persuasive is often an uphill battle because it is often asking the party addressed to give up something valuable and not easily parted with, such as money, time, and/or convictions. It is therefore critically important that a sales letter present information in a style that makes the information believable—that is, that the sales letter has the all-important characteristic of *credibility,* an essential in any sales presentation.

For this reason using "hype"—a colloquialism derived from the word *hyperbole* and meaning grossly inflated and exaggerated claims, with a strong suggestion of deliberate falsehood—is a bad idea. It may have worked once in sales and advertising, a long time ago, but the public has become far more knowledgeable and sophisticated today, and people tend to recognize hype for what it is, even when cleverly done. In fact, the fewer adjectives and adverbs you use, the more believable your letter will be. Stick with nouns and verbs as much as possible, avoid superlatives in particular as much as possible, and quantify as much as possible. And in quantifying use the most accurate figures possible and *do not round them off.* Making 937,000 into 1,000,000 or even "nearly one million" attacks credibility at once: The reader will believe 937,000—will not question it—but may smile indulgently at 1,000,000, assuming automatically that it is hype.

Use a direct style here, use imperatives, and personalize the message as much as possible. Not "Anyone who takes advantage of this offer can save a great deal of money," but "Take advantage of this offer now. You will save hundreds of dollars." *You* (the customer) is always a key word, the most important word in the language. Use the customer's name in the body of the letter, too, if you are using modern computer/word processing technology, which permits you to do this even in a form letter, for example: "Mrs. Smith, take advantage of this offer now. And ask for me when you come down to the store. I will be delighted to help you with your selection of style and color."

Be especially careful in writing a sales letter that it *appears* to be easy to read. Solid blocks of text and long, run-on sentences are formidable, so be at pains to make sentences short and direct, and break up your copy into frequent short paragraphs, with indentions at the beginning of each and spaces between paragraphs.

Mail order wisdom, accumulated over the years, has demonstrated that certain words and phrases used as or in connection with promises of benefit are especially effective in their appeal to readers and apparently never wear out (probably because most readers *want* to believe these words and phrases!). The following are some of those magic terms:

FREE	SALE
EXCLUSIVE	NEW
BE INDEPENDENT	DISCOUNT
BE THE ENVY OF YOUR FRIENDS	MARKED DOWN
BE THE FIRST TO OWN ONE	BE SUCCESSFUL

One final thing: Don't allow the message in your letter to end abruptly and indecisively, hanging uncertainly in the air. Tell the reader what you want him or her to do—come in for a personal demonstration, fill out the enclosed form, call and reserve one now, let us come to your home to demonstrate, or other action, as appropriate. If you fail to do this, many—probably most—customers will do nothing at all. Most people need to be urged and directed to do whatever it is that you want them to do.

Models following will be segregated into several classes. However, watch for these principles and factors as exemplified in the various models. (Additional remarks will be made, as appropriate, for different models.)

Sales Letters in Pursuit of Leads

Remember your objective here: You are not trying to make sales; you are trying to develop sales leads, which means finding those individuals who display some active interest in what you wish to offer, enough to merit follow-up sales effort on your part. Therefore, you must persuade the respondent to do something to exhibit that interest. That is, you are trying to "sell" the reader a serious interest in learning more about your offer.

Dear Mrs. Williams:

It's time once again, with summer almost here, to think about summer comfort. And I am delighted to be able to offer you a modern sunroom addition to your house at nearly 35 percent less than the normal cost of such an addition—if you act within the next 30 days.

The reason for the lower cost is simple: Labor is by far the major cost in construction today, and we have reduced labor costs by nearly one half. We do that by using modern prefabricated components. We do very little cutting and fitting on the job.

That saves time too. We can do the entire job within four weeks. First we come out and measure everything. Then we assemble all the standard components you need, and do most of whatever cutting and fitting is necessary here in our shop. Meanwhile our crew prepares the foundation to receive the components. Finally our installation crew assembles and installs the unit.

Just think: Even though this is late spring, you can have your new, breezy sun room in time for early summer. We arrange easy financing, and you'll be surprised at how little it costs.

A telephone call to the number above will bring our estimator out to show you samples and answer any questions you have. But you must act now because our busy season is just beginning, and we can accept new orders only for about 30 days.

Call today. There is no obligation, of course. Ask for me personally.

Cordially,

Trade magazines and journals are often free of charge to "qualified" applicants (i.e., those whose career activities make them valid prospects for the advertisers in the periodical). The publishers also rent the names of their subscribers, since all are reasonably good leads, having qualified earlier. That explains the following type of letter:

Dear Dr. Berger:

Enclosed is a sample copy of our bimonthly periodical, which brings readers the latest developments in medical electronics equipment for hospitals, clinics, and private offices. There is no charge to qualified physicians and medical administrators for this new service, but certain considerations mandate that we ask you to supply us certain information, plus a specific request for a complimentary subscription.

Enclosed, therefore, is a brief questionnaire and application for a cost-free subscription. We look forward to adding your name to our list of subscribers.

Very truly yours,

A light note and self-deprecation are sometimes used effectively, as in the following example, where an unhappy buyer confesses his sins and invites customers to exploit his mistakes:

Dear Mrs. Harmon:

If you have been waiting for a good sale to buy new furniture you are in luck. Goldner's Department Store is having the greatest July furniture sale in our history this year. But this is a pre-sale announcement, and you can take advantage of it immediately, even before July 1. You'll find that everything—but *everything*—is marked down 20 to 50 percent.

Why are we doing this? We are doing this because of an unfortunate overstock. Frankly, the furniture buyer (me) made a mistake. I completely overestimated the demand for a large number of new styles and new items, and our store has been stuck with them for months!

Of course the boss is on me to get rid of this stuff. (He cries every time he comes out on the showroom floor. If looks could kill. . . .) It's quality furniture by leading manufacturers, but we misjudged the popularity of some of the styles. (I think the manufacturers' salesmen were pretty good at what they do!)

No matter. What's done is done; we'll grit our teeth and take our losses. We must clear our showroom floors and warehouse for new fall stock. So take advantage of us and SAVE MONEY . . . lots of it. But hurry. You'll have to fight the crowds if you wait too long.

Today is not too soon.

With tears in my eyes,

However not everybody is selling merchandise:

Dear Miss Martineau:

   Because the National Association of Temporary Office Workers (NATOW) is about to launch a major membership drive this year we are offering new members—*for the next 30 days only*—the same initiation and annual membership fee that charter members paid three years ago, when NATOW was formed.
   What this means is greater opportunity for you, opportunity to sell your services at better rates, make more money, work under better conditions, and have a wider range of options from which to choose. Moreover, there are also many association activities that offer our members attractive career opportunities. There are, for example, the annual national convention, monthly meetings, association-sponsored seminars, formal and informal training courses, and many other events and services that will be valuable to you in achieving whatever career goals you have set for yourself. A brochure enclosed explains all the benefits of being a member of NATOW.
   Come down to our next meeting and coffee klatch as our guest—an announcement is enclosed. Listen to our speakers, meet other members—you'll probably find some of your own friends here—and judge for yourself.
   I look forward to meeting and talking with you personally.

Cordially,

Sales Letters in Pursuit of Direct Sales

The sales letters in pursuit of leads all asked the respondents to take some action which would be a next step and would establish that they were serious prospects. The respondent in such cases is asked to call, come in for a visit, request a copy of a newsletter or brochure, or otherwise display active interest. On the other hand, many sales letters are in pursuit of direct sales, and ask the respondent to order then and there. Such letters therefore ask for the order directly. Here is a model of such a letter:

Dear Miss Martineau:

   Because the National Association of Temporary Office Workers (NATOW) is about to launch a major membership drive this year we are offering new members—*for the next 30 days only*—the same initiation and annual membership fee that charter members paid three years ago, when NATOW was formed.

---

continued

What this means is greater opportunity for you, opportunity to sell your services at better rates, make more money, work under better conditions, and have a wider range of options from which to choose. Moreover, there are also many association activities that offer our members attractive career opportunities. There are, for example, the annual national convention, monthly meetings, association-sponsored seminars, formal and informal training courses, and many other events and services that will be valuable to you in achieving whatever career goals you have set for yourself. A brochure enclosed explains all the benefits of being a member of NATOW.

I am sure you won't want to miss this one-time opportunity to join NATOW at the same rate as did the charter members. A form is enclosed. Simply fill out the form and send it back in the envelope provided, along with your check or credit card number, and you will be enrolled immediately, with full benefits, when we receive your response.

I look forward to seeing you at our next regular meeting.

Cordially,

This was a case where the letter could have been addressed either way. That is not always the case, of course; frequently the nature of the sale or surrounding circumstances dictate the modus operandi. In the following models the nature of the sale all but mandates a sales letter asking for the order.

Dear Mrs. Wembley:

You are among the first to learn of a bright new magazine, *The Modern Image,* which will change your life! It is devoted to helping all women enhance our personal images to achieve greater career success and otherwise enrich our lives and life styles.

There is not and never has been any publication quite like this one. It's unique in many ways. Every month this new periodical will bring you brilliant and sparkling articles by leading authorities on makeup, dress, and other subjects. You'll read about new products, research studies, the latest styles for business and recreational use, interviews with successful women, photo layouts, and many other dazzling features.

We want you to have the first issue of this new magazine free. It's yours whether you subscribe or not. Simply fill out the form below and send it in. Send no money; you'll be billed later for the remaining 11 issues in six installments of only $3.97 each, if you decide you want the next 11 issues. If you don't like the first issue, just write "cancel" across the invoice when it arrives, and owe nothing.

continued

Either way, you get the first issue free and pay for only 11 issues if you decide to keep the new magazine. But I can hardly imagine how you would be willing to part with it, after you see the brilliant first issue. But you must act promptly. This offer is good only until the first issue appears on the newsstands.

With best wishes,

Dear Colonel Hill:

Due to a fortunate purchase we can offer you a sensational bargain: a 24 piece set of genuine BackSwing golf clubs, as illustrated in the enclosed brochure, for only—are you ready for this?—$189.90!

Why so low a price for this prized item? Simply because of a factory overstock. The Outdoor Sporting Goods Co., who manufacture this line, were unexpectedly unable to sell as many as they usually do in Europe due to a sudden change in the exchange rate, which priced them out of the European market. We persuaded them to let us have these fine golf clubs at a phenomenal discount by agreeing to buy the entire stock. And now we are passing the savings along to our valued customers.

We expect these clubs to sell rapidly at this price, so we urge you to act promptly. A telephone call will hold a set for you for a few days, but you can do better than that by mailing in the postage-paid order form enclosed or calling your order in by telephone.

Cordially,

Because these are sales letters, and no effort is made to hide that fact, they do not have to follow the normal style of business letters too strictly. Many devices may be employed to make these sales letters command attention and stand out in some way.

One refinement you can make is to use a headline, as many do. For example, any of the sales letters shown here might have been enhanced with a headline (usually preceding the salutation). Here are some typical headlines that might be used in the foregoing models or other sales letters (and these headlines are also good examples of promises):

AN UNPRECEDENTED SECOND CHANCE TO BE A CHARTER
MEMBER

A CHANCE TO JOIN FORCES WITH OTHER OFFICE
TEMPORARIES

ENJOY THE BENEFITS OF BELONGING
GENUINE BACKSWING GOLF CLUBS AT BARGAIN PRICES
OUR LOSS IS YOUR GAIN . . .

Many other devices are used to make the letter distinctive and so gain special attention. One sales letter soliciting our application for a credit card arrived today in the guise of a memorandum, 7 x 7 inches, with a header along these lines:

FIRST NATIONAL BANK   *MEMORANDUM*

TO: Ms. S. Holtz   Date: April 29, 1986
FROM: Henry Gordon
IN RE   Your Approved VISA or MasterCard
ACTION REQUIRED: Acceptance by July 1, 1986

The letter follows below this header, urging the respondent to complete the enclosed application and listing all the special benefits that distinguished this bank's credit cards.

Later in discussing direct-mail packages, we'll explore other devices used to dramatize offers or otherwise gain special attention, even in ordinary sales letters.

LETTER PROPOSALS

Unlike sales letters, letter proposals are not normally sent out in bulk and unsolicited—at least they do not normally arrive unexpectedly. Normally the respondent expects the proposal, having requested it or been advised that it was forthcoming.

Letter Proposals versus Formal Proposals

A letter proposal is different from a formal proposal only in that it is informal and that it is a letter (only a few pages long and in general correspondence style) rather than the multipage size, covers, binding, table of contents, and so forth of a formal proposal.

What this means is that the proposal is a special, one-of-a-kind letter, addressing a specific problem or need of the respondent, and making some specific offer to satisfy the need or solve the problem.

Situations Calling for Proposals

Proposals in general are used in sales or marketing situations that call for more formalized and extended efforts than a single call or sales letter, such as the following two general categories with a few examples of each:

1.   Proposing a custom service, in which the service itself is the main item being supplied, with any products incidental:

Interior decorating.
Renovation.
Engineering.
Landscaping.
Training.

2.   Designing something involving products, with the product(s) the main item and the service more or less incidental:

Designing layout and supplying fixtures for a retail establishment or
    other facility.
Recommending and supplying computer system.
Developing a special product—for example, a movie or automation de-
    vice.

When Letter Proposals Are Called For

Proposals result from customers' specific requests for proposals, as noted earlier, but they also result from the seller's (your) own initiative, usually following an initial meeting and discussion of a sale such as those listed here.

The size of the proposal is usually in some proportion to the size and/or complexity of the project to be undertaken. Obviously, the customer who is going to make a large investment will want to study the pros and cons of each proposal submitted. Hence it follows that a letter proposal will be used, normally, for relatively small and/or uncomplicated projects. At the same time, the project may call for providing all standard items, such as luncheonette equipment and fixtures, so that there is no complexity to the requirement, except perhaps for the diversity of items required, despite overall cost.

Why Customers Want Proposals

Each party has his or her own reasons for wanting the recommendations to be on paper, as a written proposal, rather than verbally or as a simple bid or quotation. A request for a bid or quotation requires that the customer knows precisely what he or she wants and is able to specify the requirement in detail. Frequently the customer cannot do that or may prefer to benefit from the supplier's experience and ask for recommendations and costs to be put on paper, subject to extended study and evaluation. (This is particularly true when the customer asks several suppliers to submit proposals to be evaluated competitively.)

Why You Should Want to Write a Proposal

If you have a good marketing instinct you have your own good reason for preferring to supply a written proposal: A proposal, formal or informal, large or small, is a *sales presentation*. It enables you, as the seller, to argue your case for what you offer, and to argue that case almost at leisure: It overcomes that disadvantage of face-to-face selling of the impatient or overly busy customer who does not permit you to make a full presentation. In a proposal you have the time to think out all your sales arguments and the opportunity to make your complete (written) presentation without interruption. Too, the customer may read and reread your presentation, studying it carefully, instead of relying on memory.

This means that you should *welcome* every opportunity to submit a proposal, even to the point of making a distinct effort to do so whenever you do not close the sale in a face-to-face (usually initial) meeting with the customer. The smart marketer takes the initiative in situations where it normally requires two or more presentations and negotiations to consummate a sale and advises the customer that he or she will follow up promptly with a written proposal. (No sales contact should ever be permitted to end without either an order or a definite next step planned and projected. For certain kinds of sales activity the proposal is the logical and best planned next step.)

What Belongs in a Letter Proposal

Obviously, a letter proposal is going to present a sales argument. However, you have one of two basic sales problems: In some cases you have to sell against typical resistance to change—that is, you must persuade the customer to try something new and different. In other cases, where the customer is definitely going to buy the service and/or product from someone, you must sell against competition. (In practice, some sales situations are hybrids or combinations of both circumstances.)

The letter proposal is contained in a letter of a few pages that should offer the entire presentation. However, it may be accompanied by a brochure, catalog sheet, specification sheet, or standard price list, where standard printed materials are appropriate. (That would be the case where you propose a design which uses standard, off-the-shelf components, for example, or where you enclose printed materials to document your claims.)

All the principles advocated for sales letters are equally appropriate here, with two basic differences: (1) The proposal is normally longer and more detailed than the mass-mailed form sales letter and (2) the proposal is based on knowing the customer's specific need or problem and so may focus sharply on that and ignore other, irrelevant considerations.

The fact that a letter proposal is relatively brief and informal does not alter the fact that it is a sales presentation and must include the same kind of information that a multivolume, major proposal for a multimillion dollar project would contain. The only differences lie in amount of detail and format considerations.

Sometimes the customer prescribes a format and requests information other than that listed here, although that is rarely the case with letter proposals and especially not when the customer has not requested the proposal. You may be quite informal, but you must nevertheless cover certain key points, preferably in the order presented here. However, proposals are custom presentations for custom work and so can never follow rigid rules, but should be in accordance with whatever were the original understandings and discussions that preceded and led to the proposal:

1. Introduction to background of submittal and to the proposer (you).
2. The customer's perceived need or problem.
3. The possible approaches and pros and cons of each.
4. The selected approach and rationale for it.
5. The specifics of what you will do and/or provide.
6. Costs.
7. Useful information about your own experience, qualifications, capabilities, references.

Specific formats and content are up to you, generally, but that apparent in the models that follow are suggested, insofar as they fit your own situation.

Models for Letter Proposals

Ref: Proposal for Development
of Office Automation Plan

Dear Mrs. Springer:

Following our original conversation regarding your need to automate your office functions and procedures, I did some extended research, as I promised I would. First, I reviewed your specific situation and requirements, which are basically to do that which will solve your cash flow problems.

continued

After study I concluded that your problem stems largely from the lack of coordination among three major activities, all of which relate directly to the problem—each of which, in fact contributes directly to the problem—and to each other:

1. Your accounting department, where the burden of work is in payroll and payables, needs to focus attention on financial controls such as aging payable invoices to enhance cash flow but must ensure that payments are made so as to take advantage of all discounts.

2. Your purchasing function needs to relieve the bottlenecks in processing purchase orders and following up to ensure on-time deliveries. This is necessary to reduce and eliminate, if possible, all premium prices and other extraordinary costs in making purchases under emergency conditions that require accelerated deliveries.

3. Inventory management needs to reduce the unnecessary immobilization of capital tied up in excessive, slow-moving inventory and inventory that thus becomes obsolete and loses even its original value.

Each of the affected departments and offices in your organization has one or more desktop computers and is using them effectively. However, each operates in isolation from the others, despite the fact that all the functions are interrelated, especially with regard to cash flow. This typifies the problem, and the solution lies in integrating these systems via a common database with common access and shared functions.

There are two ways to address this. One is to link all the desktop computers in a LAN (local area network) so that each is a terminal/work-station in a common system. That would require extensive work, including the purchase of at least one large hard disk system for storage of an enlarged and common database and a central printer to turn out reports for management. However, because not all your desktop computers are fully compatible with each other, certain technical problems must be solved. Moreover, such a system is not easily expandable to accommodate future growth.

The alternative is to create a LAN by installing a large system, consisting of a minicomputer, which would then utilize the various desktop computers as terminals. The technical problems are much simpler to solve in this configuration and expansion to accommodate future growth is easier, and for this reason I recommend this approach.

A second and also important consideration that impels me to recommend the second course of action is that the development of the database and other software can be done far more efficiently using a central minicomputer as the "host" computer in the system. Moreover, such models as the one illustrated in an enclosure of this proposal has all the flexibility necessary to minimize the compatibility problems inherent in linking different models together in one system.

continued

These are the general considerations and preliminary conclusions drawn. I am sure that they are correct in principle, but more intensive research and study is necessary to translate these principles into specific details of a conversion plan, the logical next step.

The cost overall for the study and the plan is estimated at $18,700. The basis for this estimate is shown in the accompanying cost analysis. The result of the study will be a plan that lists equipment, procedures, software requirements, and training requirements in sufficient detail to enable you to solicit bids or quotations from suppliers, should you choose to pursue that course later.

I am enclosing several items:

- A detailed cost analysis.
- A brochure describing the minicomputer that is typical of those I believe to be most suitable.
- Preliminary ("ballpark") cost estimates for services and equipment estimated to be necessary to implement the conversion of your office system.
- References describing other, similar installations we have designed and listing individuals you may call to verify this.

I believe that you will find this by far the most practical solution to your basic problems. I am most pleased to have the opportunity to submit this proposal.

Please feel free to call on me at your convenience for answers to any questions you may have, additional information in general, and/or a complete, detailed presentation, where you and your staff may ask any questions you wish.

Very truly yours,

Dear Mr. Warrington:

Kensington Lighting & Fixtures, Inc. is pleased to respond to your invitation to propose the most suitable fluorescent lighting fixtures for your new warehouse addition. We have had the privilege of providing industrial lighting fixtures to many area firms over the past 27 years, and we are grateful for the opportunity to offer you our recommendations. We believe they will save you considerable expense, while giving you great satisfaction.

Before preparing this proposal one of our most experienced representatives visited the locations and studied your need, as you described it and as it appeared to him, while considering most carefully the conditions under which the fixtures are to be used and the costs for various alternatives.

continued

Inasmuch as the warehouse space is almost entirely clear span and is to serve for the storage of raw materials in bulk, we judged that you would need only purely industrial fixtures, without regard to cosmetic effect and the greater cost of the latter, so we confined our considerations to lower-cost easy-to-install industrial fixtures that will save you money in installation labor, as well.

The fixtures we selected and which we propose to furnish are extremely durable, easy to install, and inexpensive, with a firm one-year guarantee. We sincerely believe that this choice represents the best value for your need, although we carry many other models in our regular line.

We judged the number of fixtures you needed by counting the AC terminations provided by your electrical contractor whom, we presume, was working from approved architect's drawings. We found 32 such connection points provided, and for the amount of space represented by the new addition, we believe that 32 4-lamp fixtures (each lamp of 40 watts), with reflectors, will provide adequate illumination. It is on that basis that we propose to supply 32 such fixtures, and our cost estimate, included here as an appendix to this proposal, reflects that.

The estimate is for the fixtures ready to hang, fitted with lamps, starters, and ballasts. It does not include solderless connectors, suspension chains, or other accessory items, nor, of course does it include installation. We can, however, supply any or all of these items and installation service, should you require it. But since you asked only for a proposal to specify and estimate the fixtures, we assumed that your plant maintenance engineer will do the installation, which is, of course, quite simple.

These fixtures are available for immediate delivery. A telephone call will bring them to you, ready to hang, within 24 hours.

I include here, also, a catalog sheet that provides a photograph of the fixtures proposed with all pertinent electrical and mechanical specifications.

Please feel free to call for more information or to discuss alternatives, should you wish to consider other types of lighting fixtures.

Thank you for the opportunity to furnish this proposal. I look forward to being of service to you.

Sincerely,

Dear Mr. Hannigan:

As I promised when we discussed your problem at the recent Education and Training convention last weekend, I did some research immediately upon getting back to my office on Monday. I found that we did,

continued

indeed, handle a similar problem several years ago for the Williamson Electrical Parts Company. They, too, were suffering the drawbacks of an overly rapid expansion—a sharp drop in productivity caused by breaking in large numbers of new employees at the same time and which was also contributed to in no small measure by the tremendous burden this placed on their supervisors.

Williamson retained us to take over the training burden from their overworked supervisors, relieving the latter so they could concentrate on maintaining productivity with the older workers.

It worked out well, for Williamson was thus able to absorb the expansion much more rapidly and they got back to full productivity in about six months. (We worked closely with John Murphy, their Director of Administration, and I am sure that John would be quite willing to talk to you and confirm what I say here.)

What is needed, Mr. Hannigan, is a three-phase program. The first phase would be a formal Task Analysis to do the basic research, establish the specific parameters of the problem, and draw up the specifications for the phase-two training program. The second phase would cover the actual development of the training program and administrative plans to conduct it. And the third, final phase would be to implement the plans by actually conducting the training.

All of this would have to be done in close coordination with your staff, of course, and all plans would be subject to review and approval by whomever you appoint to oversee the program for your company.

The schedule of main events would be approximately as follows:

1.	Task Analysis and training-design development:	30 days
2.	Training program and materials development:	60 days
3.	Training implementation:	90 days
	Total:	180 days

Costs are estimated as follows:

Task Analysis:	$11,500
Training development:	33,700
Training (our staff):	27,500
Total:	$72,700

We are prepared to get under way with this important program on a week's notice, and I am prepared to quote the above schedules and costs as firm if we consummate an agreement within the next 30 days.

Of course, I welcome any questions you may have, and will be pleased to meet with you for discussion, to make a formal presentation to you, with or without your staff, and to enter into serious negotiations immediately.

Under the circumstances I think you will agree that there is nothing to be gained by waiting, and delay is likely to be, in fact, quite costly.

Thank you for the opportunity to offer this proposal. I will be most pleased to serve your fine company in this matter.

Most cordially,

LETTERS OF TRANSMITTAL

A letter of transmittal is in most cases a rather simple letter, and in some cases even a perfunctory formality. It is used in two circumstances. One is when the letter accompanies the item being transmitted. The other is when the item is being sent under separate cover or by completely other means. The following models are, for the most part, self explanatory. (An exception follows later, and will be discussed separately at that time.)

Dear Miss Lorice:

The book you ordered, *Care and Feeding of Premature Kittens,* is enclosed here, along with descriptive literature about our many other books that we hope will interest you.

Thank you for your order. It has been our pleasure to be of service to you.

Cordially,

Dear M. J. Wilkins:

Please accept my apology for the delay in shipping your new toaster. We had just received a shipment of the latest models and had not yet unpacked and inspected them. It is our policy to protect the interests of our valued customers by inspecting *every* item before shipment, and our shipping personnel are under strict orders to adhere rigidly to that policy.

Your toaster was shipped today, and should reach you within a few days.

Thank you for your patience.

In appreciation,

Dear Marty:

We sent your order out by special express today, as you requested, and you should have it very soon. Please call me collect and let me know immediately if it fails to arrive as scheduled and in good condition.

Thank you again for your order. I am glad that we were able to help.

Regards,

Dear Mrs. Jarman:

The part you need for your new blender is enclosed here in a small parts envelope, along with instructions for installing it. I apologize for the delay in getting this to you, but it had to be special-ordered because it is a part that we do not normally keep in stock.
Thank you for your patience.

Very truly,

Dear Miss Wharton:

The membership application you requested is enclosed here, with instructions for completing it. I look forward to receiving it and to welcoming you as an active member of our organization.
Please feel free to call me personally if you have any questions or there is some other way in which I can be of service to you.
Thank you for your interest and participation.

Cordially,

SPECIAL CASES

In some cases the letter of transmittal becomes a rather important letter, and can even become a fairly lengthy one. One is the case of a letter transmitting a large and important formal proposal, especially one being sent to a government agency. (The subject of formal proposals will be covered in the next chapter, where some of the comments made here will take on added significance.)

One reason for this is that the purchasing agent or contracting official will read the letter of transmittal (it is usually addressed to that individual), but will usually not read the proposal itself. Therefore the letter of transmittal becomes your sole opportunity to address your appeal to the individual responsible, at least nominally, for the purchase, and that can become a pivot point upon which the sale hinges.

But there are other cases in which there are special messages to address to the recipient. These will become self-apparent in the models that follow.

Dear Major Mandible:

Enclosed herewith is our proposal for the reverse engineering of the MystoCoder Communications Set to produce a complete set of "as built" engineering drawings. In this proposal you will find detailed plans for security, technical management, contract administration, and cost control, all matters that were addressed carefully and stressed heavily in the RFP and in the list of evaluation criteria.

Our proposal also points out our extensive experience in this kind of work, with many similar projects carried out successfully for the U.S. Army on earlier occasions over the past 20 years.

I have been authorized by our corporation to make this offer in behalf of the corporation and to assure you that it is a firm offer for a minimum of 120 days from this date.

Should you and/or the government's staff require additional information, either spontaneously or in formal presentation, we shall be pleased to comply promptly.

Sincerely,

Dear Mr. Calcutta:

A new Mackilwainey 320A punch press is being shipped to your plant tomorrow morning to replace the Hudson AG65-7 punch press which you are returning to us.

I deeply regret that the Hudson model proved to be unsatisfactory and caused you losses in production time. It is the first time we have had any problems with this machine although we have sold hundreds of them. Of course it will be returned to us at our expense and you will be invoiced for only the difference in price between the two machines as agreed.

I am sure that you will be as pleased with the new punch press as many other of our customers have been. It is of the latest design and incorporates many new features for both safety and convenience.

Thank you for your patience and cooperation in helping us adjust this matter to your satisfaction.

Sincerely and in appreciation,

BIDS AND QUOTATIONS

Those who request bids and quotations regularly in the course of their business (especially large firms and government agencies) and firms who submit bids and quotations regularly in their marketing usually have their own standard forms for making up those bids and quotations. And, in fact, a firm is not even compelled to design such forms of their own. Major printing houses and office supplies vendors can usually supply such forms, designed specifically for many kinds of industries and businesses. In the majority of cases, therefore, bids and quotations are submitted by filling out forms, rather than by composing letters. However, should you be required to submit a bid or quotation only occasionally, and you are not supplied with a standard form to execute, the following models will guide you in preparing your submittals.

These are all cases of rather simple bids or quotations, with relatively small purchases at stake, usually, and often submitted to people the bidder knows quite well. Hence, these models tend to be rather informal and straight to the point.

Dear Mr. Mandela:

Forthright Steel Rule Dies, Inc. is pleased to supply the following quotation, as you requested in your letter of last week:

1. For fabrication of cutting die, per the drawing supplied, including all labor and materials, using standard gauge steel cutting rule: $ 378.00
2. For cutting 20,000 pieces, using stock supplied by you: $1,400.00
                                                                      Total: $1,778.00

NOTE: This quotation is based on standard work-week schedules. (Estimated time six weeks.)

Thank you for inviting our quotation. It is a privilege to respond to your request, and we will be honored to handle this requirement for you.

Cordially,

Dear Henry:

I've gone over your specifications for the new office furniture you want, and I think I can meet and probably beat any price you'll get elsewhere. The following are firm prices if you can act before the end of this month:

continued
1. Three (3) formica/walnut finish engineer desks, 30 x 60 inches, with center drawers @ $217 ea: $ 651.00
2. Three (3) Hiback matching swivel chairs, cloth finish, with padded arms @ $199 ea: 597.00
3. One (1) formica/walnut finish conference table, oval, 30 x 180 inches: 455.00
                                                    Total: $1,703.00

You will find these all top-quality in their class and at least 30 percent under their market prices. All items are in stock and available immediately.

I look forward to your order and thank you for asking for our quotation.

Regards,

Dear Mrs. Mulligan:

The Dead White Paper Co. is pleased to respond to your invitation to bid for 250,000 sheets of smooth white xerographic paper, 8½ x 11 inches, 60 lb. offset, ream wrapped, packaged in 50 cases of 10 reams each, to be delivered to your warehouse within 48 hours of an order. Our bid for this order is $1,973.50, net 30 days, 1 percent 20 days, 2 percent 10 days.

We look forward to serving your needs and thank you for the opportunity to submit our bid.

Sincerely,

Dear Mr. Wister:

The Four-Star Printing Company takes pleasure in responding to your invitation to bid for the printing and binding of 5,000 copies of your Annual Report, as specified in your request. And, as you requested, our bid includes a listing of the principal items and their cost, as follows:

1. Negatives, color separations, and plates: $3,756.00
2. Printing, 3-color process, 60,000 impressions, including makereadies and press washes: 989.00
3. Folding, binding, and cutting: 223.00
                                                    Total: $4,968.00

Thank you for giving us the opportunity to offer our bid.

Sincerely,

Dear Mr. Grissom:

In response to your invitation, ModArt Art Supplies is pleased to offer the following bid:

ITEM	UNIT PRICE	EXTENSION
24 digital logic (806) templates:	$ 7.22	$ 173.28
24 MIL STD electronic symbol templates:	6.93	166.32
12 Leroy lettering sets:	149.65	1,795.80
2 Full size Excello drafting tables:	319.75	639.50
Total:		$2,774.90

All items are in stock for immediate delivery.
Terms are net 30 days, 1 percent 10 days.
We thank you for the opportunity to submit our bid.

Sincerely,

Dear Mrs. Weston:

Harper's Office Supplies, Inc. is pleased to respond to your request for quotations on word-processing supplies. Following are our quotations on the items you listed in your request.

Olivetti MS ribbons, No. 1410 in quantities of one gross:	$73.90 per dz
Silver Reed printwheels, Courier, 10 pt, No. 6422:	19.74 ea
Tractor paper, smooth perf, white, 20 lb, 3,250 sheets:	29.99 per cs

Terms are net 30. Thank you for inviting our quotation.

Sincerely,

OTHER (GENERAL) SALES CORRESPONDENCE

There arise, of course, many special situations that do not fall neatly into any of the foregoing categories of sales correspondence but nevertheless call for action that requires correspondence relating somehow to sales. Each is an individual case requiring individual judgment to handle properly. However, it is always necessary to use tact and diplomacy in business, especially when sales are involved. In fact, even when dealing with friends or other people you know quite well you must be careful in expressing yourself, perhaps even extra-careful in those cases.

A few models following are self-explanatory.

Dear Karl:

You took me by surprise this morning when you called with a question about your bill, so I could not give you an answer immediately. I am sorry it took me so long to get back to you, but it required careful searching of a computer tape to run the problem down.

The problem was simply that your check arrived a day after we had closed the books on the July special, and the computer automatically billed you for your shipment at the regular prices, instead of at the special sale price. This time the computer was perhaps a shade too efficient! Of course, the problem is that we programmed too sharp a cut-off, failing to allow for delays in delivering mail.

Our accountant is adjusting your account, and will send you a corrected invoice at the sale price. Just discard the invoice you now have.

Sorry about the problem, Karl. I hope this straightens everything out.

Regards,

Dear Mrs. Williams:

This is to acknowledge your letter concerning your unsuccessful efforts to buy a Walkie-Wander tape player last week at the special sale we ran. I truly regret that we ran out of the item so early in the special sale. We were totally unprepared for the avalanche of buyers that descended on us Saturday morning and cleaned out our entire stock in less than four hours.

You are quite right in your belief that we should have issued rain checks to those who were still trying to buy the item when we ran out. We had not prepared rain checks because we thought we had an ample supply of the Walkie-Wander sets. (In fact, it was because we had such a large supply that we ran the sale, thinking we were overstocked on the item.)

This letter will be accepted as a rain check to buy the item at the special sale price as soon as we get more of them in, which should be in the next few days.

Please accept my personal apologies for any inconvenience caused you.

Cordially,

Dear Mr. Martinez:

Your order for a Precision Portable typewriter, along with your check, has been passed on to me for response.

Unfortunately, we do not stock or handle that typewriter. We stock the Write-Right portable typewriters, which are comparable to the Precision Portable in all respects and a little less expensive, although at least equal in quality. In fact, the Write-Right has many special features not found on any other typewriter selling at its price.

I am enclosing a catalog sheet that describes the Write-Right typewriter line, with full specifications, along with prices and technical specifications.

I am also returning your check, of course. But I would be most pleased to accept your order for one of our Write-Right models, all of which are in stock and available for immediate shipment or pickup, whichever you prefer.

I look forward to being of service to you.

Most cordially,

Dear Miss Crabtree:

At this time I cannot say with any certainty when we will be again offering a special sale on TV receivers and/or videocassette recorders. The decisions to hold such sales are dependent on many factors, many of them unpredictable.

I suggest that you watch the daily newspapers, especially the Sunday edition, for announcements. However, I will place your name on our mailing list for special sale announcements.

Thank you for your inquiry. It will be our pleasure to assist you with your purchases at some future date.

Sincerely,

Chapter 4

Other Sales/Marketing Documents

WHAT ARE "OTHER" SALES/MARKETING DOCUMENTS?

Sales letters are generally used alone or with an enclosure or two to make simple announcements, prospect for leads, remind old customers that you are still in business, and make special offers. For "more serious" sales purposes—intensive or major sales campaigns and pursuit of big-tag sales, for example—other and often somewhat larger and more elaborate sales packages are prepared and used, usually falling into two broad categories not yet discussed in any detail: formal proposals and direct-mail packages.

Both can be quite substantial, even massive, in size and complexity. Formal proposals are often thick publications, veritable tomes, which can easily run to many hundreds of pages. (Proposals for major government programs, such as space satellite development and construction, have often run to many *thousands* of pages.) Direct-mail packages are usually an assortment of items, which may include any or all of the following:

Introductory sales letters of one or more pages.
Brochures or "broadsides" (oversize circulars).
Booklets or pamphlets.
Order forms.
Other "response devices."
Catalogs or catalog sheets.
Specification sheets.
Press releases.
Advertising novelties (e.g., imprinted key chains or memo pads).

All of these will receive adequate attention in this chapter. However, we will first cover one other kind of written sales material in this chapter, for which the coverage will serve well as a preliminary to introducing those other two subjects: the traditional advertising copy, such as you find in magazines and newspapers, but also in radio and TV commercials, which are a modern extension of traditional advertising, of course.

ADVERTISING COPY

I find little to distinguish the art of writing advertising from the art of marketing, at least in principle, for the principles are the same (as reviewed briefly in an earlier discussion): Be sure you have identified the right (best possible) prospects for that which you wish to sell, promise a benefit with great emotional appeal, and present "proof" or at least good evidence that you can and will deliver on the promise.

The traditional acronym used to explain these principles is AIDA, for [get] Attention, [arouse] Interest, [generate] Desire (to buy), and [ask for] Action (the order). Unfortunately, too many advertising copywriters make these basic mistakes, perhaps under the influence of the AIDA concept:

- They spend time, energy, and money on devices that may get attention, but do nothing else to further the purpose of the copy—to persuade the prospect to whatever action the copy calls for. That is, many copy writers create attention-getting headlines or other devices that are totally irrelevant.
- They go on ego trips with clever headlines or gimmicks, all too often puns, that have only vague relationships with the message, if any, and thus sabotage the copy totally!
- They write "arty" copy (which is usually overly subtle, rather than truly artistic), possibly in pursuit of the advertising industry's CLIO awards for artistic advertising (or is that in itself an anomaly?), à la Hollywood's Oscar awards.

Advertising copy does need to get attention, but it can be designed to do so without forgetting or abandoning the objective of the advertisement and without trying to be clever. Most advertising copy has a headline and a lead, and if those are well conceived and well constructed they themselves "get attention," while they arouse interest, all at the same time.

- They base the entire message on sweet reason, unaware or unbelieving of the well-established truth that people almost invariably act out of emotional motivations, not rational ones.

Thus the advertisement for a prominent motel chain that urges the reader to "turn in" at one of their motels fails to give the reader a good *reason* to patronize that chain. Nor does that too, too cute pun even get attention; it is probably lost on most readers, who are too busy to even pause over it, much less ponder and appreciate the writer's clever wit.

The copywriter for Alka-Seltzer's famous "stomach" commercials on TV (which were acclaimed for their artistry) was closer to the mark, but still too subtle, for the campaign failed: the public simply failed to perceive the connection between the stomachs and Alka-Seltzer. And when Kool cigarettes tested a commercial that illustrated a package of the product rushing forward to burst a sturdy chain, the test audience reported that the message they got was to "stop chain smoking" (hardly what the advertiser wanted!), instead of the intended "Break the hot-smoking habit!"

Subtlety has no legitimate place in advertising because people simply do not pause over, savor, or contemplate advertising texts. Advertising copy must be as simple and straightforward as possible. Don't try to captivate the reader with clever text or interesting gimmicks; do it with captivating and believable promises of desirable benefits.

The promise of benefits can be an inverse one (i.e., the prevention or avoidance of some disaster). That's how insurance, fire alarms, door locks, and many other items are sold. That's fear motivation, and it works quite well for many kinds of goods and services, because it is a benefit, and it is most definitely emotional.

Oddly enough, even those who are advertising and marketing specialists of various kinds, those who are supposedly the experts, commit the same copy-writing crimes. One advertises in a trade journal, "Your place or mine? We'd really like to get together to discuss your advertising needs." Aside from the fact that the copy writer was trying to be oh so clever, the copy fails to reveal until almost the bottom line that they wish to sell advertising services, the stress is on what the seller (advertiser) wants, when it should be on what the seller offers to do for the reader. (The reader doesn't care what the advertiser wants, of course!) Again, no reason for calling the advertiser. Compare that with "Finally, a product that promotes sales in 5 easy steps," which then goes on to explain the steps. It could be made even stronger by changing it slightly to "... promotes sales of *your* products ...," but it does address the benefits to the customer immediately, as it ought to. And compare *that* to such poor copy as, "Ford wants to be your car company," which has been imitated by others, although it was itself a failed campaign.

The Elements of an Advertisement

The proper elements of an advertisement can easily be inferred from all of this. There should be a promise of some sort, presented in the headline or at least clearly implied there and immediately followed up with either a subhead or the first line of body copy. That should be an emotional appeal. Then it should be followed up with a rationale, offering evidence to make the promise credible. And then the reader must be instructed in what to do—fill out and mail the enclosed order form, call for your free gift, stop in your favorite drug store, come in and ask for Ed Lawson, or whatever it is you want that reader to do next.

The Myths about Advertising

There are two great myths about print advertising. One is that the copy must be short or the reader will abandon it—may even be afraid to begin it because it looks foreboding. The other is that an advertisement must have lots of white space or it won't be read for that same reason—it is (allegedly) too foreboding.

There are many, many cases that prove these to be myths based on complete misunderstanding. An advertisement that ran successfully for many years in popular magazines had a simple headline that was along the lines of I WANT YOU TO HAVE THIS WHILE THERE IS STILL TIME and was followed by a full page of solid text. (It is being imitated today by another successful advertiser.) The late Joe Karbo made a not-so-small fortune selling several hundred thousand copies of his 70-page paperback book for $10 with a full-page, solid text advertisement headlined THE LAZY MAN'S WAY TO RICHES. And those are only two of many such examples.

These kinds of advertisements were and are successful because the copy captures the reader's interest almost at once with promises the reader *wishes* to believe and finds credible. The copy is *interesting* because it *motivates* the reader, and that is what makes the difference.

A single word or two can make the difference in appeal and motivation, which means a difference in sales, of course. Maxwell Sackheim, inventor of the book-of-the-month concept and often referred to as the dean of mail order advertising, relates the case of a publisher whose book *Five Acres* was not doing well and who came to Sackheim for help. After studying the matter Sackheim recommended that the title be changed to *Five Acres and Independence,* which resulted in a rapid improvement in sales of the book.

Look for some of these elements in the models offered.

A Few Models of Advertisements

The following are all brief samples of advertising copy, small but complete examples in their introduction to an offer, with a promise, some backup rationale, and an imperative exhortation (suggestion) for action. Of course, many advertisements are no longer than these, but even those that are full-page advertisements and even longer are simply expansions of these, often with large-print headlines, photographs, testimonials, and other devices. That is, these models are themselves complete, with all necessary elements, except for some necessary details of where/how to order or follow up, and could easily be developed into much larger presentations. (Later, you will see that these principles and elements are the same as those needed to prepare the other kinds of sales copy discussed in this chapter. Only the medium and physical layouts change.)

OPPORTUNITY CALLING . . .

It's time to turn your life around and end that desperate struggle for mere existence. Start your own independent rug and furniture cleaning business. You will earn more each day than you now earn each week! No special experience or education needed. You acquire all the skills you require through our complete training IN YOUR OWN HOME, with our special E-Z-SHAMPOO equipment and instructions, plus our FREE CONSULTATION service for one full year after you enter into this fantastic program. And, best of all, it is all available on easy terms.

Call or write for FREE INFORMATION TODAY, and begin to prepare for the best years of your life.

NOW YOU CAN GET YOUR HIGH SCHOOL DIPLOMA

at home in your spare time. If circumstances prevented you from finishing high school, don't despair: You don't have to struggle through the rest of your life without this important credential. You can earn that valuable diploma—*fully accredited*—through the mail! All it takes is a few hours of your time at home working with our easy materials. And it isn't a long, drawn-out ordeal either; many of our students complete the work and get their diplomas in as little as 90 days! But you must act immediately. Fill out the coupon and get it in the mail today, and get started on what may be the most important thing you have ever done for yourself.

FABULOUS CLONES OF FAMOUS PERFUMES—FREE!

In perfumes you pay more for "names" than for the manufacturer's costs. Now you can get perfumes that are *identical* in scent to the most expensive perfumes, but cost only a fraction as much. For legal reasons, we can't name those costly perfumes that our chemists have cloned, but you'll know them at once—on first sniff! (We have asked experts to test these against their costly "originals," and the experts could not tell one from the other!)

To introduce this fantastic line we have prepared an array of seven samples which are yours free, simply for stopping into your favorite department store and visiting the cosmetic counter, where you'll get the chance to see the entire line and the pleasant surprise of learning how inexpensive these marvelous new perfumes are. Just ask for the Heavenly Scents free sample kit.

FORMAL PROPOSALS

Formal proposals are the same as informal or letter proposals, at least in principle, as explained earlier (Chapter 3). The difference is in size, format, and, of course, depth and scope of details included. Where informal proposals are in letter formats, formal proposals follow the format and organization principles of manuals and books, rather than that of business correspondence. Following is a list of the items that are generally found in a formal proposal, with some general information describing or further identifying each item, as appropriate. These are summary descriptions, and more detailed ones will be offered as we proceed to examine the anatomy of a proposal more thoroughly. Moreover, although I recommend this order of presentation shown here—and the rationale for this will become clearer as you read the detailed explanations that follow—there are cases more often than occasionally where the customer has mandated a format he or she requires you to follow or where the format advocated here is inadequate for other reasons. In both cases your proposal format must therefore be expanded or modified accordingly.

The following items and summary descriptions or definitions are therefore offered as preliminary and general guides to formal proposal format:

Cover
Title of proposal (should be descriptive or definitive of requirement or program proposed), pertinent references, if any (e.g., identification of RFP or tender to which proposal is responding), name and address of proposer, and date. (Latter is optional, not always used on cover.)
Front matter
Title page: Approximately same information as cover (sometimes paper copy of cover), with date, copyright notice, and in many cases, notice of confidential or proprietary data included.

continued

Abstract: Usually called "Executive Summary" today, nominally an abstract, generally used to summarize, highlight, and dramatize major selling points.

Table of contents: List of chapters, often includes major subheadings under chapter title listed, and often includes also list of figures and list of tables.

Preface or Foreword: Optional, may be used as desired, although its purpose is often accomplished by the executive summary and/or letter of transmittal.

Response matrix: Very useful device when RFP and required proposal are multifaceted and somewhat complex. It's a matrix of RFP requirements and proposal responses, guiding the reader to all pertinent information mandated by the customer and responded to in the proposal.

Chapter 1

Objectives: (1) Establish your identity and basic credentials and (2) demonstrate adequate understanding of the requirement.

Content: Brief introductory material identifying proposer and requirement to which proposal responds, previewing what is to come in the proposal, and summarizing the requirement in its essence. (Save details for next chapter.)

Chapter 2

Objectives: (1) Present detailed discussion/analysis of requirement; (2) establish and sell your understanding of, approach to, and capabilities to do the job (demonstrate your mastery of the problem); and (3) prepare the groundwork for next chapter.

Content: Extended discussion of requirement(s), identifying your approach (in principle), explaining and arguing the merits of your approach.

Chapter 3

Objectives: (1) Show practical implementation of approach; (2) list the specifics of what you propose to contract for; and (3) demonstrate that you can carry out the plan outlined earlier.

Content: Specific proposed program or project in detail—what, when, where, how, why, by whom, and so forth.

Chapter 4

Objectives: (1) Document your resources—facilities, staff, experience, and record of accomplishment and (2) prove that you are a *reliable* contractor, as well as a capable one.

Content: Qualifications of proposer; descriptions, lists of facilities, resources, experience, references, all supporting details.

Appendixes

Objectives: (1) Supply supplemental information of interest to only a few of your readers and (2) document and validate statements made in proposal.

Content: Additional information, if and as necessary to present material that should be appended, rather than included in body of proposal, such as copies of papers, drawings, backup statistics, slides, other such material.

The models offered to exemplify and illustrate these ideas will necessarily be brief ones for the obvious reason that even a single formal proposal is generally book-size and could not be accommodated in the space available here. However, the models will illustrate the main principles presented here.

The elements of a formal proposal have been listed here in the order of their appearance in a proposal to define the sequence and recommended format. However, for purposes of discussion the sequence followed will be somewhat different, beginning with a brief discussion and samples of titles and then going to discussions and models of the text.

Proposal Titles

Many people try to create short and "catchy" titles for books and headlines for advertisements. Regardless of any merits in that idea, it is entirely unnecessary to do this when titling a proposal: It is far more important to use a title that states clearly what the proposal is about, so there is no confusion about it. For one thing, some customers issue many RFPs, and need to be able to distinguish your proposal from others without difficulty. So keep the title as short as possible but long enough to identify it clearly and easily by virtue of the text of the title, without the need to rely on reference to the customer's request number (although that should also be furnished, when known). Here, for example, are a few typical proposal titles:

A Proposal to Research Tobacco Consumption in the Middle Atlantic States

A Proposed New Method for High-Speed Inter-Computer Communications

A Proposal to Design and Develop a Standard Navy Teleprinter

A Proposal to Develop and Deliver a Training Program in Blueprint Reading

A Proposal to Design and Develop a Management Information System for the Wendex Corporate Headquarters Central Computer

Some Format Observations

Before discussing the body of the proposal and offering models, a few observations about proposal formats are in order. Although a most general format and organization have been suggested here, a great many variations are possible. Some of these are of negligible importance and have no bearing on the outcome of the competition, while others are quite important and may very well affect the outcome. This is an appropriate time to review several of these matters briefly.

Type spacing
Most proposals are typed or printed via a word processor, which is essentially the same thing, as far as physical appearance is concerned.

There appears to be a school of thought that double-spaced copy is easier to read than single-spaced copy, and so double-spacing is quite common in proposal preparation.

There is not a great body of evidence on this matter of type spacing versus readability, but there is another school of thought that inasmuch as we all learn to read single-spaced printed material, we are conditioned to and probably more comfortable with typing that is single-spaced. At the same time, probably double-spaced copy is less formidable in its appearance, although it is doubtful that that is a factor of any importance. My own preference and recommendation is single-spaced copy or, as a second-choice alternative, one-and-one-half spaces between lines, an option available on most modern typewriters and printers. (Many printers offer even more options in spacing.)

Type sizes

Typewriters have traditionally offered two type sizes, *elite* or 10 point, and *pica* or 12 point. Today, under the influence of modern typewriters and word processing computers, these have become known as *12 pitch* (12 characters to the inch) and *10 pitch* (10 characters to the inch), respectively. This can be somewhat confusing because 10-point type equals 12-pitch type and 12-point type equals 10-pitch type. Obviously, 12-point/10-pitch (pica) type is the larger size and thus perhaps easier to read. Ordinarily, both are acceptable, but smaller sizes than 10-point (elite or 12 pitch) are to be avoided.

Chapter titles, heads, and captions

Almost all proposal writers who have not been especially trained use unimaginative generic titles, heads, and captions that contribute nothing to the effectiveness of the proposal. Most will title the first chapter *Introduction,* which appears reasonable enough, since that is the purpose of that first chapter, but it contributes little or nothing. However, a properly chosen chapter title may contribute substantially to the success of the proposal by commanding special attention, dramatizing or highlighting some key point, and/or summarizing an important sales argument. For example, a small firm in pursuit of a contract with a government agency learned that the agency was not very pleased with the performance of the incumbent contractor and would welcome a proposal that would justify replacing the incumbent with a new contractor. Accordingly, the firm titled the introductory first chapter of their proposal "A New Broom," making a clear point, of course.

The same philosophy should be applied to the selection of words for all heads and captions. Again, it is desirable to make the heads and captions short, but only when it can be done without sacrificing the message and its impact. (Actually, you should write the original draft to say it all, and then study ways to make it shorter and "punchier" without losing anything.) For example, instead of "Proposed Schedule," use something such as "A Schedule Responsive to the Need" or "A Time- and Money-Saving Schedule" as a headline to introduce a discussion of scheduling or as a caption for the schedule itself. (Of course, you must justify what the headline or caption says, and it should address an objective you have good reason to believe is important to the customer.)

In sum, there should never be a title, head, subhead, or caption that does not make some direct and *positive* contribution to the sales effort represented by the proposal.

The Introductory Chapter

The first chapter should be relatively short, in relation to the overall size of the proposal, its length consisting of probably not more than 2 or 3 percent of the total number of pages. (It can be as brief as one page, in many cases.)

Here are two models of such a chapter:

CHAPTER I

A RESPONSE THAT MATCHES THE NEED

A WELL-QUALIFIED OFFERER

Hackney & Williams Software, Inc. (HWSI) are pleased to offer Martinside Manufacturing, Inc. our services to design and develop a Management Information System (MIS) to be used throughout the Martinside organization, as specified in Martinside RFP M–87–0032. HWSI has been in software development for 14 years and numbers many major corporations and government agencies among our clients, many of whom retained us to develop the same type of program, an MIS.

Details of our experience, resumes of proposed staff, client lists, and references will be found later in this proposal.

A SPECIAL INSIGHT INTO THE REQUIREMENT

The RFP describes symptoms, stating that your internal computer reports are neither timely nor otherwise helpful in detecting and correcting problems in time to forestall disastrous consequences. It speculates that an improved or perhaps new and different computer (MIS) program is required, acknowledging that this will require first a complete analysis. We believe that this is a premature conclusion since there are several other possible causes, such as poorly designed data-collection forms or weaknesses in data-collection methods, for the production of reports that do not meet the needs of Martinside. That is, the RFP and its work statement describe *symptoms,* not necessarily causes or problems per se, and it is important that we do not confuse the two. We believe, therefore, that the initial investigation to confirm the preliminary diagnosis must consider these possibilities, and we will explore and discuss these in depth in the next chapter.

CHAPTER I

A TOTAL, ONE-STOP CAPABILITY

OVER A HALF-CENTURY OF EXPERIENCE IN YOUR SERVICE
Accurate Litho, Inc. takes pleasure in responding to your request for a proposal offering our services to produce the 1987 Magnetic Media Corporation Annual Report. Accurate Litho has been producing such Annual Reports and other fine, process-color literature for leading corporations in all industries since 1911. We are completely equipped with in-house staff specialists and facilities for typesetting, illustrating, layouts, and all other functions required to take the job from edited and approved manuscript to printed and bound copies delivered to whatever destination you specify on a guaranteed schedule.

That is not a claim. It is a pledge, and details of our facilities and resources, presented later in this proposal, will demonstrate that this is not an idle pledge.
THE SPECIAL PROBLEM WE MUST SOLVE
We have studied your statement of need most carefully, and we recognize a problem which may not have been apparent to you when you issued this request. That is the problem of a schedule that will be difficult to meet: You will not have final copy ready until the 15th of next month, but require the printed and bound product by the first day of the following month, although we will have to begin with raw manuscript to be typeset, proofread, and corrected before we can even fit copy and make layouts.

We are well aware that it has become something of a bitter joke that printers always promise delivery and rarely meet the schedule. That is not the case here. We are prepared to *guarantee* delivery on schedule, and in the next chapter of this proposal we will explain how we propose to handle this project so that we can make that guarantee and live up to it.

Notes on the Models

Note one highly significant thing about these two models of a first or introductory proposal chapter: Both highlight a specific problem or important consideration of the requirement and promise a solution, without actually revealing or defining that solution in anything approaching detailed disclosure. Instead, both promise a solution to be revealed and explained in the next chapter.

That accomplishes several important things:

It creates the necessary *transition* from the first chapter to the second one. A transition or "bridge" should always be present between all elements—sentences, paragraphs, and chapters—to continue the train of thought and build the chain of logic steadily.

Even more important than that, however, is the creation and maintenance of interest. There is an element of suspense in telling some but not all of an important matter, thus motivating the reader to hurry on to the next chapter to see what the promised outcome will be. (It is also an excellent competitive strategy.) In fact, this technique actually *dramatizes* the message and thus greatly magnifies the impact of the ideas offered.

Finally, there is one more benefit: This enables the next chapter to "start off with a bang"—to have a built-in interest factor—adding to its own effect. The second chapter should take up immediately where the first chapter ended, discussing the customer's problem or requirement.

There are many things you must persuade the customer to approve and accept in any proposal, but these are the three main "sales" your words must make:

1. Your plan or approach to solving the customer's problem and satisfying the requirement.
2. Your capability for carrying out the plan successfully.
3. Your dependability as a contractor or supplier.

Although all chapters should be written with these three main factors very much in mind, the chief focus of the second chapter is that first item listed. The second chapter begins with a full discussion of the requirement, and goes on to explain your approach to satisfying it and presenting your rationale. When you have finished this chapter, you should have prepared the customer for the next chapter: This chapter should end with a transition that telegraphs or at least foreshadows the details that will follow in the next chapter.

This chapter is thus a technical discussion, normally, elaborating on your understanding of the customer's requirement and explaining your rationale for the approach you propose, while you sell yourself in the process.

Examples can be found in the following models.

CHAPTER II

A FRANK DISCUSSION OF WHAT IS IN YOUR OWN BEST INTERESTS

FROM EXPERIENCE COMES WISDOM

Our experience in developing new management information systems (MIS), as well as troubleshooting, redesigning, and reprogramming existing ones, has taught us certain truths:

1. The possibilities for system malfunctions—that is, the number of elements that are vulnerable in most systems and so may be responsible for problems—are so numerous that it is most risky to take any-

continued

thing for granted. Every possibility must be considered and investigated before drawing conclusions.

2. It is as true as ever that the output of any system, no matter how well designed, cannot be any better than the input. Therefore, as much attention must be devoted to the data-collection forms and procedures as to the system and programs overall.

3. It is often quite easy to confuse the symptoms with the problem—that is, to identify a symptom as the problem—and so pursue the wrong objective.

4. As a consequence of these factors, it is almost always necessary—or, at least, certainly the wisest procedure—to begin each major project with a front-end analysis to ensure that we have a firm identification and definition of the problem so that we can establish our objectives accurately before investing major effort.

5. A proper problem definition is itself almost invariably an arrow pointing directly to the possible solutions or, at least, to the proper approaches to solutions.

It is, of course, very much in your own interest that we do perform this analysis, and in fairness to you, as well as to our own reputation, we could not approach this project without making this clear to you.

IDENTIFYING THE MOST ECONOMICAL SOLUTION

Your work statement is based on an assumption that a new and more efficient MIS must be designed and programmed. We have no quarrel with this, of course, should it prove necessary to pursue this course. However, even in those cases where we have found faults in the MIS to be the main cause of management-reporting problems, it has not always proved to be necessary or most efficient to develop a new system. Often it has proved entirely feasible to modify (reprogram) it, salvaging much of the original work.

The advantage of this is an obvious economy in money, but there is also an economy in time, which is often an even more important consideration.

A PRACTICAL APPROACH

In consideration of these factors HWSI proposes a two-phase approach:

Phase 1: We will conduct an initial analysis, including a 60-day study of the existing system, forms, and procedures, followed by a definitive report to you. The report will include all necessary information for a second, follow-up phase.

Phase 2: A project, based on and defined in the report on the Phase 1 study, along with a proposal listing time and cost estimates for the second phase.

In this proposal, therefore, we will estimate the procedures and costs for only the Phase 1 analysis, with specific details to be presented in the next chapter, and projecting possible Phase 2 events in only the most general of terms.

CHAPTER II

MEETING AN IMPOSSIBLE SCHEDULE SUCCESSFULLY

OUR GUARANTEE TO MEET THE DATE

Fifteen days is a difficult schedule to produce printed and bound literature starting with manuscript and glossy photos that must appear as in-text illustrations. There are many steps required, including the following major ones:

1. Set type and print galleys.
2. Proof and correct galleys.
3. Make type changes and print page proofs.
4. Make negatives, including color separations.
5. Make plates.
6. Print reports.
7. Bind and trim.

There are other steps required, however, which must be carried out in order for these to be done. Page layouts, as roughs and again as comprehensives must be made up, and finally mechanicals—final copy from which negatives and plates can be made—must be made up. And all of this must be carefully coordinated to meet even a normal schedule (which would ordinarily be six weeks for this task).

In most cases, to do all this in 15 days would be utterly impossible. Even for our own firm, accustomed to, equipped for, and specializing in "quick response" projects as we are, this task required a great deal of careful planning before we felt able to offer this proposal and pledge— actually *guarantee*—to meet the schedule. Even given the special advantages we enjoy in having most of the necessary skills and personnel available in-house at Accurate Litho, and given the special conditions we shall cite as essential to meeting the schedule date, it will be a most difficult task. It will be accomplished successfully only by the greatest of diligence and resourcefulness, which, fortunately, we are equipped and prepared to provide.

Essentially, the special conditions require your own spontaneous reviews and approvals—permission to proceed—as we proceed through the steps. That means that we will ask you to have someone with authority to approve copy come to our facility to carry out those reviews and give approval swiftly, as we go. Given that, we can guarantee success.

In the next chapter, where we present the absolute specifics of what we propose to do to meet the required delivery date, we present the total set of necessary conditions. They do not demand a great deal of Magnetic Media Corporation, however, other than on-time and as-required attendance at our plant by someone with authority to make swift reviews and give permission to go ahead so we can adhere to what will be a very tight regimen.

Notes on the Models

There are at least three major points to be made, with respect to these models of the second chapter. Despite their brevity—in the actual case they are likely to be many times longer than these samples—they illustrate the main principles, especially the following:

1. They do take up exactly where the previous chapter ended. The *transitions* from one to the other are very much in evidence.
2. They do prepare the reader to go on to the next chapter, with omens of what is to follow—*transitions* between chapters once again.
3. Each is based on a *strategy* that claims and demonstrates special attributes for what is proposed, while suggesting at least by implication that all competitive proposals ought to be examined to see if their authors have perceived the obvious problems and provided some practical means for coping with them successfully.

The Third Chapter

The third chapter, at least as defined in the format and organization recommended here, is the chapter that is usually incorporated specifically into the contract, directly or by reference. That is because it includes the absolute specific details of what you pledge to do and/or deliver to the customer, along with *when*—schedules, that is. It is, in fact, the proposal per se, where the other elements of the proposal are really ancillary to it, supporting it directly and indirectly.

For that reason, the next chapter assumes its own special importance. Where the main importance of the second chapter is that it must sell the customer on the approach and plan, the main importance of the third chapter is that it presents the specifics of what you propose to contract for—to do and/or deliver. What is here is going to be binding on you. But the reverse is true, too: Make what you are pledging to do or deliver absolutely crystal clear here to protect yourself in the event of a dispute later over what you have agreed to. That is an essential in proposal writing, and carelessness here can be costly later.

The format recommended here calls for the resumes of principal staff to be included at the end of the third chapter, since that is the chapter that is dedicated to providing the specific details. In practice, to save space, only a single resume will be included here, as part of the first model, to typify the recommended resume format. (Additional resume models would add nothing significant.)

The format shown enables you to tailor your resumes to each proposal, and yet not have to completely rewrite them for each proposal. Later, after presenting the third-chapter models, the notes will explain how this resume format enables you to do this, with guidance on how to use this format effectively.

CHAPTER III

THE INGREDIENTS OF SUCCESS

A DEDICATED PROJECT

This is to be a Special Project at HWSI. That means that a staff will be assigned directly to this project, with these project assignments their first priority, taking precedence over all other work. We can thus guarantee a continuity of effort and purpose: There will be absolutely no diversions of staff or effort from this important project.

A HIGHLY EXPERIENCED STAFF

For the first-phase work HWSI will assign two top scientists to the project.

The project director and Principal Investigator will be Dr. William Langston, a Vice President of HWSI and a veteran of more than 20 years in this field, specializing in management sciences and management information systems in industry, business, and government. He brings to this project the benefits of a distinguished academic background, as well as extensive and relevant experience in both government and private industry, where he directed a number of major MIS program developments.

Dr. Langston will be supported by Terry Willets, serving as Second Investigator. Mr. Willets, who earned his MBA in management sciences at Wynnefield Polytech, has been with HWSI for nearly 15 years and has worked on and led many MIS design programs at HWSI and elsewhere in his career. In fact, his own impressive experience and accomplishments rival those of Dr. Langston.

Fully qualified support staff will also be provided, and detailed resumes of all principal staff members will be found later in this chapter.

THE DELIVERABLE ITEM

We estimate that the report of the first-phase study will be approximately 75 pages long, including at least six flowcharts depicting the preliminary design proposed for second-phase development, as part of the final section of the report, *Recommendations*. (That may represent a redesign of the existing system, or it may represent a proposed new design, depending on the results of the study, for which full rationales will be provided.)

The report will make a full disclosure of findings, with detailed recommendations for the second-phase follow-up. These will include a critique of the present system and of its forms and procedures, with suggestions for improvement or replacement wherever and of whatever deemed necessary, and full explanations to justify all recommendations.

The report will include the information listed below and follow this general format:

Problem definition and statement of task objective.
Research and data-gathering methodology.
Narrative account of data gathering.
Presentation of raw data.
Account of data reduction methodology.
Presentation of reduced data.

continued
    Analysis and rationale.
    Conclusions.
    Recommendations.

A TIMELY SCHEDULE

Figure III-1 depicts the full schedule of events in the form of a milestone chart, which reveals exactly where, how, and what efforts are to be expended, and when each task is to start and to end. The milestone-chart format enables you to see how the several tasks relate to each other in their phase and functional relationships.

RESUMES OF KEY STAFF

The resumes of the principal staff to be assigned to this project are offered here, and their assignments to the project are guaranteed. However, in the event that some contingency impossible to foresee now interferes with that plan, HWSI guarantees to offer other staff resumes for your approval before making other staff assignments.

Dr. William Langston
Regular Position: Vice President, MIS Division
Proposed Assignment: Principal Investigator and Project Director
SUMMARY RECORD OF PROFESSIONAL ACHIEVEMENT
AND SPECIAL QUALIFICATIONS

Dr. Langston has earned a national reputation as a specialist in the design of management information systems over the 25-odd years he has been actively engaged in the profession. He earned his Ph.D. and MBA in Computer Sciences at SciTech, taught there for several years thereafter, and has been with HWSI in the position described for more than 12 years. Among the many MIS programs Dr. Langston designed was the RIDDLE system for the U.S. Navy, EPOS for the Auerbach Chemical Corporation, and MIRACLE for National Laboratories, Inc. A record of his present and former assignments follows:

1975–Present: Vice President, MIS Division, HWSI. Manages division of 22 professionals, with typical division workload of 8 projects, providing both technical and administrative leadership.
1964–75: Civilian employee U.S. Navy, Computer Systems Command, leading staff of eight system analysts and programmers.
1961–64: Assistant Professor, computer sciences, SciTech University.

CHAPTER III

THE PROGRAM TO MEET AN "IMPOSSIBLE" SCHEDULE

A PLAN FOR EFFECTIVE ACTION

To understand and appreciate the details of our program for meeting the extraordinarily difficult schedule requires an understanding of the

continued

normal production tasks and times involved for each, as exemplified here. (These are the six main tasks required for the program called for by this RFP, many of which are not really printing and binding tasks, but are editorial functions that Accurate offers as a convenience to our patrons.)

1. Set type, print galleys:	4 weeks
2. Proof and correct galleys:	3 weeks
3. Make type changes, print page proofs:	2 weeks
4. Make negatives, color separations:	6 weeks
5. Make plates:	1 week
6. Print, bind and trim:	1 week
Total:	17 weeks

Even an accelerated schedule would ordinarily mean trimming this schedule by only one third to one half the allotted time. To do this entire job in 15 days—only two weeks, that is—means trimming the normal schedule by nearly 90 percent!

These tasks are normally carried out sequentially in serial fashion, and in fact in some cases there is no alternative to serial sequencing. However, it is possible to perform some of these functions and/or portions of these functions concurrently—that is, begin the next function as an overlap—to shorten total elapsed time for the project.

There are other measures possible, too. Printing on the calendered stock called for presents a drying problem, especially with multicolor printing, so we will have to accelerate the drying process by using a special infrared drying line available in our plant.

Some of these measures mean undertaking some risk of redundant and inefficient efforts, but our plan minimizes that hazard, and Accurate Litho is willing to underwrite the risk.

The schedule presented in Figure III–1, a milestone chart, and Table III–1, a matrix of events, illustrates our proposed method for accomplishing this near-miracle. These illustrate the process of concurrent and overlapping tasks, that is, and the sharply abbreviated schedules for each.

WHAT ACCURATE LITHO PLEDGES TO DELIVER

The end-item, as identified in the RFP and confirmed here, is a 24-page annual report, printed in black plus three other colors, with eight color photographs (halftones), printed in quantity of 12,000 copies, bound and trimmed, trim size 9 × 12 inches, delivered 15 days after final copy and photographs are received. (Details of stock, binding, and other such details are included listed on one of our standard estimating forms enclosed here.)

Accurate Litho will provide experienced and capable staff (see resumes appearing at the end of this chapter) to manage this program and perform all production tasks, per the schedule, as listed in this chapter. Magnetic Media Corporation will provide its own personnel, at the Accurate Litho plant, to review and approve copy and give prompt permission to proceed.

Notes on Chapter III Models

Remember, again, that these are very much abbreviated samples of the typical formal proposal, and are used to illustrate main principles only. In the case of the first project, because it is one that consists primarily of professional services, and those of a highly specialized and custom nature, the staff and organization are of primary importance, and so the stress is made there. In printing requirements, however, the competence of the staff to carry out what are usually routine functions is ordinarily taken for granted by the customer, so the emphasis in the second case is not on the staff capabilities and qualifications (although these are not neglected), but on the problem itself. That is, the strategy in the first case was to prove the unusually great experience and competence of the staff, as demonstrated by resumes and in-text observations. In the second case the strategy is to "prove" that probably no one else is likely to be able to deliver on time by demonstrating the virtual impossibility of the schedule requirement, and then presenting, with clearly apparent confidence, a plan for getting the job done on schedule.

The resume model of the first case is built around a design to enable you to be able to tailor each resume to the proposal's specific requirements, and yet not have to completely rewrite each resume for each proposal. The items that normally have to be rewritten are the "Proposed Assignment" and the "Summary Record of Professional Achievement and Special Qualifications." Usually the remainder of the resume may be used as "boilerplate."

Of course, if you use a word processor, with these resumes in disk files, the job of tailoring them to each set of proposal requirements becomes infinitely easier and more convenient. That is true, moreover, for the proposal effort overall, especially for the fourth proposal chapter in the recommended format.

The Fourth Chapter

The main objective of the fourth chapter of the proposal is to demonstrate and build customer confidence in your reliability as a contractor, while also reinforcing and reaffirming your earlier evidence of your capabilities, as a secondary objective. Therefore, the main thrust of this chapter is presenting a record of your achievements—current and past projects of a relevant nature, along with identification of customers; special credentials, such as letters of commendation, special awards, patents, and other; and details of resources—physical facilities, personnel, corporate organization, and anything else that contributes to this objective.

Again, the models are brief, and only typify the more extensive coverage that would normally appear in most formal proposals.

CHAPTER IV

HWSI'S OUTSTANDING RECORD OF ACHIEVEMENT

FIRST, THE RIGHT EXPERIENCE FOR THE JOB

It is no exaggeration to say that our unusually appropriate qualifications for the proposed project represent distinct assets for the Martinside Manufacturing organization, since these HWSI resources will be committed to success on behalf of Martinside. Among these assets is the particularly appropriate experience of Hackney & Williams Software, Inc., as demonstrated by the following few summaries of recent HWSI projects:

A Large Government MIS: We have just completed final testing and debugging of a large management information system for the National Bureau of Standards (NBS) and demonstrated its operation to NBS, who have now accepted it. It was an unusually broadbased system for a large mainframe computer, representing a government investment of several million dollars and an eight-month effort. We are pleased to report that we delivered the product nearly 2 percent under budget and almost 30 days earlier than the stipulated deadline.

Contact to verify this: John Muller, Contracting Officer, (202) 555–1333.

A Special Problem Solved for a Customer: Modern Alchemy, Inc., a rather large midwest manufacturer of plastics and other products, has become a conglomerate in the chemical industries by acquiring 22 smaller companies over the past few years. Many of these companies had their own mainframe and/or minicomputers and management information systems, some of the systems custom-made for them, others commercial off-the-shelf programs. This polyglot assemblage made central management and reporting rather difficult for the corporate staff.

HWSI was asked to create a central MIS that would retain as many existing systems as possible, within the constraints that they had to be made compatible with the new, central MIS, and had to furnish the information that Modern Alchemy corporate staff required and specified in their RFP.

HWSI managed to create the new system and achieve the objectives by retaining and fitting into the new design nearly 90 percent of the existing systems, modifying only four of the older systems to make them compatible, and retaining the rest without change.

This was accomplished by HWSI within the budget and schedule originally proposed by HWSI.

Contact to verify this: Harry Mulligan, Executive Vice President, (312) 555–6667.

NEXT, THE RIGHT PHYSICAL RESOURCES

Hackney & Williams Software, Inc. occupies a modern six-story building of our own, in which we have over 47,000 square feet of office and laboratory space and 560 employees, including the following:

continued
- Computer engineers and scientists
- Systems analysts
- Research specialists
- Programmers
- Library scientists
- Technical writers and indexers
- Support personnel

Our laboratory facilities include a mainframe computer and a mini-computer, with appropriate peripheral equipment (tape servos, etc), and more than a dozen desktop computers.

Figure IV–1 illustrates the corporate organization, and shows where the proposed project will be established in the structure. Note that it is assigned a position that assures it a high degree of visibility by top corporate management, a reflection of the importance we assign to this project.

Figures IV–2 through IV–6 are copies of unsolicited letters of commendation from customers who chose to thus express their appreciation for the way in which we conducted their projects and satisfied their needs.

CHAPTER IV

ACCURATE LITHO'S UNUSUALLY COMPLETE FACILITY AND ORGANIZATION

A TOTAL PUBLICATIONS ORGANIZATION AND PHYSICAL PLANT

Few printers maintain as complete an organization and set of physical facilities as those of Accurate Litho. For one thing, few printing plants have their own facilities for making the color negatives and separations for process color printing; most vend this part of the work to specialists. And few have a complete graphics arts and editorial staff on-premises full time, ready to support all publications requirements.

Within our modern three-story building is a complete printing and binding plant on the ground floor. This plant occupies 8,400 square feet on one level, with both large web presses and small sheet-fed presses, a 36-inch camera and dark room, and a complete bindery. The second and third floors, constituting another 14,600 square feet, house 234 employees in business offices and editorial offices.

Among the many similar projects we have handled in the recent past were these:

125,000 copies of American Tool Steel Corporation's annual report, similar to that referred to here, delivered four weeks after arrival of camera-ready text and photographs. Contact at American Tool Steel: Tony Morgan, (206) 555–9990.

> continued
>
>   3,000 copies of 456-page manual for United Technical Services Corporation, including 38 process color photos, sewn bindings and paper covers, produced in six weeks. Contact: Barry Greenbaum, (415) 555-8677.
>
>   Figure IV-1 is an organization chart, showing the entire Accurate Litho corporate structure. Figure IV-2 is a typical workflow diagram, reflecting our normal processes. Figures IV-3 and IV-4 are certificates of commendation from the U.S. Navy for an earlier project in which we met difficult deadlines.

Front Matter of Proposals

The two items of front matter that need special discussion here are the Executive Summary and the Response Matrix. Ordinarily, the use of an Executive Summary obviates any need for a Foreword, Preface, or Abstract in the front matter. The Response Matrix is the other important item requiring special discussion, although brief mention will be made also of the letter of transmittal used normally in submitting a formal proposal.

The Executive Summary

The Executive Summary is nominally supplied for the benefit of those executives in the customer's organization who would normally not, for whatever reason, plod through the entire proposal. This implies rather clearly that it (the Executive Summary) is an abstract of the proposal. However, the shrewd proposal writer will utilize the Executive Summary to summarize the most persuasive highlights of the proposal (i.e., the major benefits and other arguments for the selection of the proposer as the awardee.)

   The typical Executive Summary found in most proposals, therefore, is a crisp—sometimes even staccato—recital of major arguments, in brisk telegraphic style designed for impact via style as well as via content. The models will reflect that:

> **EXECUTIVE SUMMARY**
>
>   A contract award to Hackney & Williams Software, Inc. (HWSI) represents many benefits and advantages to Martinside Manufacturing, Inc., such as the following examples:
> - Fourteen years of highly specialized and totally relevant MIS experience.
> - An insight that anticipates possible false starts and therefore prevents them through preventive measures.

---

continued
- One of the nation's leading experts in management sciences and systems leading the project, supported by another expert of almost equal credentials.
- HWSI's perfect record of on-time and within-budget performance in 374 prior projects.
- Program-installation backup support (guaranteed) should any problems surface.
- Proximity of contractor's corporate offices.

EXECUTIVE SUMMARY

Accurate Litho offers Magnetic Media Corporation many exclusive advantages in this proposal, owing to Accurate Litho's facilities and capabilities. The following are points which, we believe, must be considered carefully and thoughtfully in selecting an awardee for this contract:

1. Accurate Litho offers a highly unusual—probably unique—set of publications capabilities under one roof.
2. Owing to this remarkably comprehensive and complete set of capabilities, it is likely that Accurate Litho is the only contractor who can deliver on schedule.
3. Accurate Litho offers a concrete, detailed, and specific plan to meet the schedule.
4. Accurate Litho *guarantees* to meet the schedule, under the conditions set forth.
5. Magnetic Media is justified in having faith in Accurate Litho's promise, for reasons set forth in this proposal.

Notes on Models

One way to make the models even more effective is to follow each statement with a notation of where in the proposal the reader may find details of what the item claims. But that leads us to the Response Matrix, which does that and more, although it is helpful to also note the chapters/pages/paragraphs that offer the details of the items.

The Response Matrix

Unfortunately, many customers miss important points in reading proposals, and so fail to credit the proposal writer with having supplied adequate information and/or responding to the RFP request for specific data. In many cases this alone can cost you the contract you should have won.

The Response Matrix offers you a convenient and effective way to solve—even avoid—this problem. Simply put, the Response Matrix is a table that lists all the items the customer has requested in the RFP and specifies where in the proposal the requested information is supplied. That is, a Response Matrix is designed to help the reader verify the total responsiveness of your proposal and so maximize your technical score, where there is systematic scoring, and to maximize the effect of your technical proposal in all cases. In general, it is a table in which are listed the requirements specified in the RFP (and derived from the checklists prepared earlier), and assuming the general form of Figure 4-1.

In many cases such matrixes can run to many pages, and so the significance of noting this partial page as "Sheet 1," or, if you prefer, "Page 1." The right-hand column is normally left blank for the convenience of the customer who, it is hoped, will use it to note your complete compliance with all requirements.

It is usually advisable also to introduce this matrix and explain its purpose, along the lines of the following statement:

The Response Matrix, Figure 4-1, is offered for convenience in verifying that this proposal is completely responsive to all requests and specifications in the RFP, either implied or explicit, and to evaluating the proposal accordingly.

SPECIFICATION SHEETS

In this technological age it has become a practice in many cases to provide specifications of items to describe them objectively. A list of specifications is no place to use marketing hyperbole and to make vague claims of excellence. It is, rather, a presentation that must have an objective and factual tone and present verifiable facts. A failure to be objective and factual in tone nullifies any influence the specifications might have in their use as part of the marketing package. The list of specifications is intended to convey the information that the prospective buyer needs to review in reaching a buying decision—the evidence

FIGURE 4-1 Response Matrix, Sheet 1

RFP/SOW (page)	Description	Proposal (page)	Notes
p. 3	Proximity to customer	p. 5	
pp. 7, 9, 10	Staff qualifications	pp. 12–16	
p. 14	Schedule requirement	pp. 18–23	

or proof required to support the advertiser's basic promise. (Moreover, inasmuch as the specifications do purport to be totally factual, a lack of caution here might actually constitute an illegal misrepresentation of facts.)

On the other hand, it is a legitimate (and common) practice to be selective in what is and what is not included in any list of specifications. You are not required to make the list of specifications absolutely complete. The specifications sheet may include those items that are beneficial as marketing assets, and exclude those that represent liabilities, rather than assets. Moreover, it is a common and legitimate practice to squeeze the specifications as far as they will go without violating truth. (In some cases it requires exacting laboratory work to validate the claims made in the specifications.) That is why, for example, a statement of specifications can justifiably claim some extreme that has little or no practical value to the user but is still true and at least nominally a mark of high quality.

Specification sheets may or may not be technical, depending on the nature of the item described. That is, the specifications for a high-quality stereo or highly sophisticated personal computer might be technical and complex, using many scientific electrical and electronic terms to describe the item, while a specification sheet for a pocket calculator or "boom box" stereo would be considerably simpler.

On the other hand, the specifications for a chair or table would not ordinarily be very technical, but would tend to be confined to a description of the materials and physical dimensions, possibly with some description of fasteners or other information pertinent to the construction of the item.

It is not only the nature of the item that determines how technical the specification sheet will be; the nature of the reader for whom the specification sheet is intended has a great deal to do with it too. That is, manufacturers realize that the average consumer is not able to even understand, much less make good use of, highly technical data, and so even a specification sheet for a computer will not be highly complex or painstakingly detailed in scientific and engineering terms when it is destined to be distributed by a retailer or in a mailout to consumers. On the other hand, if a computer manufacturer was preparing specification sheets to be sent out to other manufacturers or technical/professional specialists—engineers and consultants, for example—there would almost certainly be some rather esoteric and even mathematical technical data because these intended readers would want a complete definition with all the technical details provided. (Examples might be MTBF—mean time between failures—and MTTR—mean time to repair—figures, derived from suitable engineering studies when the specifications are of electronic equipment. Other kinds of items might have other cryptic figures such as "Rockwell hardness," none of them of interest to the lay person.)

The size of the specification sheet depends on the amount or volume of data supplied and the nature of the data. Whereas a specification sheet for some uses might well consume an entire sheet or even several sheets, many specifications contain only a few lines of information. The term *specification sheet* is therefore used generically here, for it may constitute an entire brochure of technical details or it may be considerably less than a "sheet." For example, the specifications included in a little brochure that accompanies one telephone retailing for about $40 are quite brief because they are addressed to the user, who could not benefit from reading more technical data. (It will be found among the models as the specifications for the "Tone Phone.")

You must, then, use your own judgment as to what information is needed for an objective and accurate description of the item. We are going to assume that the intended reader is an average consumer, not a scientist or other technical specialist of any kind (a reasonable assumption to make for our purposes here), and structure our models accordingly.

Formats and Styles

Formats and styles of specification sheets vary widely, from quite formal, tabular organization, to informal text descriptions, to various combinations or hybrids. Again, the choice of format is dependent principally on the depth of detail and the reader for whom the information is intended.

The flexibility of style is reflected by the several models shown here.

A Few Models

Following are several brief models (specifications for ordinary consumer items are rarely much more than a few lines) and a few longer ones for somewhat more complex and costly items.

CLASSIC CAPTAIN'S CHAIR DESCRIPTION

Material:	All solid seasoned walnut
Finish:	Natural—stained and french polished
Fasteners:	Tenon pegs, corner blocks, and glue (no metal used)
Weight:	14 lbs
Special features:	Contoured seat

THE TONE-PHONE

Pulse dialing rate:	10 pp
Interdigital pause:	820ms
Redial memory capacity:	32 digits in pulse mode
	31 digits in touch tone mode
	Standard DTMF
Telephone connections:	Modular connectors (USOC type RJ–11)

THE GEE WHIZ DESKTOP COMPUTER

Microprocessor:	Intel 8086–2 8 MHZ
Memory:	128/256/640k RAM; 8k ROM
Storage:	Dual DS/DD 5- /4–in drives, 360k ea
I/O ports:	Keyboard, monitor, serial and parallel printer/modem
Video out:	Monochrome or color, w/graphics
Resolution:	604 × 480 pixels
Keyboard:	Detachable, 83 keys, 10 programmable function keys, numeric pad
Included software:	Diagnostic disk, Gee Whiz wp, Gee-Whiz dbms
OS:	MS-DOS 2.11
Price:	Basic (128k) system w/dual drives, monochrome monitor, 128k RAM: $2,739
Options:	RGB color monitor, $875; 256k RAM expansion, $485; additional 128k increments, $430 ea; tutorial software, $35; GWBASIC, $60; 1,500 MS-DOS programs available
Service:	Gee-Whiz factory service available at 183 locations in U.S.

CATALOG SHEETS

Catalog sheets are similar to specification sheets in that they describe items and the characteristics of the items. But whereas specifications purport to be totally objective and must be so, catalog sheets are advertising or sales presentations and are thus not so bound; they may employ all the devices necessary to and commonly practiced in sales and advertising.

Catalog sheets are not necessarily bound into catalogs and may, in fact, bear no relationship to an actual catalog. They may be simple flyers or circulars, called catalog sheets simply because they resemble the pages found in a catalog.

They thus may be in color, more often than not include drawings or photos, and otherwise bear all the characteristics of any other printed sales presentation. The principal feature that distinguishes them as catalog sheets, rather than as pure circulars, is the part or order numbers supplied to identify the items advertised.

The catalog sheet for a well-known computer diskette, for example, has a color photograph of the product and the following copy:

---

100 percent error-free   5-¼", 8" & preformatted diskettes
Critically certified   Lifetime warranty
Critically certified, each and every _____ diskette is tested to meet or

continued
exceed the most demanding ANSI, ECMA, ISO, and IBM standards. Unique coating technique with longer-lasting lubricant improves signal resolution. Advanced polishing method assures a smooth, even recording surface for longer head life. Because they are tested throughout the production process, you can be sure _____ diskettes are of the highest quality and dependability on the market. Backed by manufacturer's lifetime warranty.

This paragraph is then followed by a table that lists the diskettes (24 different ones), with a part or order number for each and with prices for orders of different quantities.

A Few Models

AM/FM Cube Cassette Player

Entertaining combination: AM/FM radio and cassette recorder/player with automatic stop, LED digital clock, 24-hour alarm, day/month calendar, illuminated dial, AC/DC/battery operation.   Shipping weight 3 lbs. $34.99. **Order number AR-348.**

Automatic Dialer and Calculator

Hold it to mouthpiece, and it dials your numbers for you!
Local and long-distance calls no problem: stores 84 numbers of up to 32 digits each.

This month only: Save over $10 on this calculator and automatic dialer that fits into your shirt pocket. Code up to 84 numbers with your own choices of names and/or initials. This little beauty also has a built-in clock and timer, memory, and automatic shut-off, too. Built to sell for $45.00 but offered this month only at the special sale price of only $34.95. **Order Number TD-192 (W).**

President's Chair—Stainproof fabric with genuine leather trim, gas-powered lift, and super-smooth ball casters. Strong welded construction, choice of decorator colors, unconditionally guaranteed for full year. We challenge you to beat this price anywhere for a chair of this quality. **Order President Chair 795–DSO–2. Special price: $217.50.**

Schoolhouse Wall Clock—Authentic reproduction of the famous 19th century schoolhouse clocks. Polished octagon-shaped pine with cherrywood finish, polished brass pendulum. Large black Arabic numerals on white dialface behind brass-trimmed glass door, quartz-controlled movement, accurate within 30 seconds per year! With or without chimes, battery operated (C battery operates clock for up to one full year).

454-CH-2443: Clock w/o chimes, List $69.85, Sale price: $48.65
454-CH-2444: Clock w/chimes, List $79.85, Sale price: $58.65

Men's Fashion Slacks—Cuffless, summer weight, permanent press, designer colors, guaranteed unconditionally. Return these beautiful slacks for full credit or refund if you are not absolutely delighted with them. They are a special buy (manufacturer's overstock), originally manufactured to retail for $29.95. You won't see this bargain very often. Better stock up now while you can!

Choice of brown, black, blue, green. $14.95 each; 2 pairs for $27.85; 3 pairs for $39.90.

No. AASL-243-87: Color: ____ Waist: ____ Inseam: ____ No. Prs.: ____ Color(s) of additional pairs: _____

DIRECT-MAIL PACKAGES

Marketing by direct mail is a lusty activity which is still growing and becoming a virtual industry in itself, currently accounting for many billions of annual sales. (One acknowledged expert puts the figure at $150 billion annually, and this is only for sales made directly via mail. It does not include sales concluded via other means but initiated from leads generated by direct-mail methods.)

Direct mail advertising requires and sustains many support services such as mailing list managers and brokers, consultants, copywriters, advertising agencies, mailing services, printers, and others and is served by several trade publications. It has also generated its own argot, naturally. But there is some confusion in the terminology used, and it is not easy to discriminate among the relevant terms *direct marketing* (also often referred to as *direct-response marketing*), *direct mail*, and *mail order*. Some believe these are alternate terms for the same thing or, at least, that direct mail and mail order are simply two of the many ways to market directly or by "direct response." Others, purists, distinguish sharply among the terms. Those who so discriminate between terms designate as mail order the practice of advertising in what are usually considered to be (and often actually designated as) mail order sections of periodicals and even of radio and TV stations, urging the prospects to order directly by mail or telephone. They consider direct mail to be a different field because it entails soliciting orders by mailing out packages of literature to thousands of names on mailing lists—rather than by advertising in the media. And while these are two of several ways of marketing directly (in-store demonstrations, door-to-door selling, and selling at seminars or public lectures are some other direct-marketing methods), many use the terms direct mail and direct marketing interchangeably and are usually referring to direct mail when they use the term direct marketing.

We have already discussed advertising, sales letters, and some other elements usually found in direct-mail packages. Here we will concern ourselves with some of the other materials used in direct-mail solicitations and with the makeup of such packages.

The Elements of a Direct-Mail Package

The direct-mail package typically includes many of the elements already described and exemplified earlier. Most include at least the following items:

> Sales letter.
> Brochure and/or circular or broadside.
> Order form.
> Return envelope.

In many cases direct-mail packages include still other items that have been discussed earlier, such as specification sheets and catalog sheets. But direct-mail packages also often include more specialized items. One that has been used frequently in the past few years is a little brochure or miniletter that is folded and says on the outside something along these lines: "Do not open unless you have decided not to order." Inside is an additional sales argument and an iteration of the main selling points. This is intended as a sort of reverse sales psychology, written with the knowledge that curiosity will impel a great many people to read what is inside that novel enclosure, whether or not they have yet decided how they will react to the offer generally.

Other devices are used to command attention and motivate the reader. Many packages include a plastic card, closely resembling a normal credit card. Insurance companies and others who offer what is essentially a subscription service, such as a travel club or automobile club, often use these. But the package may also contain novelty items, many of them having practical uses. The National Pen Corporation, for example, usually includes a sample pen or pencil—one of their products—in the envelope. (They manufacture pens and pencils imprinted with the purchaser's copy, to be used by the purchaser as advertising giveaway items.) A company that sells plastic sheets to be used in 3-ring binders as protective covers for documents encloses a sample sheet with their mailers.

Printers also usually enclose samples of their work, as do others when that is a practical and appropriate action.

The Philosophy of the Direct-Mail Package

Three points should be made about direct mail, and all must be kept firmly in mind to develop effective direct-mail materials and packages:

1.   The direct-mail package is advertising material, of course, and thus should follow the same principles as in all other kinds of advertising. It has several advantages over media advertising. One is that you can take a great deal of space—thousands of words and supporting illustrations—to make your presentation and appeal. Another is that you can target prospects far more precisely with direct mail. And still another is that you can conduct tests and gauge results far more rapidly and precisely before making the major commitment to "roll out" or invest in the main effort. That latter is a large factor in reducing risk in doing business via mail and other direct methods.

2.   The sales letter is central in the direct-mail package and should be a complete presentation in itself. All the other elements elaborate on and reinforce the basic points made in the letter. The assumption is that the respondent will read the sales letter, but not necessarily anything else. Hence you need to tell your whole story in the letter, but still try to make the points that will induce the reader to turn to the other enclosures for reinforcement of your sales appeals.

3.   One direct-mail cliche that appears to be true enough nevertheless is a bit of doggerel that says: "The more you tell the more you sell." And that "more" you should tell is reflected in both the amount of detail you provide and in the reinforcement and repetition of important motivational points. That will become more and more apparent as we go on to discuss the direct-mail elements not presented earlier in these pages.

Despite the fact that in the usual direct-mail package you have ample room—thousands of words—in which to present your sales appeal, you must sell as vigorously as though you had only a two- or three-inch advertisement space in which to do the job. You can employ several pages and thousands of words to make your presentation, but you can't compel the reader to suffer through copy that is boring or otherwise completely lackluster. You must somehow induce the reader to stay with you by making it appear to be worth his or her time to do so.

Among the many myths of advertising is the one that condemns wordiness in advertising copy, but brevity is not its own virtue; it does not create sales when you fail to capture the reader's interest. On the other hand it has been amply demonstrated that readers will devour every word of even the lengthiest copy when the copy interests them—when it *strikes a nerve* by helping the reader perceive that his or her personal fears or desires are at stake. "The more you tell the more you sell" aphorism works, but it works only when you manage to persuade the prospect to *read* all you tell.

Keeping Your Eye on the Ball

Capturing and sustaining interest is only one ingredient of success. It is not, of itself, enough; there are other caveats. *Interest* is one thing; *motivation* is another. TV viewers watched the famous Alka Seltzer stomach commercials with great interest because the commercials were entertaining and amusing. But they were a dismal failure because they did not *motivate* viewers to buy Alka Seltzer. And that was simply because they failed to make the viewers understand *why* they should buy Alka Seltzer—what it would do for them. The copywriter took his or her eye off the ball and forgot to motivate the viewer. Sales presentations that fail to move the respondent to a buying action are always complete failures, no matter how well written, how artistic, or how entertaining. (The successor commercials, still in use, used fear motivation, and used it quite successfully.)

It's easy to allow yourself to be decoyed into taking your eye off the ball—forgetting to focus on selling the product, on motivating the reader to order. The terrible urge to be oh-so-clever is a common trap for copywriters. Developing sales copy is not the art of writing; it is the art of persuasion.

Another deadly mistake many copywriters make is becoming subtle. (In fact, those Alka Seltzer commercials were guilty of that "crime"; they were far too subtle.) Rarely do readers study or pore over advertising copy, so they are not likely to grasp any meaning that is not unmistakably obvious. Subtlety that conceals your meaning and intent nullifies your copy almost 100 percent as far as motivating a prospect to buy is concerned.

Another kind of subtlety that is practiced widely and profitably is the use of euphemisms. In an age when undertakers have become morticians and janitors have become maintenance engineers, sellers of secondhand Chevrolets and Fords sell "used cars," but sellers of second-hand Continentals and Jaguars are more likely to sell "previously owned" cars. For those spending a great deal of money for a luxury automobile, "previously owned" is a great deal more palatable adjective than "used" is, and does not obscure the meaning. For the same reason, use "inexpensive" or "less costly," instead of "cheap," when you are making a price appeal. But also use such terms as "higher quality" or "upscale," rather than "more expensive" (unless you are referring to a competitive product!) when you are making a quality appeal.

THE SALES LETTER

There is only one important difference between the sales letter discussed in an earlier chapter and the one referred to in this chapter: The earlier examples were of sales letters that are expected to stand alone; here we are referring to sales letters that are the focus of entire packages of sales literature. That is, these latter sales letters may refer to other enclosures, such as brochures, response envelopes, and order forms, and are actually introducing an entire package of literature, representing a multielement presentation.

Depending on individual circumstances, this sales letter may be one, two, or more pages long. Figure 4-2 is an example of such a letter.

Unlike the sales letters illustrated in an earlier chapter, sales letters introducing a direct-mail presentation are not usually addressed to the individual by name (although that has been changing recently, with desktop computers making it possible for even the small office to address each letter individually). The sample shown in the figure is classic, however, and a model of those still very much in use today. Note especially the free use of headlines, underscores, circling of items, and inserts made by hand with a bold writing instrument. That is very much the style in use for many years and to be found yet in the mail every day.

Figure 4-2 A Typical Direct-Mail Sales Letter

EXCELSIOR ELECTRONICS, INC.
4222 Lincoln Drive
Pleasantville, OH 44444

NEVER AGAIN A FORGOTTEN AND BURNED ROAST OR SPOILED DISH WITH THIS FANTASTIC NEW COOKING TIMER: IT TAKES THE GUESSWORK OUT OF COOKING AND MINDS THE COOKING FOR YOU!!
(and it's an AM/FM radio, kitchen clock, and alarm clock, too)

The Computer Age brings this fantastic new *high-tech* unit to you. It minds the kitchen for you while you go about doing other things. You can even have the built-in radio playing your favorite music while the Cook's Helper keeps track of the time and signals you when time's up.

AVAILABLE IN 7 DECORATOR COLORS

This beautiful and compact unit, available in ⑦ beautiful decorator colors (white, yellow, red, blue, green, orange, and beige), can be placed on a counter top or fastened conveniently out of the way to the underside of one of your kitchen cabinets or on a wall, using the special easy-mount brackets supplied. It is *any one can do it!* only 4 × 5 × 8 inches, and so takes up practically no room at all, even in small kitchens. And yet it is so modern and so attractively styled that your friends will all want to know where you got it!

IT HAS FEATURES GALORE

Among its many features is a means for adjusting the kind and intensity of the signal it sends you when time is up. That can be adjusted from a subtle chiming note to an insistent ring or buzz. The timer may

continued

also be used to turn the radio on or off automatically at some future time. It also has its own electrical outlet which you can use to turn another appliance on or off at some preset time—to start your coffee in the morning, for example.

FANTASTIC DISCOUNT PRICE

This is easily the hottest item we've handled in years, and on-hand supplies will not last long, especially at the low-low price we've set for this item: It was built to sell for $49.95, but we've persuaded the manufacturer to help us introduce this new item at a special price. If you act within 21 days, you can have your own Cook's Helper (not more than two to a customer, under this special deal) for only $29.95.

BONUS FREE GIFTS YOURS TO KEEP

And even that is not the only good news. To encourage you to act promptly, if your order is received within 10 days, you will get two gifts: A set of aluminum measuring spoons and a mystery gift, also of use in your kitchen. Moreover, this unit is sold with a 100 percent money-back guarantee. You can return it within two weeks without explanation for full refund and keep the free gifts.

Obviously, you can't go wrong here, no matter what you do, for our ironclad money-back guarantee protects you completely. But you must act NOW to be sure of getting your own Cook's Helper, for this item is going very fast.

FAST ACTION IS IMPORTANT

Just fill out the handy order form enclosed and get it in the mail with your check or money order for immediate delivery of your very own Cook's Helper kitchen timer/radio/clock. And be sure to tell us what color you want while we have a complete selection still available.

Cordially,

Ben Carter

Ben Carter
President

P.S. To show you how eager we are to send you one of these beautiful and useful new high-tech kitchen marvels, here is another SPECIAL OFFER: The first 250 people who get their orders in will get still another FREE SURPRISE GIFT, a kitchen item you won't want to be without. But remember, you must act immediately to qualify for this EXTRA FREE GIFT.

Note the stress the letter makes on action now. That's because so many people procrastinate. I still get inquiries and even orders in response to offers I made several years ago and have not made since. This is not an unusual phenomenon, but is rather typical. (Some mail-order dealers have referred to this as the "drag.") But for everyone who responds many months and even years later, there are dozens who mean to respond but never "get around to it" or are simply indecisive and never do reach the decision to respond.

Those are lost sales. Therefore the urging to act now and the inducements to act promptly. Such inducements greatly increase sales because they prod the undecideds into acting.

Inducements to Act Promptly

Inducements to act promptly take many forms, although all fall into a few general classes, as follows:

Bonus offers: These are usually offers to provide a free gift to each respondent who sends in an order. (The large mail-order firm, Fingerhut, takes this even further by providing both an identified gift and a surprise gift with each order.) In some cases, where the gift is too expensive to give away, the offer is made to sell the gift for a price well below cost.

Discounts: Many entrepreneurs offer a substantial discount for prompt action, knowing that relatively few of those who do not act promptly will ever act at all. This is a simple device. It merely offers the respondent a cash discount on either the basic offer or something related to it—perhaps a book, clock, radio, or some other relatively expensive item.

Package deals: These are a variant or hybrid of the discount and bonus inducements. The offer is to sell a combination of items at a special low price.

No-risk guarantees: Often the inducement to act is an ironclad guarantee that the item may be returned for full refund if the buyer is not satisfied. Or, as a variant, a "send no money, we'll bill you" offer is made, still with that same no-risk guarantee. And several mail-order sellers have emulated the example of one of the more innovative mail-order experts, the late Joe Karbo, by guaranteeing to hold the customer's check for 30 days and returning the original check if the customer is not satisfied and sends the item back.

An Atypical Sales Letter

Despite the popularity of those attention-grabbers illustrated in Figure 4-2, not every direct-mail sales letter uses or should use those devices. I found an exception in my post-office box this morning. It is a one-page letter from a rather well-known organization, a straightforward letter with a conventional and dignified typed appearance and no circles, handwritten notations, or other tricks of the trade. It presents an image suited to the proposition, which is to sell me a set of 12 Lee Iacocca autobiographical tapes, a product that clearly is not to be loudly huckstered but must be sold in a dignified manner.

The letter is addressed to me personally. It even addresses me as "Mr. Holtz" twice in the text. It is marked, above the salutation *PERSONAL AND CONFIDENTIAL,* a notation that showed clearly through the oversize window of the envelope, which also revealed the visible letterhead imprint, "Office of the President."

Overall, this is an economy package. The letter is about two thirds of a page, the final portion of the page used as the order form (or "response device," as many in the trade refer to it). The order form asks me to "simply sign here"—leaving me a blank space for my signature—and offers me the option of canceling the invoice and returning the item within 30 days if I am not satisfied. But the package does include a letter-size (number 9) prepaid return envelope. (The trade refers to a response envelope as a BRE, for business reply envelope.) It includes, also, a four-page brochure, completing a simple package.

There is a jarring note: I might have been more impressed by the personal address had the envelope been mailed first class. I found it a little difficult to take "personal and confidential" seriously in what was obviously bulk mail, sent for 12.5 cents, rather than the 22 cents of first-class mail.

There are other errors. One is to address me as "Hrh Communications," instead of the correct "HRH Communications, Inc." It reflects some carelessness on the part of whoever compiled the mailing list and can be a fatal error, since many people are highly sensitive about their business names as well as about their personal names. Less serious, but still an indication of carelessness, are spelling errors in the address.

The most serious error is that the letter fails to give me an immediate reason for being interested in the proposition at all, much less motivate me to actually order the tapes. The lead is weak. It invites me to try what the writer refers to as an "exciting new audiocassette program" (exciting in his opinion, not by virtue of any evidence to indicate that) for 30 days without cost or obligation. Presumably it is that latter offer that is supposed to capture my interest and begin to motivate me. But a "no cost or obligation" offer is appealing only if there is some desire for the item on the part of the prospect. It's a help in closing but not in opening a sales argument. The motivator, what the tapes will do to help me increase my success, appears later and even then is barely hinted at rather than made plain. (The writer appears to assume that everyone will want these tapes because of the magic name of the author.) And buried near the end of the letter is what would probably be by far the strongest motivator if it were used properly—*up front and dramatized*—the suggestion that these tapes contain information to help listeners avoid the obstacles that impede or prevent success.

Despite these shortcomings, there are many situations where the sales letter ought to be completely conventional and shun all those special attention-getting devices. This is not to say that even the most dignified and "quiet" sales letter should not sell vigorously and emphatically. In fact, it is by no means certain that all those attention-getting dramatics of sales-letter tricks do any more for the sale than does a good sales argument—an appealing motivator with effective closers.

Figure 4–3 illustrates this type of sales letter. Note that it does not fail to sell: It follows sales principles faithfully, although without all the flourishes of the more aggressive huckstering style of other sales letters. In fact, it includes at least three motivations:

1.   It begins and focuses primarily on the usually effective fear motivation by pointing out the inherent high risks of mail-order ventures and then offering a degree of insurance against failure.

2.   It uses gain motivation, explaining how membership offers help in succeeding and listing a number of specific benefits.

3.   It uses the exclusivity and privilege motivation twice in the exclusivity and privilege of membership and the exclusivity and privilege of sharing in many insider tips and trade secrets.

Figure 4–3 A Low-Key Sales Letter

SOCIETY OF MAIL ORDER DEALERS
P.O. Box 10000
Chicago, IL 60601
Working together for everyone's success

**HERE'S HOW TO AVOID THE FATAL ERRORS
AND VIRTUALLY GUARANTEE YOUR SUCCESS
IN THE MAIL-ORDER BUSINESS**

Harold W. Marten
365 National Bank Building
Cleveland, OH 45442

Dear Mr. Marten:

  Wouldn't you like to take the risk out of your mail-order business? Of course you would. And you can. You can take most of the risk out of it almost immediately by joining with your fellow mail-order dealers—*highly successful* mail-order entrepreneurs—and learning the secrets of their success so that you can apply these priceless insider tips to your own venture.

  It's easy to do just that now. Membership in the exclusive SMOD—Society of Mail-Order Dealers—is being expanded to accept into our ranks just a few new mail-order dealers who have been recommended by members or otherwise considered qualified for membership. As an active member of SMOD you will receive many business and professional benefits, including (but not limited to) the following:

  ■A monthly newsletter (tabloid style) of 16 to 24 pages full of news, suggestions, ideas, and other valuable information from **SMOD** National Headquarters.

continued
■A meeting of your local chapter every month where you meet and chat with your fellow members, listen to helpful presentations, and participate in planning for the future.

■An annual National Convention, a full week of meeting member dealers from all over the country, attending professional seminars and social events, learning of the latest developments and techniques in the Exhibit Hall, and gathering up a briefcaseful of useful literature.

■Many other special events sponsored by both your local chapter and National Headquarters.

■The right to use the prestigious SMOD logo on your stationery and in your advertising.

■Access to legal counsel and support from the SMOD National Headquarters staff.

■Access to cooperative mailings, cooperative purchases, and other money-saving joint activities, many of which would not even be possible for many of our members to undertake alone.

Elsewhere in the enclosed package of SMOD literature you will find descriptions of SMOD organization and activities, statements by executives of many member firms (you will find both the largest and smallest mail-order firms among our members), and many other details of why you should join SMOD TODAY.

Cordially,

J. Wilson Miner
President, SMOD

This letter is relatively brief, given the commitment asked, but its brevity is probably an asset as long as it is amply supported by other enclosures. Many readers would not take the time to read a four- or five-page letter, but would read a brief one and review enclosed brochures, order forms, and other ancillary material.

An Example

A package currently on my desk from the Newsletter Association is introduced by and includes a six-page letter, using a typeset seven-line headline above the generic and impersonal salutation "Dear Newsletter Colleague." The body of the letter is typed, probably via a word processor and printer, uses many underlines, and ends in a lengthy postscript.

The letter's main appeal is to the desire for gain, promising the reader the expert guidance and access to information that will produce success. It then goes on to list many services, activities, and benefits in detail, including a money-back guarantee and bonus books.

The half-page postscript offers reprises of the bonus offers and adds the offer of other bonus publications. It is a rather lengthy letter, but since it appeals rather effectively to a most basic interest—success in what is usually a hazardous and difficult business venture—it probably works well.

However, despite the lengthy letter and the details provided therein, the package includes a rather substantial quantity of other support materials:

- A two-page order form with testimonials and selling arguments, printed on extra-heavy paper stock.
- A postage-paid return envelope (BRE).
- "Teaser copy" on the carrier envelope (a number 10 window envelope), covering virtually all available space on both front and back, pressing hard with both fear and gain motivational appeals.
- A small brochure—a reduced reproduction of a one-page testimonial letter from a member.
- A four-page typeset brochure listing the alleged pitfalls in newsletter publishing.
- A small brochure (with proportionately small type) presenting information on the association's planned next annual conference.

Note that this mailing contains not one but three brochures. (In fact, the order form itself is really a brochure.) This is quite a package, especially for a mailing in a number 10 envelope, but these orders do not represent casual purchases because membership in this association is not cheap. The cheapest membership is $250 annually, with a possible maximum of $1,650 annually. It takes a fair amount of marketing material to elicit an order for even $250 from a prospect, let alone $1,650. That is presumably the reason for the lengthy letter and the several brochures, although most direct-mail packages include a brochure or two. Brochures and sales letters are a mainstay of direct mail, virtually obligatory ingredients of the package.

BROCHURES

Brochure is a relatively broad and general term. It can be and is applied to quite a wide variety of materials, from simple leaflets of a few hundred words to slender folders that may be inserted in an ordinary number 10 business envelope to quite elaborate bound publications of many thousands of words, and even to "broadsides"—folded advertising enclosures that unfold to 11×17 or 17×23 inches or even larger size "flats."

Brochures may be bound with staples, with spiral wire or plastic spines, with commercial binding posts or similar fasteners, or by having their spines glued with "hot melt" in what is called perfect binding, the way rack-displayed paperback books are bound. However, if brochures are a diverse and loosely related family of printed materials in their sizes and other physical characteristics, they are almost equally diverse and loosely related to each other in the purposes and objectives for which they were created.

Each Brochure Should Have a Specific Objective

The term *brochuremanship* has been coined to refer to the practice of gilding the lily when writing any kind of descriptive paper about a subject. This assumes that every brochure is written to sell something—to indoctrinate and persuade, if not to sell in the literal sense. That is not always the case, although every brochure should have a clear and specific goal. Many brochures are created simply to inform, to advise, or to record information, as in the case of brochures written to document and make official an organization's personnel policies and purchasing procedures or to describe the symptoms of a common disease. And even in the case that concerns us, brochures that are part of direct-mail packages, not all brochures make a direct effort to sell or persuade. Instead, each brochure may support a single one of the several goals and objectives that an effective sales effort must achieve.

To review these briefly, an effective sales effort must first interest and motivate the prospect with the promise(s) of benefits that are much to be desired. But then the presentation (direct-mail package, in this case) must "prove" that you can and will deliver the benefit if the prospect sends you the order. That means that you must establish credibility on at least two levels: the logic of the benefit(s) resulting from the purchase (for example, prove that your diet tablets work) and the faith in your own honesty and dependability (prove that you will deliver the product and the result promised).

It is to achieve these objectives that the developer of the package on my desk included several brochures. One is a testimonial letter. Another is a reinforcement of the fear motivation—the risks and pitfalls that the association will help the respondent to avoid. Another builds the image of a large and capable (sheltering) organization. Each makes its own contribution. Each is an element in an *integrated package* that represents a *complete system.*

Developing the Brochure

One thing you must think about in developing brochures (or other elements) to go into a direct-mail package is how *much* motivation and proof you need. Or, perhaps expressed more clearly: How much selling do you have to do to get the order?

The size of the order—the commitment or amount of money you ask—is a major factor in finding an answer to this question. Certainly you do not need a $1.50 (cost) package of materials to close orders for a $10 calculator. You will be out of business quite soon if you operate on that basis. On the other hand, it is equally obvious that you are not going to get many $1,000 orders with a $1.50 direct-mail package. That modus operandi will also soon have you seeking a job or another kind of enterprise.

It is another case of "the more you tell . . ." A simple one-page letter brought me in enough $6 orders for a manual to encourage me to continue, but adding a four-page brochure to the letter more than tripled the orders. And there is no doubt that the one-page letter and the four-page brochure were more effective than a five-page letter or five-page brochure alone would have been. "The more you tell . . ." does not refer to number of words alone, but to the general impact of the direct-mail package overall. Far better to enclose several brief pieces in a package than one or two lengthy pieces because multiple pieces are usually more effective in direct-mail advertising. Unless you are lucky enough to truly captivate most of your readers with your opening—something that does happen, but only occasionally—most readers will not struggle all the way through a lengthy piece of advertising matter. Somehow a number of briefer pieces is far less formidable in appearance and is therefore far more palatable. If the reader has even a passing interest in your offer, he or she is far more likely to at least skim through and glance at the several items than to pore over a lengthy letter or brochure. For this reason, as well as for the other reasons cited, in many cases (e.g., where the selling proposition demands or at least justifies a relatively elaborate package of materials) there is great benefit in using several brief brochures, each focusing on a different major point, each with its own headline and lead.

There are, however, many occasions in which a single general brochure is required, a fact recognized in the following models. Of course, while many brochures are simple folders containing nothing but text and headlines, many others are quite elaborate with drawings, photographs, multicolor printing, and even special effects such as die-cut windows and foldouts. In the models that follow only headlines and text will be presented, with the clear understanding that the actual brochure may include any of the foregoing embellishments and refinements.

Model of a General Brochure

Headline:

MARKETING SERVICES
FOR THE TELECOMMUNICATIONS INDUSTRY
How to Get Rapid Results in This Dynamic New Industry

Body copy:

Why Hire Outside Services?

---

continued

There are at least three good reasons for going outside your own organization for marketing support:

To gain objectivity. The outside consultant or contract specialist brings a fresh and unbiased view to your situation and needs, something those who are close to the problem have difficulty in achieving.

To avoid undue staff pressures. Requiring your own staff to mount extra effort when they are already burdened with a full workload is not in the best interests of your management, for they do not produce their best work under such extreme pressure. The outside consultant is able to concentrate full attention on the problem.

To bring special skills to bear. Telecommunications, especially in the modern sense with all the high-tech developments of recent years, is a highly specialized field. You are likely to have difficulty in finding true expertise in this field among your own staff. It's a job for a specialist, and you usually have to contract out to find one.

Why Choose George Watkins?

With a background as sales and marketing manager for a half-dozen well-known manufacturers of telecommunications equipment, I have full knowledge of the field—over 20 years' worth—in terms of technology, equipment, markets, and competition. (Specific details of this background made available on a confidential basis on request.) This is the kind of expert help I offer you.

How I Work

Every job I work on is a custom job, tailored to my client's needs and convenience. However, the following are the typical arrangements, depending on the circumstances of the individual case:

Defined Project. In this arrangement we agree on what is to be done, produced as end-product(s), schedules, and costs. (You identify the need or problem, I estimate the time and cost, and we discuss and negotiate an agreement.)

Open-Ended Assignment. In this arrangement you retain my services, on a daily or hourly basis and on your premises or on mine, for as long as you perceive the need. You may terminate those services at any time on minimum notice.

Task Assignment. You may retain my services on a task-by-task basis or for single tasks as you see the need. We negotiate each task informally.

General Retainer. In this arrangement you are assured of priority demand for my services by paying me a monthly retainer (which accumulates, if not used each month) for some minimum number of hours or days per year.

A FEW PAST PROJECTS
(Abstracts of illustrative past projects.)

Models of Special-Purpose Brochures

**WHAT DELIGHTED USERS HAVE TO SAY
ABOUT *MERCHANDISING TODAY***
(Original correspondence on file in our offices and available for inspection.)

"Boosted sales 32 percent."—RBF, Halifax, NS

"I get at least two good ideas a month from this great newsletter, and most of those ideas either save me money or produce extra sales."—GG, Topeka, KS

"*Merchandising Today* paid for itself and showed me a profit with the very first issue. I never knew how much I didn't know about merchandising!"—HS, Philadelphia, PA

"One item in last month's issue of your newsletter alone was worth the entire year's subscription price and reading time."—PG, San Francisco, CA

"Please renew my *Merchandising Today* subscription for three more years. If you had a lifetime subscription rate I'd subscribe for it."—BS, Pocatello, ID

"Enclosed is payment for four additional subscriptions for my four store managers. I couldn't begin to teach them how to retail as well as your newsletter does."—HGH, New York, NY

"A friend of mine sent me a copy of *Merchandising Today,* and I fell in love with it at once. Why shouldn't I, when it has so many priceless ideas in it? Enclosed is payment for my two-year subscription."—BB, Olean, NY

"Sorry I didn't subscribe sooner. Please send me as many back issues as possible and bill whatever it costs."—HH, Bakersville, PA

***PROFESSIONAL SOFTWARE* PROGRAMS ARE DIFFERENT;
THEY ARE TAILORED TO THE PROFESSIONAL SPECIALTIES**

PROFESSIONAL SOFTWARE specializes in programs designed especially to help meet the needs and solve the problems of physicians, lawyers, architects, engineers, dentists, and other independent professionals. Among the many general classes of programs for your personal computer systems are those that provide such functions as the following:

- Conventional word processing, with special speller programs with technical terms for various professions.
- General accounting and payroll systems.
- Inventory management and reporting systems.
- Patient and client recordkeeping.
- Automatic billing.

continued

- Generating and sending out of statements.
- Late notice and collection letter distribution.
- Communication with central databases, such as the National Library of Medicine's MEDLARS and the Department of Education ERIC systems.
- Library file maintenance.
- Indexing and cataloging systems.

In most cases we have special programs (as listed in enclosed catalog) for each profession, so that the word processor for physicians lists thousands of medical terms in its built-in dictionary/speller, while that for architects lists construction and building design terms and that for lawyers lists legal terms.

The same principle applies to the communications programs, the library programs, and the other special programs. Each of our programs is designed for a specific profession. You no longer need adapt your way of doing things to the software programs available; we adapted the programs to your needs. But we have gone even beyond that: We offer many programs designed for specialists within a profession, such as obstetricians and surgeons in the medical profession and corporate lawyers and criminal lawyers in the legal profession.

All programs are available in a variety of PC and PC-compatible formats and are fully supported via our toll-free number. That is what makes these programs different: You are never stuck because of technical or applications difficulties. Our specialists are available every day, all day to take your call and help you solve your problems.

We guarantee our software, as we do all our products.

APPLICATION NOTES FOR THE DUST MASTER

Our special Dust Master, that little battery-operated, handy-Andy vacuum cleaner, has many obvious uses. But here are a few less-obvious ones that our customers have told us about.

Crackers in bed: "My husband and I munch in bed watching TV almost every night, and the result is crumbs in bed. Who can sleep in crumbs? I use our handy Dust Master almost every night to clean up those crumbs before we turn in."—Hattie G., Monroe, LA

Cleaning my room: "Maybe it's not what the Dust Master was intended for, but I swipe it when Mom is out and do a quickie sweep up of my carpet so Mom isn't after me any more about keeping my room clean."—Cookie W., Pine Bluff, AR

Our new car: "The Dust Master is far handier than the car vac that needs a cord connected to the cigarette lighter. We use it to vac out the car almost every Sunday."—Mary K., Bryn Mawr, PA

Lamp shades: "The Dust Master is absolutely fantastic for keeping fabric lamp shades clean. I rarely have to clean one with cleaner fluid now."—Stephanie M., Cicero, IL

continued

Dog hair: "Our dog sheds pretty badly, but we now keep up with it without trouble by following him around with our Dust Master."—Betty M., San Diego, CA

After dinner: "Nothing gets up the crumbs on the good table cloth after dinner like the Dust Master does. I have reduced my tablecloth laundering by about 75 percent by using the Dust Master."—Laura Z., Stockton, CA

In the wood shop: "I borrow my wife's Dust Master (when she's not looking) to clean up the basement floor after I spend time in my woodworking shop. Now we have no more arguments about the poor job I do of sweeping up."—Henry G., Missoula, MT

Barber shop clean-up: "I cut my husband's hair at home (we object to paying $7.50 for a haircut), and it gets all over everything, no matter how many cloths I use. I use my Dust Master to clean the hair clippings up off the chair, floor, and my husband too!"—Mildred N., Brooklyn, NY

Chapter 5

Collection Letters

COLLECTION LETTERS ARE NORMALLY PART OF A PROGRESSIVE SYSTEM

The need to send out letters prompting or soliciting payment is a common one. It is a need not only for profit-making business firms but also for many nonprofit organizations, such as associations and government agencies. (In fact, even federal government agencies are beginning to adopt some of the commercial collection tactics to redeem unpaid student and business loans made or guaranteed by the government.)

In many ways collection letters are the most difficult to write, for it is necessary to find and strike a proper balance between extremes in being courteous and being businesslike. Going to an extreme in one direction may suggest to the other party that you don't really mean business, while an extreme in the other direction is likely to become offensive and unnecessarily cost you the patronage of the other party.

There are, of course, some extreme cases when you no longer want the patronage of the other party except on a cash basis, if at all. However, you can't know that in the beginning. The unpaid obligation may be simply an oversight requiring a gentle reminder, or it may be that the respondent is simply a little late in making the payment but will make it without excessive lateness, once reminded. Too sharp a tone in the first reminder may prove highly offensive and anger the other party, causing you to lose his or her patronage. And, of course, a doctor does not want to lose a patient unnecessarily, any more than a lawyer wishes to lose a client, a department store a customer, or an association a member.

For this reason collection letters are ordinarily of many kinds, usually making up a system of letters that begin with gentle and even subtle reminders and only gradually become less forgiving and more insistent on payment. The hope underlying such a system is that the first letter or two will bring payment so that further correspondence will not be needed and the respondent will not be offended or angered. On the other hand, the assumption in escalating the severity of the tone in the demands for payment reflects a growing conviction that the other party needs to be dealt with firmly if payment is to be elicited. And if continued efforts bring no results, the assumption then becomes that the party does not intend to pay, and is probably not worth having as a patron, at least not as an account to which credit must be extended. At this point, but only at this point, the main objective is to induce the payment without very much concern (if any) for continued patronage by the respondent.

COLLECTION LETTERS ARE USUALLY FORM LETTERS

Most who bill numerous accounts regularly use form letters in the name of efficiency. It would simply be impractical for anyone to compose individually hundreds or even dozens of collection letters every week or two. (While most accounts are billed monthly, past-due accounts often require notices sent out more frequently.) Until now, such letters tended to be preprinted forms. Even when truly individualized letters were required they were generally typed individually but following a form established for the purpose.

Today, with word processing computers in even the smallest offices, it is possible to automate the process so that *every* letter is individually typed and addressed, although still following a form. The forms are, however, recorded on a computer disk, and a simple command causes the computer to type out the desired ones, properly addressed to the individuals.

Designing Your Own System

It is entirely feasible to develop your own system of collection letters by using the models included here to design your own standard letters and recording them on disks in your own system. (More suggestions about this will be offered later.)

THE FIRST NOTICE

The first notice sent out may be a bill (usually referred to as an invoice by business firms), if the bill was not handed to the patron at the time of the exchange or included with the merchandise. It is a more or less standard practice with most organizations who bill regularly to send a monthly statement out to patrons listing the status of the account—usually acknowledging payment received since the last statement and listing balance due.

This is usually a simple form, often with the word *Statement* appearing at its head. However, firms who do relatively little billing may not even have such a form, but may use a standardized invoice form (available from most office-supply sources) with the word *Statement* typed in, in place of the word *Invoice,* as shown in Figure 5–1. (An even simpler method of those who do little billing is to use a letterhead with the word *Statement* typed in.)

Figure 5-1 Invoice Form Used as a Statement

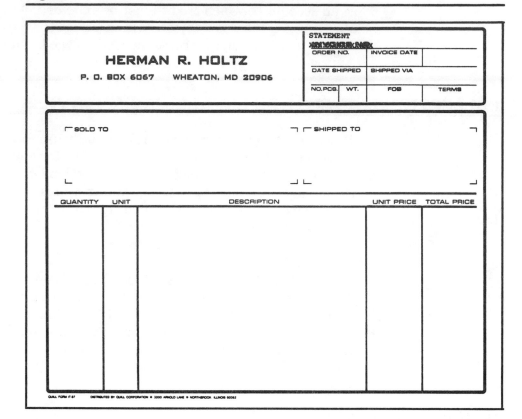

It is not only business firms who use statements as initial reminders of payment due (and many send such statements out as a routine to every patron, regardless of the status of the account). It is quite common for professionals and others charging for personal services—doctors, dentists, lawyers, hairdressers, and others—to send out statements every month as first notices.

Of course, because a statement is a completely objective and routine form—it doesn't really deserve to be called a letter—no one can take offense at it, even if they have already paid the bill, while it still serves to remind the respondent of the obligation if the bill has not been paid.

A First Notice *Can* Be a Letter

Despite the popularity and widespread use of statement forms as a first reminder of payment due, there are some who prefer to use some sort of letter as a first notice or reminder. However, since second notices (when they are the first actual *letter* sent out) rarely make reference to an original statement or first notice, the models for those letters (presented here as models of a second notice) are usually suitable for use also as first notices.

It is from this point on, after a first notice has been sent out and the respondent has failed to pay the bill or make some appropriate response within some reasonable time, that the reminders should begin to escalate, although usually still with great discretion and courtesy initially. In most cases it is not yet time to "get tough."

THE SECOND NOTICE

There is quite an enormous diversity in the kinds of creditors sending out collection letters, including but not restricted to the following:

Doctors, dentists, other professionals.
Retailers, such as department stores.
Credit card companies.
Banks.
Utilities.
Loan companies.
Schools (correspondence and other).
Associations.
Mail-order vendors.
Book clubs.
Printers.
Country clubs.
Wholesalers (and other suppliers to businesses).
Construction contractors (and tradespeople of various kinds).

There is also a large diversity in the kinds of conditions and situations surrounding or characterizing the obligation. In some cases the entire balance owing is due, whereas in others only an installment is currently due. Sometimes the amount owing is in dispute, while in others the entire bill is in dispute. In still other cases the dispute is over whether the merchandise or service is satisfactory and whether the bill is properly due therefore. And in some cases the customer has paid part of the bill, but not all, so the past-due notice is worded to ask for the balance, which should have been paid earlier.

The following collection of models represents an effort to provide an example of most of these typical situations, with a suggested method for responding to each.

A Set of Second-Notice Models

As in the case of first notices, second notices of payment past due are not always letters literally. Many creditors use other forms and formats for reminding their patrons that there are payments overdue. A few "get tough" almost immediately with printed forms headed by a headline that says something such as SECOND NOTICE! or PAST DUE! when the first notice has not produced payment, but most are still rather gentle at this point, especially when dealing with a patron who has ordinarily made payments faithfully on time. In some cases the creditor sends a copy of the original bill or of the most recent statement as a reference and attaches a sticker or note bearing a brief message, such as one of the following:

Just a friendly reminder that this account is past due. Your prompt remittance would be greatly appreciated. Thanks.

You have probably overlooked it but your payment of $_____ is past due. If there is any question regarding your account, please call. Thank you in advance for your prompt attention to this and for your valued patronage.

Some stores use a card instead of a letter for a second-notice reminder, with a mild statement, such as that in the sticker-note above, and a listing of the payment due, sometimes with the overall balance also listed. (Some even use a series of such cards instead of a series of letters, escalating the severity of tone as described here.)

Following are a number of typical second-notice (and in some cases first-notice) collection letters that are, in fact, letters rather than other devices. In most cases the text suggests whether the addressee is an individual or an organization and whether the amount owing is a personal or a business obligation. In others many of the models are so general as to be useful for many situations. Note however that when a notice is sent to a company or other large organization, it is not necessary to be quite so conciliatory because other businesspeople understand the need to send such notices and do not take offense usually, even when they have already paid the invoices.

Dear Mrs. Williams:

We note that there remains a small balance of $35.93 on your account, which has now become overdue.

May we expect your attention to this within the next few days?

Thank you for your continued patronage and for your help in clearing this small matter up quickly.

Sincerely,

P.S. If payment has been made, please disregard this notice.

Dear Mr. Braun:

There still remains a substantial balance owing us for recent shipments to your plant, as shown in the attached copies of the original invoices. We would deeply appreciate your timely remittance of payment for these invoices, as agreed upon by you in opening your account with us.

Thank you for your cooperation.

Very truly yours,

Dear Mr. George:

Perhaps it has escaped your attention that there is still an outstanding balance of $62.00 owing for your new hearing aid, with which you were recently fitted in our offices.

We thank you for your patronage of our establishment, but we must ask you to help us by making a prompt remittance to clear up this now overdue account.

Thank you for your understanding and cooperation.

Sincerely,

Dear Mrs. Henry:

It has been brought to my attention that we have no record of payment for last month's shipment of office supplies sent to your plant. If you will check your most recent statement I believe you will find that you have overlooked this obligation.

Won't you please help us get this matter cleared up by an early remittance?

Thank you.

Very truly,

Dear Major Martini:

Our records do not indicate receipt of the July installment on your account. Our computer shows an amount owing currently of $176.89. It is necessary to remit that amount immediately to bring your account up to date.

I look forward to receiving your remittance promptly. (If you have remitted your payment in the meanwhile, please disregard this notice.)

Sincerely,

Dear Miss Warrington:

Since we do not normally carry open accounts nor even have a credit or billing department, our extension of deferred payment to you last month was a special courtesy, with the understanding that you would make your remittance promptly upon invoicing.

An invoice was sent to you two weeks ago, and we have so far not received payment. May we expect payment immediately so that we may now close the books on this abnormal situation?

Thank you in advance for cooperation in clearing this up.

Sincerely,

Dear Mr. Wenger:

Enclosed is a copy of last month's statement for printing, showing a balance due of $329.47. We have, as of this date, not received this.

It has always been our policy to extend credit for a maximum of 30 days, and we have always made this clear when granting open accounts to our customers.

Can we count on you to clear this up promptly?

Thank you for your help.

Sincerely,

FOLLOW-UP NOTICES

When a second notice fails to produce the desired results, follow-up collection letters begin to become increasingly more insistent and less conciliatory, although there is a distinct difference between the approach to individual consumers and that to business firms. In the models follow-ing, which show a growing impatience with the delinquency, it is gener-ally apparent which is addressed to an individual consumer and which to an executive in a business organization of some kind. (In many cases, especially when several earlier notices have failed to bring results, the letter will bear a sticker or rubber stamp that says boldly and often in bright red ink: OVERDUE, DELINQUENT ACCOUNT, FINAL NO-TICE, or other such expression to dramatize the message. Moreover, the tone of the letters becomes steadily more aggressive and forecasts serious consequences for failing to pay the bill. And, in many cases, be-gins to inflict some of those penalties.

Models of Follow-Up Notices

Dear Mrs. White:

Frankly, we are puzzled. You have been a customer of Edgar's Depart-ment Store for many years, and maintained an account in good stand-ing for most of those years until recently. Now there is an unexplained and mystifying delinquency, and you have failed to respond to previous notices sent you regarding your charge account.

Is there some problem which prevents you from making payments on your account as in the past?

Won't you please stop in and discuss this with us so that we may work together to find some way to help you bring your account up to date.

Sincerely,

Dear Mrs. Whilliker:

You have failed to respond to our previous correspondence, and your account is now seriously delinquent, with $287.53 in overdue install-ments. This can have serious consequences for you and your credit rat-ing. We have tried to be patient, but we must insist that you attend to this matter now so that we shall not have to demand payment in full of the entire account ($967.68) or take other further action to resolve this matter.

Sincerely,

Dear Dr. German:

Your account is now unacceptably in arrears, and I must advise you that this is our Final Notice. Unless a minimum payment of $123.45 is received from you within 10 days we shall be forced to turn this entire account of $654.55 over for collection.

I sincerely hope that you will remit payment so that we will not find it necessary to do that.

Very truly yours,

Dear Mr. Bockwinhkle:

Your company's account is now $1,235.65 over your $5,000 credit limit, and we have not received a payment from you in several months, despite our several notices requesting payment. Accordingly, we must advise you that for the present, until the account is brought up to date, shipments to you must be on a COD basis.

I regret that we must do this, and I hope that you will understand our position.

Sincerely,

Dear Mr. Bertram:

Your account is in a delinquent status, as we have advised you several times in recent correspondence. The total owing is now $412.43, plus service charges.

Much as we value your patronage, as we do that of every customer, we cannot permit your delinquency to continue. We must advise you that effective January 17, we shall turn this account over for collection. That means that it will be automatically recorded as a delinquent account by the credit bureaus.

You can avoid this by paying this account in full before that date or making other satisfactory arrangements with us regarding your delinquency.

I sincerely hope that you will do that.

Very truly yours,

Dear Mr. Wallace:

It disturbs us that an old customer such as you should not only become delinquent in your account for the first time since we began to do business, but that you should also fail to respond to our inquiries. Obviously, like you, we have to collect what is due us if we are to pay our own bills and remain in business.

Perhaps you are having difficulties, and perhaps we can help in some way. But if you are having difficulties we cannot help unless you respond to our inquiries and talk to us.

Won't you give me a call personally so that we can discuss this and work something out to resolve the problem?

Sincerely,

Dear Mrs. Winston:

We have written you several times regarding your account with us, which is seriously past due. So far we have received no response from you.

Your credit rating is a valuable asset, and may even be critical to your ability to conduct your own business successfully. We certainly do not wish to do anything to impair your credit standing.

Please help us resolve this matter satisfactorily by remitting payment in full promptly or, if that is not possible, coming in to see me or calling me so that we can discuss ways to settle this matter.

Sincerely,

Dear Mrs. Beale:

So far you have simply ignored several letters asking you to get in touch with me about your seriously delinquent charge account. (The complete balance owing and now overdue is $197.49.)

This leaves me no choice but to turn this entire matter over to our attorneys for whatever legal action they think proper.

I will wait until February 9 to do this, to give you one final chance to respond in some way so that we can clear this up. I hope that you will do so so that we can avoid taking any unpleasant further action.

Sincerely,

SPECIAL COLLECTION PROBLEMS AND SITUATIONS

Collection problems are not always a simple matter of trying to collect delinquent accounts from people who are either slow in paying or are failing completely to pay at all. Sometimes there are special problems and situations surrounding claims for payment, and these complicate the situation. For example, in some cases there may be a dispute over the amount owed or whether anything is owed at all. This can arise from a challenge to the accuracy of the billing. A customer may claim that you failed to credit a payment or a return, that he or she was overcharged for an item, or that it was on sale and the regular price was charged. In fact, the possibility that you made a mistake somehow in the billing or in issuing a proper credit is one of the several reasons to be cautious and courteous in the initial requests for payment. Perhaps people and not computers make mistakes, but there are mistakes made nevertheless whose effects tend to be more severe today because we put too much faith in computerized systems, all but certain that the system cannot err. But even more common than accounting errors—and such errors are really not too common today—is the problem of payments and bills crossing in the mail, so that the customer is outraged to be notified of delinquency or assessed a special late charge when he or she did, in fact, pay the bill on time.

Still another problem that arises is that of the delinquent debtor who submits an unacceptably small payment without having gotten your agreement in advance that you would accept a small amount as a satisfactory installment on the debt. Or, as a variant of this, the problem sometimes arises when a debtor tries to settle an account by compromise by offering a partial payment and asking you to accept this as a settlement of the entire claim.

Form letters can be used to cope with many of the problems that arise out of such situations. The following models demonstrate how this can be done, and each model is worded to reflect the type of special problem it is designed to help you cope with. As in the case of the other collection letters in the system, initial efforts are made to handle the matter pleasantly and at low stress. Only when and if these methods fail is the pressure raised.

Models of Collection Letters for Special Situations

Dear Mr. Sandusky:

Thank you for your payment of $_____ received on July 9. This payment reduces your outstanding balance to $_____. We do appreciate your efforts to bring this overdue account up to date, but we hope you will make an effort to clear up the final balance within the next few days.

continued
We look forward to receiving your final payment by the end of this month at the latest.
Thank you for your cooperation.

Sincerely,

Dear Mrs. Holcomb:

I have had our accountant check your account records carefully, and he reports that there is no record of the $_____ payment you believe you made last month. Perhaps you have confused this with a payment you made to someone else.

Won't you please check your own records and see whether you can find a canceled check for that amount? A copy of a canceled check would be convincing evidence that we did receive the payment and possibly failed to record it. However, in the absence of such evidence of payment we must rely on our own records and insist that you make a payment of at least $_____ to eliminate the delinquency in your account.

Sincerely,

Dear Colonel Weldon:

We have been having difficulty in verifying the return of a defective _____ which you reported to us. We are unable to issue a credit until we verify the return of that shipment. If you can send us a copy of your receipt for that shipment it will help greatly. And, for the moment at least, we will suspend our demand for payment of that merchandise.

Therefore, we have for now reduced the amount of your currently due bill to $_____ and will look forward to receiving your check in that amount.

I apologize for any inconvenience we may have caused you.

Very truly yours,

Dear Ms. Smythe:

You were quite correct in your claim of an overcharge. Inadvertent although it was, we did overcharge you $_____ for your _____.

The total of your account now owing is therefore $_____, as you stated in your letter, and your check for that amount will bring your account completely up to date.

Sincerely,

Dear Mrs. Carrone:

I am sorry to hear that the knockdown TV stand delivered to you did not have a complete set of parts for its assembly. You may either bring the entire package back to the store for exchange or you may bring in a list of missing parts and give the list to the department manager, along with this letter. He will see to it that you get the parts you need.

I will advise our accounting department that they may expect your payment as soon as we have made this exchange for you. Please accept my apology for any inconvenience you have suffered.

Yours truly,

SITUATIONS REQUIRING PERSONAL LETTERS

The examples of collection problems we have looked at called for or at least could usually be handled by form letters, and it is true enough that probably 95 percent of your collection problems can be handled with form letters. But occasionally there arises a special situation that demands a personal letter to be resolved properly. There are no hard and fast rules for handling these situations because there are too many imponderables—unpredictable circumstances and considerations—possible. However, a few models are presented here to illustrate the principle of such cases and some methods for coping successfully with them.

Dear Mr. Halaby:

We traced the mix-up in your account to a computer error. We then made the proper adjustments, and your account records have been brought up to date. We are pleased to acknowledge that your account is and was current, and not delinquent, as we mistakenly claimed.

continued

We apologize for the error, which is entirely our fault, and hope that you were not caused undue inconvenience by this.

Sincerely,

Dear Mr. Magid:

Although our accounting department has sent you several statements and notices that your account is seriously delinquent, we have not heard from you in response. Mr. Munday, our credit manager, knowing of our long personal relationship, has asked me to write you about this.

Perhaps you are having business or even personal difficulties, as we all do at times. Or perhaps there is some other reason that you have permitted your account with us to become past due. That is a most unusual condition for you. In all the years we have done business together I cannot recall this ever happening before. Therefore my special concern about your business and personal welfare.

Whatever the problem is, it won't right itself. It is therefore important that we talk about this. Won't you write or call me personally? I am sure that together we can and will work things out and solve whatever problem exists concerning this.

Most truly yours,

Dear Mrs. Walters:

Your account has been referred to me for my personal attention because you are a long-time valued patron of our store, and the store manager is sure that you would not register a complaint if it were not justified. However, he reported to me that he has had some difficulty understanding just what the nature of your complaint is so that he can do something about it. He says that you can't or won't tell him just why you insisted on a cancellation of your contract to pay for a sewing machine you purchased here.

It is my understanding that you returned the sewing machine after you had had it for some time, that you made no explanation of why you were returning it other than that it was "no good," and that you not only refused to make further payments on the machine but that you demanded a refund of earlier payments.

continued

I am sure you had some reason for your actions, but as of now we do not know exactly what that reason was.

You are an established and valued customer, and if, indeed, the machine is defective we will see to it that a full refund is made or the machine replaced with another one, even if we have to absorb the loss. However, we do need your help with this, so that we can go back to the manufacturer with the problem. Won't you please call or come in and see me personally?

Thank you for your help with this difficult matter, and please accept my personal apologies for any inconvenience or distress this experience has caused you.

Very truly yours,

Dear Mr. Pearson:

The manager of our electronics service department has advised me of your refusal to honor our bill for $67.55 for parts and service to your television receiver. According to the information I have received, your position is that you have been complaining about the receiver almost from the first day you bought it in our store, and it has taken us over a year to straighten the problem out properly.

In reviewing our records I find that we have made four service calls at your home to service this TV, and that we brought it into our shop on two occasions, the last one nearly six months ago. No charge was made to you on any of these occasions, although the warranty on your set covers parts for one full year, but it covers labor for only 90 days.

In short, Mr. Pearson, we accommodated you with both parts and labor for a full year. According to our records we also offered to exchange your TV for another, but you declined that.

In all fairness to us, Mr. Pearson, you cannot expect us to go on furnishing service free of charge. This last service call was most definitely more than a year after you bought the set, and so we are entitled to be paid for our work. Still, I do understand your feelings in this matter, and I want to consider them. Therefore, I have instructed our service manager to reduce this bill by one third to $45.00. Please remit that amount and we will mark the bill paid in full.

I hope that this will resolve everything for both of us.

Sincerely,

■ **Chapter 6**

Letters of Agreement (Informal Contracts)

CONTRACTS AND AGREEMENTS

In law—by formal legal definitions, that is—contracts and agreements are not quite the same thing, and presumably a great deal could depend on the legal differences in the event of a contract dispute and subsequent litigation. In practice, at least for those everyday business situations that do not require or justify the expense of formal legal services, the differences are academic and of little consequence. An agreement between two or among more than two parties to do something specific is a contract and ordinarily enforceable. There must be an offer and an acceptance.

There are certain other conditions necessary, as any good law professor will hasten to tell you. What is agreed to must be within the law, the contracting parties must be of legal age and competent to enter into agreements in all other respects, and there must be a "consideration."

An agreement need not necessarily be signed by both/all parties to be a binding and enforceable contract (with certain specific exceptions), although the lack of signatures may make it more difficult to resolve subsequent disputes arising out of the agreement. For example, a purchase order is usually signed by only the issuing party, rather than by both, and constitutes an agreement. (There are exceptions: In some cases the party to whom the purchase order is issued is asked to acknowledge receipt and acceptance of the purchase order by signing and returning one copy to the issuer.)

Technically, an agreement consists of an offer and an acceptance, which then gives it the force of a contract. A purchase order is an offer to buy something, usually at a price specified in the purchase order. The other party's acceptance of the order—supplying the items or services specified in the purchase order—completes the agreement.

Actually, the contract or agreement need not even be in writing to be binding and enforceable (again with certain notable exceptions, where the law demands an agreement in writing); the fact that the agreement was entered into and exists, even as a verbal commitment, makes it a binding contract. However, in the event of a later dispute as to what the precise promises and agreements were, it can become quite difficult to enforce a verbal agreement or adjudicate a dispute because it becomes difficult to establish the precise terms of the agreement when the references are only to the memories and representations of the parties. Therefore, except for minor agreements that entail little or no risk of problems difficult to solve, it is wise to specify the agreement in writing and have all parties sign to affirm their knowledge and agreement.

In short, the main objective of a written agreement or contract is or should be, at least nominally, to define and describe the terms of the agreement so that it is not necessary to rely on human memory, which is usually somewhat faulty when the personal interests of each party are at stake.

Formal Contracts

Lawyers drawing up formal contracts have different objectives than do business people and other lay persons who turn their hands to drafting agreements. The lay person is (properly and rightfully) concerned primarily with defining the agreement—what each party has agreed to do—so that there is a clear understanding of the agreement in its entirety. The lawyer is (properly and rightfully) concerned with clarity of definition, but also with enforceability—with ensuring that his or her client will have adequate legal protection in the event of a dispute concerning the contract. And to do that the lawyer relies not only on a knowledge of the relevant laws per se, but also to a large extent on precedents—on models of language and form that have been established as standards through usage and accepted by the courts in the past. That is the chief reason for the tortuous legal phraseology, with its strange Latin words and other terms rarely used or heard outside of legal documents and courtrooms. Only slowly is the legal profession willing to risk the use of the modern and simplified language that represents departure from old customs and so engages the hazard of possible new interpretations that may endanger enforceability or recovery in event of disputes.

Informal Contracts

Of course, I will not attempt here to suggest the use of formal or legal phrases in drafting agreements. Aside from being entirely unqualified to do so, I have as my principal purpose the goal of offering guidance and suggestions for only those informal (or, at best, semiformal) agreements and contracts nonlawyers—businesspeople and others—would draft themselves.

As John Cotton Howell states plainly in his *The Guide to Business Contracts* (Citizen's Law Library, 1979), "You don't need a lawyer to negotiate and prepare business contracts for you." And he thus introduces the truth that every transaction we enter into, even buying a morning newspaper, involves a contractual exchange. However, aside from that technicality and on a more practical scale, we do draft a great many contracts without the use of lawyers, as a practical necessity, creating rather informal (but no less binding) agreements.

Among the many kinds of situations calling for such informal agreements are the following. Each example refers to a relatively small-scale commitment; anything to be undertaken on a major scale and/or with major investments and risks would almost surely involve protracted negotiations with formal legal services for all parties and multipage contracts loaded with those technical terms and interminably long clauses. But here are a few typical situations suitable for informal written agreements:

Retention of temporary or contract employees.
Award of a small contract to carry out a project of some sort, such as writing a custom computer program.
Retention of a consultant or other professional to provide services.
Agreement to provide special or custom-made items.
Agreement to coventure in an enterprise.
Agreement to co-bid.
Agreement to subcontract.
Agreement to liquidate assets.
Conditional sale.
Agreement to invest.
Agreement to sell some asset.
Commission agreement.
Lease or rental agreement.
Sublease.
Publication release or permission form.
Agreement to represent or be represented.

Reasons for Drafting Informal Agreements

There are two principal reasons for drafting letter contracts and similar informal contracts and agreements. One is to avoid both the expense and time involved in bringing in legal talent. That is an important reason. But the other, and in many ways even more important reason, is to avoid scuttling the entire transaction.

Unfortunately, that very practice lawyers normally employ of making contracts and agreements "bombproof" for their clients is often directly in conflict with good sales and marketing policy. Instead of making it easy for the prospective customer or client to do business with you, it makes it difficult. Confronted with the necessity to negotiate with a lawyer—which also means bringing a lawyer of his or her own into the negotiation of a rather small contract and often haggling over possible problems that are, in fact, unlikely to even materialize—prospects often opt to abandon the negotiation entirely. Even when no lawyer is physically present the lawyer's handiwork can have the same effect:

Confronted with a document thick with "whereases" and "party of the second part" phrases, the prospect often flees hastily.

It is therefore purely in the interests of marketing and sales success that contracting should be kept as simple, as straightforward, and as painless as possible.

The Forms of Informal and Semiformal Agreements

Purchase orders, which are used for many of these situations, may be printed forms, or they may be simple letterheads such as that of Figure 6–1. Those who issue purchase orders only infrequently tend to utilize this simple form, although standard purchase-order forms are readily available from most stationers and office suppliers.

Where this is used to make a simple purchase—an order of ordinary office supplies, for example—there is no need to request the respondent to accept the offer formally by signing and returning a copy. However, when the offer is to buy some special custom-made item or service, the buyer may be entering into some risk, at least that of losing valuable time, if the respondent does not confirm that he or she accepts the order and will fill it. In such case it is wise to request that the respondent sign and return a copy of the order as a promise to fill it. That, for all practical purposes, then constitutes a contract because both parties have agreed to do certain things for each other: One will supply some goods or services, and the other will pay some agreed upon sum of money in exchange. Figure 6–2 is an example of such a purchase-order/agreement. Here there is a custom service required, there is a definite time element that is critical to the purchaser, and the purchaser wants a definite commitment by the supplier to meet the schedule as well as perform the services at the price quoted. Therefore it is important to the purchaser to get a signed agreement. However, the services are routine printing and binding services (nothing extraordinary about them), despite being custom services, and have been quoted earlier by the printer. Therefore, a purchase order is adequate to serve the purpose here.

Letters of Agreement

Many situations do not lend themselves to such a simple solution because the agreement is somewhat more complicated or unique and requires a fairly comprehensive description and explanation. A number of models following illustrate a variety of such situations. The models themselves range from simple letters expressing agreement or acceptance to semiformal contract forms, usually on letterheads and usually constituting not more than a single page.

FIGURE 6–1 Informal Letterhead Purchase Order

HRH COMMUNICATIONS, INC.
P.O. Box 6067
Silver Spring, MD 20906

PURCHASE ORDER

May 29, 1986

TO: Business Support Services, Inc.
    705 Butternut Avenue
    Royal Oak, MI 48073

    Six (6) each multi-strike ribbons for Silver-Reed EXP 550.

Herman Holtz

Models of Letter Agreements

Letter agreements are normally on the letterhead of the seller or buyer. For example, a consultant or supplier of any other custom-designed service or product is likely to offer a client his or her own agreement form, preprinted on his/her letterhead or, at least, boilerplated so that it can be typed up quickly on a letterhead. Sometimes the client prefers that

FIGURE 6–2 Letterhead Purchase Order with Acknowledgment Copy

HRH COMMUNICATIONS, INC.
P.O. Box 6067
Silver Spring, MD 20906

PURCHASE ORDER

May 29, 1986

TO: Hunnicut Lithographic Corp.
    112 W. Georges Lane
    Heartburn, OH 55555

     Print and bind 5,000 copies of enclosed Windmill
Corporation Annual Report, per quotation submitted
earlier, to be delivered not later than 7/12/86.
                                                    $1,768.92

Please sign and return one copy of this order as acknowledgment
and agreement to supply items specified.

_____
For HRH Communications, Inc.

_____
For Hunnicut Lithographic Corp.

the agreement be on the client's letterhead. The seller may then offer the client a copy of the form to be retyped on the client's stationery. Therefore, the agreement, even if a standard form, may appear finally on the letterhead of either party.

It should be understood, of course, that none of this is represented to be qualified legal advice and that the forms suggested here may or may not stand up to legal tests in a court of law. The presumption on which these models are based is that there is honest intent between or among the parties (and an infinite number of "whereases" and "wherefores" will not suffice to make the transaction bombproof), and the principal purpose of the written document is to avoid the trap of being forced to rely on memory for precise promises and agreements.

In general, then, the contract should do the following:

Identify the contracting parties.
State the date the agreement was entered into.
State specifically what each party promises to do and, where appropriate, when it is to be done.
Define the consideration. (Actually, this is simply what one of the signatories, usually the one paying or otherwise compensating the other, is to do, so it is a somewhat redundant listing here.)
Identify the signers.

The following models are self-explanatory, and are usually typed on the letterhead of one of the contracting parties, as explained here. They range from simple memoranda of understanding to relatively structured, although brief and more or less informal, agreements that tend to follow the general form of classic contracts.

MEMO: Agreement to Purchase

Date:_____

John Doe of Mulberry Lane, Wichita, Kansas, agrees to purchase and Jane Roe, of Roes Acres, Hayseed, Oklahoma, agrees to sell 5,000 pounds of sugar cane for the sum of One Thousand Six Hundred and Fifty dollars ($1,650), said sugar cane to be ready for delivery by June 30, 1988, and transaction to be completed by July 10, 1988. Receipt of Five Hundred dollars ($500) deposit is hereby acknowledged, balance to be due and paid on delivery.

_____   _____
John Doe   Jane Roe

Assignment

I, Walter Miranda, of Harvest Hill, Seattle, Washington, for and in consideration of Eight Thousand dollars ($8,000) paid to me by Henry Willows of Riverbank, Colorado, receipt of which is hereby acknowledged, sell, assign, and transfer to Henry Willows a debt owing me

---

continued
from the Tractor Drive Corporation for services rendered of Nine Thousand Two Hundred and Fifty dollars ($9,250), with full power to collect and discharge or sell and assign the same asset.

I certify that this sum of $9,250 is justly due as stated.

Dated:_____

_____
Walter Miranda

Howard Hodgkins will provide to the Excellence Corporation such personal services as are necessary to develop a first issue and detailed model of an 8-page monthly customer newsletter for the Corporation.

The Excellence Corporation will provide all office facilities and resources—desk space, typing services, access to office copiers, and to corporate information and personnel—necessary for those portions of the work Mr. Hodgkins deems necessary to be carried out on the Corporation's premises.

The Corporation will pay Mr. Hodgkins $650 per day, and Mr. Hodgkins guarantees completion of the work within 30 days from date at a cost not to exceed $12,000 in fees for his services.

Final payment and completion of the project will be subject to final review and acceptance of the product developed by Mr. Hodgkins.

This constitutes the entire agreement between Howard Hodgkins and the Excellence Corporation.

Date:_____   Date:_____

_____   _____
For Excellence Corporation   For Howard Hodgkins

The following constitutes the entire agreement between Energetic Sales, Inc. (ESI) and Hightech Chips Corp. (HCC).

ESI agrees to represent HCC in the markets in all 50 United States and U.S. possessions and to apply its best efforts to generate sales of HCC products in all markets presently served by ESI. ESI agrees that they will neither represent nor sell the products of any other manufacturer or vendor of electronic chips.

continued
    HCC agrees that ESI will be the sole marketing representative of HCC and will service all HCC accounts other than those already established as of this date as house accounts, per the attached list.

    ESI will be commissioned at one third of the HCC list prices, as published in the HCC official catalog, except for such special arrangements as ESI and HCC shall agree upon and enter into.

    This agreement is valid for an indefinite period, with annual options, and may be discontinued by mutual consent or upon payment of liquidated damages, which shall consist of the equal of ESI commissions for the highest 90-day period of the previous year.

    This agreement is valid and binding immediately upon signing by the legal representatives of both parties.

_____   _____
for Energetic Sales, Inc.   Date

_____   _____
for Hightech Chips Corp.   Date

    Harry's Department Stores Corp. of New York City, New York, hereby authorizes FastTalking Auctioneers, Inc. of Closeout, New York, to sell at public auction the entire contents of Harry's Department Stores in Blue Sky, Pennsylvania; Mountaintop, West Virginia; and Fishnet, Maryland.

    FastTalking Auctioneers, Inc. agrees to advertise all sales at their own expense and conduct all sales to completion not later than September 30, 1989.

    FastTalking Auctioneers, Inc. will require a minimum of three bids for each item sold, except as otherwise agreed to by Harry's Department Stores Corp. and shall retain twenty (20) percent of all proceeds derived therefrom as their commission on sales. Other than this, FastTalking Auctioneers, Inc. is to have complete control of all sales, advertising of sales, and all related activity.

    This is the entire agreement between Harry's Department Stores Corp. and FastTalking Auctioneers, Inc.

_____   _____
for Harry's Department Stores, Inc.   Date

_____   _____
for FastTalking Auctioneers, Inc.   Date

_____   _____
Witness   Witness

READY-MADE CONTRACTS AND AGREEMENTS

As in the case of invoices and purchase orders, there are many types of contracts and agreements that can be purchased in standardized, ready-made form. Printers, stationers, office suppliers, and even ordinary department stores today sell standardized, fill-in-the-blanks forms for entering into separation and divorce agreements, leasing equipment or buildings, issuing a bill of sale, and for sundry other purposes requiring some written agreement or legal document. (You can also buy ready-made forms for writing a will, adopting bylaws for an organization or corporation, filing for bankruptcy, and for many other such needs.) Some of these are legalistic, with all the proper Latin terms and legal injunctions, having been created by lawyers; others are quite simplistic and in everyday language, having been adapted to everyday use by editors and writers, in the philosophy espoused here.

It is, of course, very much in your interest to take advantage of such forms when they suit your purpose. But bear in mind the caveats offered earlier: An overly ponderous and cabalistic agreement is no less so merely because it is a preprinted standard form. If it is difficult for lay people to understand or is intimidating in its general impact, it may very well blow up the entire transaction for those reasons alone.

It is thus wise to review the wide choice of competing forms carefully before adopting one and choose one that appears easiest to understand and least intimidating but still serves all your needs.

Even when you choose one of many competing forms you are under no compulsion to use the form as is. You may modify it by striking out clauses or words that do not apply, by changing wording, and by adding words, clauses, and even whole paragraphs. (It is usual practice to have all parties to a contract initial every such change or addition to prove that every party to the contract has approved each change or addition and to make it a binding commitment.) This is, in fact, a common practice even in those cases where one of the parties enters into contracts regularly and so has his or her own standard contract forms. While some organizations have a standard form that rarely varies, others are in enterprises that involve individual negotiations in each case, and thus almost always must modify their "standard contract" to fit the individual case.

OTHER SPECIAL CASES

There are other special cases, such as one in which the contract itself is a simple form that includes other documents or other information "by reference." One example of this is the case where a buyer—client, that is—has requested proposals, bids, or quotations and selected one of the proposals, bids, or quotations as the winner. In such cases it is more or less customary to incorporate the original proposal, bid, or quotation as the "schedule"—list of specific items or services to be provided, along with dates of other time elements—as an integral part of the contract. That is, the contract invokes the earlier submittal as a part of the contract "by reference."

That's not all of it. In the case of government (and in that of many large corporations who do business regularly in this manner) the simple contract form (which may be a single sheet, as in the case of the Federal Standard Form 33), the contract also invokes a number of standard procurement regulations—actually legal statutes, in the case of governments—also "by reference."

In fact, in the case of the Federal Standard Form 33 and similar cases, the seller is required to sign the form and submit it with the proposal or bid, and the contract may be made effective and binding by the buyer by the simple expedient of accepting it—by countersigning the form. That is, the seller has already signed a contract in advance, the specific terms of which are embodied in his or her proposal or other submittal (bid or quotation). All that remains to make the contract an enforceable legal instrument is the buyer's authorized signature. (It is at least for this reason—the need to have a bid or proposal document that can be included in the contract by reference—that bidders and proposers are asked to supply formal amendments to their bids and proposals to document agreements made in negotiations prior to contract awards.)

In other cases, where the buyer does not have a standard form for the purpose, the inclusion "by reference" may still be accomplished easily through the agency of a simple letter that accepts the seller's original submittal and makes it the schedule—details—of the contract.

Following are a few models of such letters.

MODELS OF LETTERS INVOKING PROPOSALS, BIDS, OR QUOTATIONS BY REFERENCE

Ref: Your quotation of 11/30/87

Dear Mr. Mulligatawny:

   This is to advise you of our acceptance of your quotation submitted in response to our RFQ No. H-65-74-87, for 4,500 Widgy-Widgets, Size 12, to be delivered on or before October 25 of this year. Please accept this letter as our contractual commitment.

Sincerely,

Dear Mrs. Harrison:

Your proposal No. W676-A-87-A, as amended following our meeting with you on June 3, 1987, is hereby formally accepted by Hyperion Corporation. Please sign the copy of this letter and return it to us to confirm your formal acceptance.

Sincerely,

John W. Martin
President

Accepted as specified herewith.

_____

Joan M. Harrison, President
Electronic Futures, Inc.

Dear Mr. Watkins:

Your bid of January 8, 1988, is hereby accepted, along with all terms and conditions specified therein, making it a binding obligation and creating a contract between us, as specified in the bid terms.

Work may begin immediately, subject to schedule commitments specified in the subject bid submittal.

Please sign and return one copy of this letter.

Sincerely,

Harold M. Beatty

Accepted for Nuts & Bolts, Inc.

_____

■ PART II

REPORTS

CLASSES AND CATEGORIES OF REPORTS

Our society generates a great deal of "paper" today—documents and publications of many kinds—and both the volume and diversity of such items is increasing steadily. Not the least of the items making up this potpourri is a collection of documents classified generally as reports.

Public corporations and even many government agencies are required to prepare and publish a document called an Annual Report. Financial departments (specifically, controllers) of most large organizations (and even of small organizations) must produce a variety of financial reports, such as profit and loss (P&L) statements, balance sheets, statements of net worth, and sundry others. Leaders of special projects, especially when those are custom jobs for customers, are usually required to produce a routine monthly progress report on each project and often special interim reports at key points, as well as a final report on completion of the project. Managers responsible for supplies and materials must produce inventory reports of various kinds, which must complement and balance production reports prepared by production managers. And those responsible for quality control, inspection, sales, advertising, publicity, and other functions must all produce their own reports. Usually these are on a monthly basis, but in many cases, such as that of sales and marketing, reports are often required on a weekly or even on a daily basis. (Salesmen, for example, are often required to produce a daily "call report" accounting for each day's sales efforts.)

PURPOSES AND OBJECTIVES OF REPORTS

Reports can be intended for different readers and different uses. The purpose of reports in a typical business organization is to keep management informed of all current conditions and to alert management to any special conditions or events, such as unaccounted-for gaps in the inventory, financial emergencies, dwindling profits, serious schedule slippages, or other events (problems, especially) that should command the attention of management. And where a special project is concerned, reports are often prepared for the customer's eyes, as required by contract.

On the other hand, annual reports are usually for the benefit of investors—stockholders—and prospective investors, although they are also useful tools to support marketing and even public relations and are often distributed freely for that reason.

Reports may be intended for the general public, too, especially when they are ordered, funded, and produced by public organizations, such as government agencies and nonprofit corporations of various kinds. Legislative bodies often order studies made and reports produced as necessary input for the consideration of public problems and possible legislation.

In organizations where reports are ordered for use of management, decisions are based generally on the information provided, although frequently the report triggers a special investigation or research (or at least a staff meeting) by management before they make a decision. The reports intended primarily for such use are of great importance since they are the chief means, in many cases, for high-level executives in an organization to become and remain aware of conditions in the "line" levels of the organization—the levels of production, sales, and other shirt-sleeve working levels.

In general, then, reports are an important part of business and career activity for a great many people, but there are many kinds of reports, many uses and sources of information for use in reports, and many methods for developing them. The diversity and importance of reports in business and career life are great enough to justify a separately identified Part for the subject.

Chapter 7

Reports, Various

A FEW COMMON PRINCIPLES

Although there are a great many different kinds of reports generated for many different applications in organizations, there are a few principles and guidelines that are or should be common to all or nearly all reports. Those guidelines are based on the premise that a report is at least ordinarily (with perhaps an occasional exception) a recital of factual information and not a sales argument. If a report is to be persuasive, that persuasion should be the consequence of reliable information that is logically organized and leads to reasonable conclusions, not of emotional argument. In fact, most, if not all, reports ought to exhibit these characteristics.

1. Each report must have a clearly understood purpose or objective—to report progress or status routinely, to report one or more special problems, to support an argument for or against something, to furnish special information, to furnish routine information, or other. No report can be very effective if the author of the report does not have a clear understanding of the need or purpose the report is to satisfy.

2. The information must be complete, accurate, and organized coherently in a manner appropriate to the purpose of the report.

3. The information must be presented in simple and straightforward language so that it is a clear recital of facts and, where appropriate, conclusions and recommendations drawn from and based on those facts. (In the latter case, it is essential that the rationale or logical chain of reasoning be furnished too.)

INFORMATIONAL VERSUS ANALYTICAL REPORTS

Several types of reports have been identified already, classified in terms of the kinds of data they report on, such as inventory, finances, production, and so forth. They may also be classified and categorized by their purposes or objectives and the way they handle the data included in them. That is, each report is normally either informational or analytical; the report simply narrates factual data in a given order and organization or it offers analysis of the data with conclusions drawn from the analysis and, in some cases, with recommendations based on the conclusions. And at the same time, reports may be formal, following some prescribed and standardized format, or they may be informal, relatively casual documents.

THE COMPUTER AS REPORT WRITER

One reason for the vast increase in paper today is the computer, especially the personal or desktop computer which has now made it possible for even the smallest offices to enjoy the benefits of the digital revolution. A great many of today's reports are simply collections of statistical data tabulated and printed out by the computer automatically or on special command. (This is especially true where the data is essentially numerical, as in inventory, purchasing, sales, and accounting.)

Despite this, a great deal of report writing must be done by humans, with and without the help of the computer. Even where the computer produces most of the report, as is true in many cases, a human must still organize the information, verify its accuracy and completeness, perform analyses, draw conclusions, affirm the accuracy and completeness, and prepare the textual elements of the report. (Relatively few reports, except purely routine statistical tabulations, are distributed without some text and human input.)

TYPES AND SOURCES OF INFORMATION FOR REPORTS

Reports often include and may, as just noted, consist principally of statistical or quantitative data—figures. These may be figures that are simply reported or cited (quoted from other sources), or they may be figures derived from other data and developed for citation in the report. But this is true for other, descriptive or narrative data also. The sources for both kinds of data are many:

One frequently used method for gathering information is library research, or the study of previously prepared documents, published or otherwise. These may include notes, logs, diaries, clippings of items and articles from periodicals, files, official records, books, correspondence, audiotapes, videotapes, slides, film clips, and/or other already recorded sources.

Another commonly used method is interrogation of or interviews with knowledgeable individuals who are likely to be able to make useful contributions. This need not be confined to experts or key executives. In some cases the most valuable or most relevant information is derived from mass interviews or questionnaires—surveys and polls. (Or the primary purpose of the report may be the gathering, recording, and analysis of mass opinion expressed by some group or body of people.)

Still another and most important source of data in investigatory reports is your personal observation. In fact, this and interrogation are often the primary sources of critical new information, with other data constituting background information for purposes of reference and orientation of the new data.

DISCUSSIONS OF DIFFERENT SOURCES

In many cases you have no choice of sources; you must use whatever is available. But there are other situations in which you have alternative sources available for research and data gathering, and you can choose among them. Or you may have data already at hand from many sources, offering relevant information that is replicated by each source, and you must decide which data/source is best to use.

Personal Observation

In general, the best—most accurate and most reliable—information is that which is based on your personal observations. This should be the most recent, most thoroughly detailed, most easily verified, most thoroughly annotated, and most objective information. It is always wise to do whatever you can to verify or validate any information you gather or are offered, so, when there is even a slight reason for doubt, try to verify data by personal observation if at all possible; sometimes that is the only acceptable verification. (For example, in a case where I was personally preparing a report on a radically new and different type of radar equipment, the engineer in charge of the project challenged certain statements I made as being obviously untrue. He remained unconvinced even when I demonstrated logically that what I said was logically and inescapably true, due to the revolutionary nature of this radar design. Finally, it was necessary to transport him to the site a number of miles away, where the equipment was in operation, so that he could verify my statements for himself.) And even then be aware that it is possible to be mistaken about that which you have personally seen or thought you have seen.

Library Research

In a great many cases library research for much of the data is an absolute necessity because it would be impractical, if not impossible, to try to gather all the information you need by other methods, especially when the nature of the report is such that it requires historical data. In such cases you may and often do have the option of several alternative sources. You should therefore employ some rational principle for choosing which source/data to use, such as that noted earlier. Compare the alternative sources and select that or those which you find or believe to be most recent, objective, detailed, verifiable, annotated, and dependable.

And, if time permits, compare the information from one source with that from other sources to determine whether there are substantial differences in what is reported as facts, conclusions, or recommendations. (Similarity among the sources should increase your confidence in the data, while wide differences or discrepancies among the sources should arouse your suspicions and lead you to serious efforts to verify and validate your data.)

Interviews of Individuals

Reports often must be based, at least in part, on interviews of individuals who are in a position to furnish useful and reliable information from their own records and memories. There are a few principles or "rules" that you should follow with respect to conducting such interviews. These are guidelines that most experienced interviewers believe to be important:

- Do your homework. Learn as much as you can about the individual you have arranged to interview. It's bad form to ask questions or display ignorance about things you could have (and should have) learned in advance of the interview. (In fact, it's a good idea to do this research before requesting the interview, for it often helps persuade the interviewee to cooperate.)
- Know exactly what information you want. A busy person will become impatient with you if you are obviously on a fishing trip or floundering about without direction. Make up a set of specific questions in advance, and use these as a general outline.
- Be completely open. Let the interviewee know just what your main purpose or objective is—what specific information you are seeking and for what reason.
- Take notes as unobtrusively as possible. Focus all or nearly all your attention on the interviewee and what he or she is saying. Look him or her straight in the eye and show your complete attention.
- Use a tape recorder, if possible, but never assume that it is permissible to use a tape recorder. Be sure to ask the interviewee's permission (preferably in advance, when arranging the interview). Many people are uncomfortable in having a conversation recorded.
- Ask permission to quote the interviewee directly in your report. That's a matter of courtesy, even when you have the legal right to quote directly, as when you are both employees of the same organization and the report is to be used only internally. Better yet, get the permission in writing. And if the report is for general publication, you must get that permission in writing.
- Be careful of your accuracy in quoting or citing the information that you are reporting or using. Call back and double check anything of which you are not certain.

Mass Interviews and Surveys

Many reports are based on the opinions or reactions of some group of individuals, such as the employees of some organization, a group of students, a group who are all in the same profession, a segment of the general public, or some group selected on the basis of some commonality. This is then a survey or poll, although *poll* indicates a simple count, whereas *survey* suggests a more wide-ranging sampling of opinion or reporting.

Such data gathering may be carried out by interviewing individuals personally—face to face—and recording the responses on some sort of recording form or master scoring sheet or by asking interviewees to complete questionnaires and then compiling the data.

There are hazards in conducting such investigations. One is that many individuals who are polled or surveyed tend to tell the interviewer what they think the interviewer wants to hear, rather than what they truly believe. Another, kindred, hazard is that many interviewees are ashamed or for some other reason reluctant to express their true feelings and so answer questions with what they believe are acceptable responses. And still another is that many individuals will follow a set pattern of "I don't know," "I have no opinion about that," or similar noncommittal responses. And related to that last-named hazard, the fear of having or at least of admitting to having a firm opinion, is the tendency of many respondents to choose the middle-road or apparently most neutral position possible.

It is possible to combat these problems to some extent, if you give some thought to them in advance when preparing the questionnaire. (And you should be working from a prepared set of questions whether you are asking the respondents the questions personally or having them complete a written questionnaire.) Admittedly there are problems with essay-type questionnaires, too, as there are with multiple-choice/check-off types. (For one thing, it is difficult to score, amass figures from, and evaluate essay-type questionnaires because there is little or no uniformity among the responses.) However, there are a few guidelines that will be offered here and that should help when constructing a questionnaire of any kind.

Be aware, too, that certain questionnaires are, in fact, "opinionnaires," in that they are purely reflections of respondents' opinions, which may or may not have any factual significance. This is not necessarily a negative factor, however, for there are cases in which respondents' opinions are the data you want, but be sure that it is what you want when constructing your questionnaire.

Questionnaire Formats

In constructing a questionnaire, whether you are planning to ask the questions directly (face to face) or have the respondents complete a written questionnaire, you should be conscious of the hazards enumerated here and plan your questionnaire format so as to minimize the problems. Here, for example, are a few dos and don'ts for questionnaire construction:

If at all possible, do not require the respondent to identify himself or herself. If the respondent does not have to give his or her name, he or she is likely to be far less inhibited in responding and thus less likely to evade revealing true opinions or convictions.

Don't make it easy for the respondent to make a noncommittal or neutral response. If yours is a multiple-choice or check-off format, don't offer "I don't know" or "No opinion" choices, for these are virtual invitations to escape taking a firm position.

For the same reason, don't offer easy opportunities to take the middle road. Don't offer such choices as High, Low, Medium, or a choice on a scale of from 1 to 10, for that is again an invitation to escape by being neutral.

If you use a multiple-choice or check-off format, provide only choices that reflect definite opinions so that the respondent is forced to take a stand of some sort if he or she answers the question. (And a failure to answer a question is not really any worse than a noncommittal or neutral answer, so you lose nothing by so structuring the questionnaire.)

Try to construct questions—items to be answered by the respondent—so that you get the *type* of response you want—*opinion*, if that is what you want, or the respondent's report of *fact*, if that is what you want.

Of course, respondents must answer factually to certain types of questions: Are you married? Do you own your home? Which of the following age groups are you in? On the other hand the respondent must express an *opinion* when asked such questions as the following: Do you think the income tax is fair? Do you approve of night clubs?

ORGANIZATION OF A REPORT

Different kinds of reports are organized differently, and a great many variations of format and organization are possible. However, the following are among the most basic and commonly encountered schemes of organization. They are useful for reports of various kinds (and for other documents also), and nearly all report requirements can be accommodated by using one of these formats or an adaptation of one of these:

Chronological: Which can be historical—from the beginning to the present—or the reverse, from the present to the beginning.

Order of importance: From the most trivial or peripheral information to the most important or reverse.

Evolutionary: From the seminal to the current state or reverse. (Roughly similar to chronological, but not bound strictly by chronology but by logical development or evolution, since most things do not develop in straight lines but pursue somewhat erratic courses.)

Therein lies something of a hazard, calling for writing skill. If the report is to show the evolution of something and that evolution is, characteristically, not strictly chronological, you must exercise great care that you do not lose your reader in the recital. It is quite easy to do so if you switch organizational patterns without warning.

The hazard lies in mixing methodologies. If you choose to use a chronological sequence, do so and stick with it, without more than passing attention to evolutionary considerations. Or, if you choose to present the evolutionary history, be sure to subordinate chronological data. It is difficult to change horses—switch format/organizational lines—in midstream without causing confusion. Unless you are an especially skilled writer, it is best to avoid doing this entirely; choose the pattern of organization and stick to it strictly.

Aside from that, a report, like any other written presentation, has an introduction, a body, and a conclusion or ending. But each of these essential and obligatory elements merits individual consideration because it may comprehend a number of considerations.

Introduction to Report

The introduction should orient the reader and prepare him or her for what is to come. As a minimum an introduction ought to identify the report (give its formal name and, if that **does** not itself define the nature and purpose of the report, explain that also); indicate something of the background of the report; summarize a few brief facts about it, such as the method of investigation; and indicate something of the basis for or sources of the information.

Other items that might be included in the introduction, depending on whether the report is formal or informal, written to some standardized or official format, or other circumstances, include at least these:

Authorization for or sponsoring entity of the report.
Scope and limits of the report.
Summary of problem or other reason for the report.
Preview of report, giving information on its organization and, in some cases, projecting a précis of conclusions and recommendations that will be found.
Definition or glossary of special terms used.
Acknowledgments of sources and contributions.
Formal abstract of report.

Body of Report

Typically, the body of a report elaborates on the introduction, presenting the data collected, often with a narrative account of how it was collected, even to the extent of explaining collection methods and sources, problems encountered and how they were handled, and whatever else is suitable for describing and qualifying the information gathered. There is likely to be some explanation, too, of how the information is organized, and a statement as to how complete or adequate the information is deemed to be.

Conclusion

If the report is of such a nature that it merely presents the data collected without attempting to analyze it or draw conclusions therefrom, the report may organize the data in several different ways (as some models will show shortly), quite likely with the aid of charts or graphs of one kind or another to assist the reader in viewing the data from different perspectives and understanding their basic significance.

On the other hand, if it is to be an analytical report, the body will ordinarily include a detailed explanation of what has been done with the data and suitable discussions of how the data was manipulated or processed, how it was reorganized and analyzed, what conclusions were drawn, and what recommendations are made as a result. The rationale is presented to demonstrate the validity of those conclusions and recommendations.

Conclusions and Recommendations

Conclusions drawn from the data and its analysis must follow conventional principles of logical reasoning. Bear in mind, however, that the reasoning to a conclusion must follow one of two general patterns or orders, inductive or deductive.

Deductive reasoning, which is probably more familiar to most of us than is inductive reasoning whether we know it by that name or not, consists primarily of matching observations to known or inferred principles to reach a conclusion. For example, the argument that it walks like a duck, quacks like a duck, and looks like a duck, so it must be a duck is an example of deductive reasoning. Inductive reasoning follows the opposite logical path and might proceed that since every duck known walks, quacks, and has a sameness of appearance, those characteristics are the test of whether a given creature is a duck or not. That is, deductive reasoning examines general facts (or principles) to enunciate a special fact, while inductive reasoning examines specific facts to establish a general fact (or principle). A natural law, such as that of the lever, for example, is discovered and defined through inductive reasoning, and that law is then put to work in deductive reasoning to create a practical application, such as the pulley or crane.

And so, in reaching and expressing a conclusion in a report, it is necessary to know precisely what you wish to achieve with the report—to see what general principles of fact may be induced from the data or what specific facts may be deduced from the data.

PREPARATION FOR REPORT WRITING

Report writing ordinarily requires a fair amount of preparation. Even before the data is collected and organized you should have had some sort of generalized outline for your report. In fact, it would be difficult to know how to organize or even collect the data suitably without having at least a general idea of the report format you will use.

Possible sections or functional elements of such an outline are offered here. Which of these are useful and appropriate to your own report depends on factors peculiar to your own need, so you may choose from among the listed items or add to them, as you perceive you own need. But before studying the possible sections or chapters of your report, decide on the following:

---

1. What is the specific or generic title of your report?
2. What does the report address?
   - [ ] A specific problem   [ ] A general need
   - [ ] _____   [ ] _____
3. What is the specific objective or purpose of the report?
   - [ ] Solve a problem   [ ] Identify a problem
   - [ ] Inform   [ ] Analyze
   - [ ] Offer arguments pro   [ ] Offer arguments con
   - [ ] Establish a record   [ ] Define
   - [ ] Advise   [ ] Refute
   - [ ] Offer conclusions   [ ] Offer recommendations
   - [ ] _____   [ ] _____

Answering these preliminary questions will help you choose the most appropriate items for your outline from among the following possibilities.

Introduction.
Background.
Statement/definition of problem.
Analysis of problem.
Description of present design/procedure/method.
Critique of present design/procedure/method: advantages and disadvantages.
Alternatives.
Expected results.
Narrative of data gathering.
Description of data gathered and used here.
Organization of data for this report.
Examination of data.
Method of data reduction.
Method of data analysis use here (e.g., statistical disciplines/methods/procedures).

Conclusions.
Recommendations.
Proposed design/procedure/method.

These topics and suggested chapter or section headings cover a majority of the subjects to which sections of your report may be addressed, although there may well be other appropriate topics to address. (Note that these are generally parallel to the items offered in the preceding checklists.) Select those which appear most appropriate to your own needs and use them to assemble the most appropriate preliminary outline to serve you as a guide in your data gathering and initial organization.

THE PRESENTATION

A report is a presentation. It is intended to convey meaning—*messages*—and no matter how well organized the data is, no matter how effectively the data has been analyzed, no matter how accurately the conclusions have been drawn, and no matter how wisely the recommendations have been thought out before being made, the report must rely for its effectiveness overall on how well the information is presented to the reader.

There are two main criteria for judging the report as a presentation: One is the measure of how effectively the report *communicates* or makes its meanings and messages clear to the reader. The other is the measure of how persuasive it is in inducing the reader to understand and believe precisely what it states.

These considerations are not entirely unrelated to each other, for language that is ponderous or otherwise difficult to understand arouses a degree of skepticism as to its validity by virtue of its nature. Such language inherently conveys an impression of evasiveness or reluctance to make plain statements of fact. Somehow the very nature of the language suggests that the author is either not at all clear in what he or she wishes to say or is trying to lend a false impression. Clear, forceful, and direct statements, on the other hand, tend to be more believable of themselves simply because they convey an aura of sincerity and honesty. However, that is not the only route to believability; there are other factors that affect believability and clarity of writing, and these effects can be achieved as the result of distinct and deliberate methodologies that can be learned.

The Noun-Verb Rule

One major characteristic of the proper language that is as appropriate for reports as it is for proposals and other literature—and perhaps even more necessary to and appropriate for reports—is objectivity. A report by its very nature must not only *appear* to be unbiased, but must strive to *be* completely objective. It must be devoted primarily to the presentation of facts and must make it clear that it is expressing someone's opinion when that is the case, but in all other cases make it clear that it is reporting facts and/or objective conclusions based on facts, not opinions.

One way to support your effort to be as objective as possible is to observe the noun-verb rule, which is simply that of restricting your reporting to nouns and verbs, holding the use of adjectives and adverbs to the absolute minimum possible. Modifiers should be used, in reporting factual data, only when they are necessary to definitions or descriptions. Referring to a "red automobile" (when it is necessary to mention the fact that it is red) is using a modifier (red) to report a fact, whereas referring to it as a "flashy" or "flashy red automobile" is expressing an opinion. In fact, "red automobile" may be considered to be a compound noun, rather than a noun and adjective, so that the noun-verb rule is not violated nor an exception taken to it even in this case.

Aids to Presentation

"Writing" should not be used in the literal sense here. The goal of all writing, including the writing of reports, is communication of information and ideas, and words alone are not sufficient to do the job. There are many ideas that cannot be communicated effectively by words alone, at least not by straight description. And there are also many ideas that cannot be communicated effectively by words at all, or at least not nearly as effectively as they can be communicated by or with the use of some sort of presentation aids.

There are two general types or classes of aids: Verbal aids—aids based on the use of words alone, although not as straight description—and graphic aids—pictorial representations of some sort. And within each of these there are subclasses of aids to expression and conveyance of meaning:

Verbal aids:
    Examples.
    Analogies.
    Imagery.
Graphic aids:
    Photographs.
    Line drawings.
    Charts and graphs.
    Other illustrations.

The key to using the right materials and tools for presentation lies in being able to understand the reader's viewpoint and the possible difficulties he or she may have in visualizing what you wish to present, a quality called *empathy*.

Verbal Aids

Examples—"for instances"—are probably the simplest form of verbal aids. They are normally used when a principle has been presented, and it is necessary to help the reader understand the significance of the principle by showing how it works in practice—by showing a typical *application*. Gresham's law (that bad money tends to drive the good money out of circulation) is almost impossible for the lay person to understand without examples to show that people tend to hoard the more reliable currency and hasten to divest themselves of unreliable currency while they still can spend it.

Analogies are often needed. When the typical example would still be so far beyond the everyday experience of the average reader that it would not be helpful as an explanation or aid to understanding, an example that is an *analogy* is constructed. The gold standard is far easier for the noneconomist to grasp when it is explained in the analogy of (what happens to be also historical fact) the individual storing gold in a public warehouse and using the receipts for his gold as transferrable exchange of ownership of the gold—a primitive form of paper money, in effect.

Imagery is simply the use of words to paint images in the reader's mind. It can be a far-ranging subject in itself, but briefly it includes some of what I have enjoined you against—adjectives and adverbs—as well as other forms: analogies, in some cases, and imaginative descriptions of all kinds.

Graphic Aids

The whole idea of graphic aids revolves around the alleged and probably apocryphal quotation from Confucius that a single picture is worth a thousand words. Perhaps Confucius did not actually say that, and perhaps it is not a literal truth even if he did say it, but it ought to be, for it is a truth in principle. It is a truth in principle at least in those cases where the objective is to paint an image in the brain of the reader, either to help the reader view precisely what the writer wishes the reader to view or to help the reader understand an abstraction. Consider, for example, how you would induce a reader to see in mind's eye that very chair you remember from your childhood without using a photograph or some aid almost equally graphic and detailed.

A line drawing might suffice—and it might not—to help the reader visualize that chair, depending on how complex an image you wish to convey and the amount of detail necessary to present that image. You might very well need something a bit more sophisticated, if not a photograph then a type of drawing called a *rendering*, which can offer shadings, detail, and nuances not possible in simple line drawings. (Such a drawing is often used as an "artist's concept" to help readers visualize a proposed building or other item yet to be constructed.)

On the other hand, explaining abstract concepts or dramatizing quantitative relationships is often aided more by such illustrative devices as charts and graphs of various kinds. Consider the case of basing some example or explanation on a mathematical concept, such as that of the Pythagorean theorem, which states that in a right triangle the sum of the squares of the opposite two sides is equal to the square of the hypotenuse. That is very nearly impossible to even convey, much less explain, without some graphic aid, usually a line drawing of a right triangle with labels identifying the three sides, the angle, and the squares of each side.

Still another simple but useful line drawing is the flowchart or block diagram, used most commonly to show relationships, interdependencies, and sequences of events. (Computer programmers, engineers, and other technical designers use such charts quite frequently.)

Examples of these kinds of charts and graphic aids are illustrated later in this chapter (in models of reports).

Forms and Formats

Much as in the case of proposals (and there are many similarities between proposals and reports) reports can be either formal or informal and so can be presented in formal or informal formats. Even so, a variety of formats are used commonly for both formal and informal reports. In general, an informal report can be in the form of a letter or memorandum, and it can be of any length. A formal report is more likely to follow some prescribed format—and there are many such formats—and to have front matter, including a cover page, title page, table of contents, and abstract. It may also have a foreword or preface. And in some cases the abstract is in the form of a 3×5-inch card intended for insertion into library card files with suitable notations, such as a number assigned under the Dewey decimal system, to facilitate library indexing. And in the case of government and other large organizations the report may include a half-dozen such index cards for multiple filings.

Finally, formal reports are likely to include such items as bibliographies, footnotes, appendixes, and indexes, items not likely to appear in informal or letter reports and reports offered as memoranda. (Guidance in constructing and using such refinements, as well as for physical formats, is offered in a later chapter.)

MODELS OF REPORTS

Many of the principles and practices discussed in the previous pages are shown in the following models, which illustrate a few typical reports, beginning with the simplest informal ones and then offering more formal reports.

DATE: April 22, 1988
TO: Harry W. Headman, VP Marketing
FROM: Peter Underling, Sales Manager
SUBJECT: Weekly Sales Report

The new sales campaign, launched last week, has demonstrated immediate success, with a marked increase in both dollar volume of sales (nearly 15 percent over the previous week) and in number of new accounts won from our competitors. (See computer printout attached for exact figures.)

Our special offer of a dozen toothbrushes free for every $100 worth of any other merchandise ordered was very well received by our customers, especially the small neighborhood stores to whom this offer was especially addressed. However, the best news is that this special offer enabled us to open 27 new accounts last week, many of them merchants we had tried to win over in the past without success.

In light of this I recommend that we extend this offer indefinitely. (You will recall that we planned to make this offer for the month of April only because April is traditionally a slow month for us.) I believe that if we continue this offer through the rest of Spring and Summer we will succeed in adding dozens of new accounts.

March 2, 1987

Mr. Honorable P. Worthy
President
Traditional Mercantile Corporation
Small Corners, OH 55445   Ref: First monthly report on Contr. 87-B-74A

Dear Mr. Worthy:

This is the first of six monthly progress reports on our research into changes in rural markets for Traditional Mercantile Company products. For the record, to place this informal report into proper perspective, your company, Traditional Mercantile Corporation, has suffered a steady decline in rural markets over the past 35 years. Prior to that time and for over 40 years, Traditional Mercantile Corporation had enjoyed a steadily growing catalog/mail-order business in rural markets throughout the United States, selling general consumer merchandise. The contract between us (cited above by reference) provides that we, Motivational Research Associates, Inc. (MRAI), will (1) conduct research into the base causes of the continuing decline in orders and (2) report on these causes, with recommendations to your corporation of measures to reverse this trend and restore the business volume and growth pattern your company enjoyed before the decline began.

continued

We have agreed to provide six monthly progress reports to keep you posted on our research/investigation and such related considerations as problems encountered and plans for coming months. Not later than 90 days after the final (sixth) month of the contract we are to provide you with a formal final report with the complete project history, data collected, conclusions drawn, and specific recommendations for reversing the sales and marketing trend you are now experiencing.

In this first month we have investigated typical rural markets, each in a different area of the United States. The investigations were conducted in the following six rural counties, after determining that this would give us a good demographic cross-section of the United States:

Greenwillow, Maine	Cattlecountry, Texas
Seawater, New Jersey	Hillanddale, Montana
Coastline, Georgia	Balmybreezes, California

Our main effort in each of these counties was to determine what changes of the past four decades would have affected these counties as markets for general consumer merchandise.

We found, as we suspected we would, that many changes have taken place in all rural areas of the United States since World War II (which war and post-war period appears to have been a seminal period in the development of today's America). The following are the most significant ones, we believe, as far as the objectives of this project are concerned:

1.   Virtually everyone in the United States, but especially rural dwellers, has become far more mobile today, with few families lacking a modern automobile and a very large percentage of families having two and even three automobiles in the family.

2.   The same thing may be said for telephones, radios, and television receivers. Except for those few living in the most remote areas, everyone has such conveniences today and uses them freely.

3.   Equally popular and nearly universal has been the proliferation in credit cards of many kinds and in their use. Millions of families who never could or would have bought on credit before now enjoy and exercise almost unlimited credit.

4.   These factors have contributed to an apparently growing trend of local merchants taking orders by telephone, "charging" orders, and delivering purchases to customers who have ordered by telephone.

5.   This ability to buy even before one has the cash available, coupled with the eagerness of local merchants to deliver immediately, appears to have brought about some hitherto uncharacteristic impatience on the part of rural consumers. They appear less willing to wait many days for delivery and now seek faster (usually local) sources to satisfy their wants.

6.   This latter problem has been made even more serious by the decline in mail services.

(Points 4, 5, and 6 made here are or are based on premises which we propose to investigate in future months.)

continued
This appears to add up to a general decline of rural dwellers' dependence on the traditional catalog sales method of doing business in rural areas. However, this is only the initial data collected, and it is much too soon to draw any conclusions. In fact, although we suspected that we would find some of these trends to be the case, the scope and intensity of these changes appears to be far greater than we suspected originally, and we think it wise to change our original plans somewhat and expand this investigation into a great many more areas of the United States, especially those areas where postwar growth has been the greatest and thus presumably should offer you great increases in your sales volume.

We therefore plan to conduct a similar study in 24 other counties throughout the United States, about two thirds of them rural and the remainder urban, so that the latter will act as something of a control—a reference—for the other portion of the research data so gathered.

If there are questions regarding any of this we will be pleased to discuss and/or otherwise respond to your request for more information.

Very truly yours,

Walter G. Warner
Project Manager

March 2, 1987

Mr. Honorable P. Worthy
President
Traditional Mercantile Corporation
Small Corners, OH 55445
Reference: Progress Report, per Contract 87-B-74A,
                    transmittal of

Dear Mr. Worthy:

Enclosed is the first of six monthly progress reports, in triplicate, per the contract cited here. We believe that we have succeeded in identifying a number of key factors relevant to the marketing study and analysis that is the subject of the contract, and that we now have an even clearer insight into the proper avenues of investigation.

Please feel free to call on me personally for any additional information or discussion of any points made in this report.

Sincerely,

Walter G. Warner
Project Manager

Encl: Three (3) copies of Monthly Progress Report No. 1, per Contract 87-B-74A

Progress Report No. 1
For February 1987

A MARKETING STUDY

Performed for
Traditional Mercantile Corporation

by
Motivational Research Associates (MRAI)
of Chicago, Illinois

March 2, 1987

TABLE OF CONTENTS

continued

I: BACKGROUND DETAIL

1.0 Summary of the Problem

Traditional Mercantile Corporation has suffered a steady decline in rural markets over the past 35 years. Prior to that time and for over 40 years, Traditional Mercantile Corporation had enjoyed a steadily growing catalog/mail-order business in rural markets throughout the United States, selling general consumer merchandise.

1.1 The Main Objective of the Study

Motivational Research Associates, Inc. (MRAI) (1) is conducting research into the base causes of the continuing decline in orders and (2) will report on these causes, with recommendations to Traditional Mercantile Corporation of measures to reverse this trend and restore the business volume and growth pattern your company enjoyed before the decline began.

1.2 What MRAI Is to Deliver

MRAI will provide six monthly progress reports to keep the Corporation advised on all efforts, findings, measures taken in our research/investigation and such related considerations as problems encountered and plans for coming months. Not later than 90 days after the final (sixth) month of the contract MRAI will provide the Corporation with a formal final report with the complete project history, data collected, conclusions drawn, and specific recommendations for reversing the sales and marketing trend the Corporation is now experiencing.

1.3 First Premises

As was the case with other major catalog firms, Traditional Mercantile Corporation's original market was primarily a rural one, and flourished in a day when rural dwellers were not mobile in the sense of the term today because few had even the relatively primitive automobiles. Moreover, at that time relatively few rural areas had electricity and telephone lines in common use, and so found it convenient to do a great deal of their everyday shopping for consumer items via the mails. And the Great Depression of the 1930s militated against this situation changing much for economic reasons, even when advancing technology was making change possible, at least technically.

This much was established and accepted fact. However, from this we inferred a beginning premise that these conditions no longer prevail, that great changes had begun to take place in the postwar period (after World War II, that is), once wartime shortages began to be replaced by the resurgent commercial industries and economic prosperity had returned.

It appeared to us that this change had come about and had seriously (and adversely) affected the traditional markets of Traditional Mercantile Corporation. Our initial investigation, therefore, was designed to test this theory and see what changes had, in fact, occurred in those usual markets of the Corporation.

continued

II: INITIAL (AND PRIMARY) RESEARCH EFFORTS

In the first month we have investigated typical rural markets of the type where Traditional Mercantile Corporation had always enjoyed its greatest success in earlier years. The counties selected (drawn from the Corporation's old sales records of its best markets) were each in a different area of the United States, chosen to represent what we thought would be a representative sample. The investigations were conducted in the following six rural counties, after determining that this would give us a good demographic cross-section of the United States:

Greenwillow, Maine   Cattlecountry, Texas
Seawater, New Jersey   Hillanddale, Montana
Coastline, Georgia   Balmybreezes, California

Our main effort in each of these counties was to determine what changes of the past four decades would have affected these counties as markets for general consumer merchandise.

2.0 Early Findings

We found, as we suspected we would, that many changes have taken place in all rural areas of the United States since World War II (which war and postwar period appears to have been a seminal period in the economic development of today's America). The following are the most significant ones, we believe, as far as the objectives of this project are concerned:

1.   Virtually everyone in the United States, but especially the rural dweller, has become far more mobile today, with few families lacking a modern automobile and a very large percentage of families having two and even three automobiles in the family.

2.   The same thing may be said for telephones, radios, and television receivers. Except for those few living in the most remote areas or suffering abject poverty, everyone has such conveniences today and uses them freely.

3.   Equally popular and nearly universal has been the proliferation in credit cards of many kinds and in their use. Millions of families who never could or would have bought on credit before now enjoy and exercise almost unlimited credit.

2.1 Method of Investigation

Two general methods were used to conduct these investigations:

a. Field researchers visited these counties and conducted interviews, filling out questionnaires (data sheets) as they did so. The questionnaires were divided into two parts. One part collected factual data, such as number of automobiles, telephones, radios, television sets in house; average number of shopping trips to nearby cities versus volume of buying locally versus volume of buying by mail or telephone; and other such quantitative information. The other part was an attitude survey to determine how respondents felt about various methods of shopping, eagerness or reluctance to travel to cities, and other such factors that bear on buying habits.

b. This data was compared with parallel data gathered from the U.S. Census Bureau and state and local government records (e.g., the

continued

state's motor vehicle administration). The latter data was used to verify data gathered by our field investigators, and it did, in fact, confirm the data we had gathered in the field.

2.2 Early Data Collected

This data is reflected in the following charts. The first chart is a plot to show the increasing growth of modern conveniences and communications—automobiles, telephones, radio, and TV—over the years of Traditional Mercantile Corporation's existence. Note that the Great Depression of the 1930s results in a dip in the curve, but it picks up steadily after World War II and the end of the economic depression until it levels out very close to the 100-percent level. (This is a logical and predictable result.)

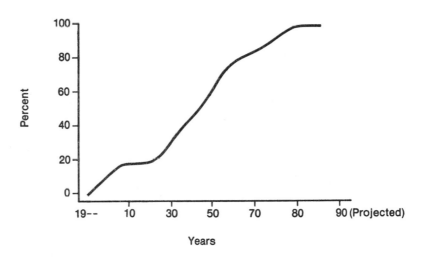

Growing percentage of rural residents driving automobiles

The second figure is a bar chart showing the effects of economic depression and modern developments on catalog shopping. Note that the depression years curtail catalog shopping because they curtailed buying generally. And even when World War II put everyone back to work, including the farmers, the lack of consumer goods was reflected in catalog-shopping patterns until commercial industry returned to its prewar status, producing a great increase in consumerism generally. But the swiftly growing popularity and number of automobiles and the excellent superhighways that led straight to the great cities from the farms produced the result shown here: Rural catalog shopping declined.

continued

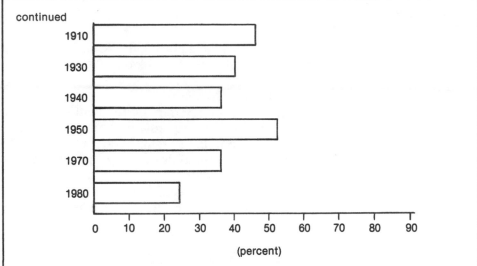

(percent)

Catalog shoppers as percentage of rural families

III: A FEW CONCLUSIONS

At least a few preliminary conclusions can be drawn as a second set of premises:

1.   These factors have contributed to an apparently growing trend of local merchants taking orders by telephone, "charging" orders, and delivering purchases to customers who have ordered by telephone.

2.   This ability to buy even before one has the cash available, coupled with the eagerness of local merchants to deliver immediately, appears to have brought about some hitherto uncharacteristic impatience on the part of rural consumers. They appear less willing to wait many days for delivery and now seek faster (usually local) sources to satisfy their wants.

3.   This latter problem has been made even more serious by the decline in mail services, and reliance on the Postal Service is in many respects a handicap in conducting a catalog/mail-order business.

IV: PLANS FOR COMING MONTH

This appears to add up to a general decline of rural dwellers' dependence on the traditional catalog sales method of doing business in rural areas. However, this is only the initial data collected, and it is much too soon to draw any firm conclusions. In fact, although we suspected that we would find some of these trends to be the case, the scope and intensity of these changes appears to be far greater than we suspected originally, and we think it wise to change our original plans somewhat and expand this investigation into a great many more areas of the United States, especially those areas where postwar growth has been the greatest and thus logically should offer you the potential for great increases, rather than decline, in your sales volume.

We therefore plan to conduct a similar study in 24 other counties throughout the United States, about two thirds of them rural but the remainder urban, so that the latter will act as something of a control—a reference—for the other portion of the research data so gathered.

PART III

MISCELLANEOUS DOCUMENTS AND DATA

THE COVERAGE IN THIS PART

The chapters included in this final part offer two general types of information and guidance: Suggestions for writing the less often needed kinds of business writing and helpful reference material. The foregoing chapters have addressed often felt writing needs, some of them rarely if ever addressed in depth by books on office correspondence and business writing (e.g., proposals and reports). But there are many other writing needs that are less often encountered and also rarely if ever addressed in popular literature on business writing. These fall logically into a "miscellaneous" class, although they have the common feature of being general and occasional requirements of administration, public information, and some other miscellany, rather than of marketing or other "line" functions dealing with customers and customer-prospects.

In the arena of general administrative needs there is the need to develop and write such things as purchasing guidelines and rules, personnel policy manuals, general company policy guides, company memoranda, and in-house newsletters, to name just a few of the common needs of managers and administrators. Public information needs require more specialized information and guidance for those not familiar with such things as news releases, press kits, product releases, public statements, speeches, and other such items.

These are among the categories that will be covered in the remaining chapters that make up the third part of this book. But there are a few other miscellaneous matters to be handled in these final chapters, offering information and guidance promised several times in earlier chapters. One chapter, for example, will offer some general guidance in formats for letters and several other kinds of written products and suggestions for using a word processor to facilitate and speed up your writing work. The last chapter will offer general administrative guidance in setting up this entire system of business writing in your organization and may very well serve you in itself as a manual for managing in-house writing chores of all kinds or even of those that affect your own department and mission.

It is not by chance that this latter material was saved for last. It was saved for last in order to provide you with a ready reference to these less often needed instructions and especially to items you might wish to look up and refresh your memory on from time to time, rather than being compelled to search through all the chapters to look up a format or a word processing tip.

Chapter 8

General Administrative Writing Needs

SOME CLASSES OF ADMINISTRATIVE NEEDS

Administration in the typical organization usually includes such functions as those of purchasing, accounting, and personnel management at the minimum. Most other functions fall elsewhere—for example, inventory management is likely to be a production department responsibility. However, in some cases, notably where there is a physically separate corporate headquarters of a multibranch or multidivision corporation, all or nearly all of the organization's functions are administrative because the corporate headquarters is itself usually a basically administrative organization. But in this case we shall consider the three major functions listed—accounting, purchasing, and personnel—as the major and principal administrative functions commonly encountered everywhere. Each will be treated briefly in this chapter, with appropriate models.

PURCHASE PROCEDURES

In most organizations, including government agencies, purchasing is managed and authorized at more than one level of purchase size, as well as at more than one level of management. Typically there are three levels of purchases: small, spontaneous, and informal purchases; small formal purchases; and large or major purchases. The small, spontaneous purchases are usually made out of petty cash funds (called imprest funds in governments, usually) and accounted for or justified by a petty cash slip or an expense account. The small formal purchases are purchases made by purchase order usually (although sometimes formal contracts are used even for small, formal purchases) with budgeted funds authorized in advance. And formal purchases are almost invariably made via formal contracts, with funds budgeted and authorized in advance. The distinguishing differences among these are almost invariably price or size of purchase.

Typically, purchasing in a company, especially in one that does a great deal of purchasing, such as a manufacturer, wholesale distributor, or retailer, is a major function that must be controlled most carefully. In such companies profit and loss—the very survival of the company—is closely related to and even dependent on the wisdom and judiciousness of the purchasing function because profitability depends on the margin between cost and selling price, as well as on other cost factors, with cost the major factor in the profit and loss ratio.

But even companies that do not do a great deal of purchasing on a regular basis, such as services organizations, occasionally make such major purchases as real estate, construction, fleets of vehicles, or large computers, so they also find it necessary to exercise close control over purchasing to ensure that the organization's self-interests are safe-guarded when making purchases.

It should also be noted that in many large organizations ceilings are established on the size of the purchases various managers are permitted to authorize. For example, a low-level or "line" manager might be per-mitted to authorize $500 purchases, a middle-management executive might be permitted $5,000, and a top executive $25,000. For larger pur-chases than that approval of the chief executive or even of the board of directors might be required. The policies and procedures governing these matters would (and do) vary widely with different organizations.

A Typical Policy/Procedures Manual

In the case of a truly major purchase, such as that of a building, the principals of the organization and/or the directors are sure to be directly involved. But the principals cannot be directly involved and responsible for the day-to-day purchasing, even when some of the purchases are quite substantial. And yet it is necessary to control purchasing so that it is carried out in the manner that reflects the will of the principals. Hence, policy must be set for the guidance of individuals within the or-ganization. And those policies generally include fixed rules or guidelines to advise everyone what the rules for purchasing are. A brief example of a purchasing manual is offered here. This might be appropriate for a small company, and the values expressed were chosen with that in mind.

A Sample Purchasing Manual for a Small Corporation

THE AJAX METAL PRODUCTS CORPORATION
PURCHASING POLICY AND PROCEDURES
July 25, 1981

1.0 General Policy

---

continued

The basic purchasing policy of this corporation is to utilize competitive bidding to the maximum degree practicable in all procurement by the corporation, except as otherwise provided here. Competitive bidding is defined for this purpose as getting a minimum of three bids or proposals for each major purchase, as specified in the following paragraphs.

1.1 Classes of Purchases

Purchasing by and for this corporation is established at three defined levels:

a. Casual purchases.

b. Small purchases.

c. Major purchases.

1.2 Definitions

1.2.1 Casual purchases are made to satisfy spontaneous needs for goods and services not to exceed $100 each, to be paid for with petty cash funds and documented via petty cash voucher or personal expense account, with a proper receipt in both cases.

1.2.2 Small purchases are purchases not in excess of $1,000, requiring only three verbal bids or informal written bids, and documented via purchase order, but using duly authorized and budgeted general funds.

1.2.3 Major purchases are those in excess of $1,000 but not greater than $25,000. Such purchases shall be made only subject to the following procedures and restrictions:

a. The purchase shall have been approved by the corporation's Executive Vice President, the President, or the Controller.

b. A budget shall have been established and authorized for the purchase.

c. A solicitation shall be issued (advertised) and a minimum of three formal (written) bids or proposals received and evaluated by a selection committee established for the purpose.

d. Bids or proposals shall be evaluated by a committee or board consisting of not fewer than three (3) members who shall utilize an objective rating scheme and render a written recommendation and justification for that recommendation.

e. The written recommendation and justification for the final selection shall be made and submitted to the Controller, with a request for negotiation of a formal contract.

2.0 Purchasing Authority

Authority to initiate and consummate purchases is established as follows:

2.1 Casual purchases

Casual purchases may be authorized and approved by all supervisors and line managers.

2.2 Small purchases

Small purchases may be authorized and approved by middle managers, provided suitable budgeted funds are available and subject to the provisions of paragraph 1.2.2.

2.3 Major purchases

continued

Major purchases may be authorized and approved by all senior executives and/or by decision of the board of directors, provided suitable budgeted funds are available and subject to the provisions of paragraphs 1.2.3, *a, b, c, d,* and *e.*

3.0 Initiation of Purchases

The form of a purchase request varies with the type and size of the purchase, as follows:

3.1 Casual Purchases

Casual purchases may be requested verbally or informally in writing by anyone and authorized as noted in paragraphs 1.2.1 and 2.2.

3.2 Small Purchases

Small purchases, as defined in paragraph 1.2.2 may be requested by anyone with defined purchasing authority, but they must be requested by formal letter or memorandum (a Purchase Request standard form is acceptable, but not required) to the Office of Purchasing, signed by the appropriate authority (as in paragraph 2.2), with proper citation of authorized and approved budgeted funds. The request must include an item description or other specification of the goods and/or services to be solicited or a Statement of Work, as appropriate, the type of agreement contemplated (purchase order or type of contract), the response required (quotation, bid, or proposal) and other provisions and requirements of the purchase, as appropriate.

3.3 Major Purchases

Major purchases, as defined in paragraph 1.2.3 must be requested formally and addressed to the Office of Purchasing, using a standard Purchase Request with identification of approved budget funding and authorizaton, per paragraphs 1.2.3 and 2.3. The request must include an item description or other specification of the goods and/or services to be purchased or a Statement of Work, as appropriate, the type of agreement contemplated (purchase order or type of contract), the response required (quotation, bid, or proposal), and other provisions and requirements of the purchase, as appropriate.

4.0 Exceptions

Exceptions to these procedures and policies may be made when unusual circumstances justify exceptions, but they may be made only with a written statement of authorization from the President, Chairman of the Board, or Senior Executive Vice President of the Corporation.

Signed:

_____

Alexander Dewright
Senior Executive Vice President

Other Data Often Included

This small model reflects only the most basic data to be found in a written purchase procedure. In the actual case, even the smallest written procedure and policy statement for purchasing would be somewhat more expansive than this. Other information that would often be included, depending on certain factors in each individual case (e.g., size and nature of the organization and the amount and diversity of its purchasing) is reflected in the following list of items often included in purchasing directives:

- The purchasing manual may include reproductions or at least descriptions of forms used—petty cash vouchers, purchase orders, expense vouchers, and contract forms. These might be reproductions of blank forms or forms that have been properly executed, as examples.

- In the case of large organizations it might also include reproductions of pages of governing regulations, and in the case of governments those would normally cite public laws governing purchases with public money.

- It might also cite classes of goods (e.g., supply groups) which is a common practice among governments because governments buy such a wide diversity of goods and services.

- It would include or incorporate by reference a number of specifications or the terms *best efforts* and *good commercial quality* as standards by which to specify goods and services.

- It might also cite some specific procedures required to initiate and validate or authorize a purchase, which might include certain standard forms or memoranda of some type.

- There may be definitions and types of responses to call for—quotations, bids, and proposals—depending on needs and purposes and supplying at least general guidelines for these.

- It may include types of contractual vehicles possible (with definitions)—Fixed-Price contracts, Basic Ordering Agreements, Time and Material contracts, Cost-Reimbursement contracts, Annual Supply Agreements, Indefinite-Quantity contracts, Call contracts, Task Order contracts, and others, with guidance or suggestions on which are most suitable for various needs and purposes.

- Finally, it would probably include at least some legal information about contracts, appeal procedures, cancellations, transfers and assignments, and related considerations.

PURCHASE REQUESTS

A purchase request may be addressed to the approving authority and have been made out as an application for approval and authorization of the requested purchase. On the other hand, once approved and authorized by the proper authority, it is usually sent on to the purchasing agent or contracting official as a request for purchasing services, for the purchasing function is one of providing services to others in the organization. Perhaps more literally a purchase request is an *order* to the purchasing official to provide the administrative services necessary to complete the purchase.

The services normally required of the purchasing agent include several steps:

1. Review the purchase request and verify that all is in order as required in the organization. (In large organizations, such as government agencies, purchasing officials tend to be either lawyers or accountants and often are both, since those are the two major aspects of the job.)
2. Issue solicitations and/or advertise the requirement so as to get an adequate number of quotations, bids, or proposals.
3. Officiate in receiving responses and seeing to it that adequate and proper evaluations are made to select an awardee.
4. Make the award and consummate the purchase.

Like purchase procedures, purchase requests can take many forms, depending on the organization and related factors. In the federal system, for example, a purchase request that would be sent to the Contracting Officer would include all the items listed here: the allocation of funds (the Contracting Officer would almost surely take steps, such as consulting the agency's budget office to verify that the funds cited are available and properly authorized for the expenditure) and would verify the satisfaction of all other requirements, legal and policy-wise (for each agency has internal policies, some of which are set by the Contracting Officer, in fact, and which vary from one agency to another). And the purchasing officer in any situation would be likely to look long and hard at the purchase specifications: the item description and/or statement of work, the response asked for, the type of contract suggested, the other forms and papers enclosed for bidders and proposers to fill out and sign, and the reality of the deadline for submission of offers.

There are at least these general considerations involved in reviewing the purchase request:

1. Verifying that the request meets all the requirements of the organization's rules and regulations for making purchases.
2. Verifying that the vendors solicited are presented with a clear description of the goods and/or services required and that the terms are at least within reason.
3. Evaluating the fairness—objectivity—of the request to ensure that all vendors have an equal opportunity to pursue and win the award.
4. Verifying that the type contract suggested is appropriate.

In some cases the purchasing official may invite the requestor to suggest names of potential contractors to whom a copy of the solicitation should be sent, but some purchasing agents are opposed to this, believing that the procurement will be more objective—fairer—if the requestor has no voice in who is invited to respond.

In many ways the most difficult part of the job for both the requestor and the purchasing official is the specification of what is required—the item description and/or statement of work (or SOW, as it is often referred to).

SPECIFICATION OF THE REQUIREMENT

Most purchasing officials would prefer to make all purchases through competitive bids, with the award going to the lowest bidder. That makes the entire procedure swift and simple, while it assures the purchaser of the lowest price.

This is a practicable way of buying when it is possible to specify what is wanted with enough precision to ensure that the item(s)—products or services—will be the same or at least equivalent to each other no matter who furnishes them. And that is the sticking point: It is not always a simple matter to make that specification precise enough to ensure that the only significant difference among competitive offerings will be the price. That is to say, the specification must be clear enough so that the customer can inspect the delivered item and verify beyond doubt whether the item is or is not precisely what was ordered—whether, that is, the supplier has fulfilled the contract faithfully. And this consideration often applies to services as well as to products and materials. Therefore the term *item* used here refers to services, as well as to products and materials.

There are several ways in which an item to be furnished can be specified to potential bidders. Here are the most common ways:

1. Specifying the item according to well-known characteristics and unequivocal standards, such as "white, granulated cane sugar in 2 lb. boxes," "yellow enameled, No. 2 lead pencils, using cedar wood, with erasers and brass ferrules," or "painting with two coats of latex, water-based paint."
2. Specifying the item by naming a well-known brand and calling for that or its equivalent, such as "IBM Selectric Mod II typewriter or equivalent."
3. Citing a well-known industry standard, such as the U.S. Pharmacopeia or some military standard in specifying the product desired.
4. Writing a special item description for the procurement.
5. Using some hybrid of the above measures.

STATEMENT OF WORK (SOW)

It is not always possible to offer a specification that is unequivocal. In some cases the customer requires R&D—innovative research and development—or other original and exploratory engineering work. In other cases no one, not the customer nor the bidders, really knows what is possible, but the customer is willing to invest in original research (and basic *scientific* research is somewhat different from the engineering R&D type of research).

In such cases as these there is no "item description." There is, instead, a statement of work—an SOW—that is the basis for a request for proposals (RFP). In this case, instead of asking the prospective bidders to quote prices for furnishing a clearly specified end-item, the purchaser (customer) must describe the need or problem (and often is able to describe only symptoms) and is compelled to *ask* the potential supplier what he/she (the supplier) *suggests* as a solution to the customer's problem or need.

CONSIDERATIONS IN WRITING A STATEMENT OF WORK (SOW)

The need for a statement of work (SOW) creates quite a different situation than one in which an item description can be used. It is a situation in which you, as the customer, appeal to the prospective suppliers as experts, seeking to elicit from each a *proposal*—a plan—for solving the problem. Writing such a statement properly calls for some skill, and the purchasing official is often not in a good position to determine whether the SOW is well written—whether, that is, it is likely to produce the desired results, especially when the work required is specialized in some way. (Presumably, the SOW is written by one or more company specialists who have at least an expertise in the general field of which the proposed work is a part.)

There are two extremes to be avoided in writing an SOW. Inasmuch as the overall objective is to asssess and evaluate proposed alternative solutions, the statement should be such as to encourage the proposer to think out the problem and offer his or her best advice. Unfortunately, the mistake some writers of such statements make is to attempt to dictate the solution desired, which inhibits innovative and creative thinking by the proposer. This extreme should thus be avoided.

The other extreme to be avoided is that of making the statement of the problem too vague and general, thus tending to elicit nonresponsive proposals.

Ideally, then, the SOW should be written in such a way as to fall approximately midway between these extremes. However, this is not to say that the SOW should not specify certain constraints and requirements. You must explain these if you expect to receive fully responsive proposals. Moreover, to be truly useful the proposal must explain the plan offered so as to enable you, as the customer, to evaluate all the proposals with some rational basis for selecting one as best.

A Model of an SOW

Following is a brief model of an SOW, illustrating the main points made here. It lays out specific major tasks in general as phases of work, primarily in terms of defining the objective of each major phase of work and a specific objective for the project overall but does not attempt to dictate to the proposer all the minutiae of each task, thus encouraging the proposer to flesh out the overall description with details of how he or she proposes to carry out the work. It also suggests a schedule to make the respondent aware of the general time scale within which the customer wants the project completed but does not insist that the job be done precisely according to the schedule offered. (In many cases, when it is necessary, a deadline is defined, however.)

STATEMENT OF WORK

A MODERN PROBLEM

The increasing complexity of modern systems, especially automated equipment systems using electronics and computer chips, has imposed an ever-greater burden of training to produce maintenance technicians. It has come to a point where it is difficult to find qualified technicians, and the cost of training technicians in these systems (at least in the classical sense of technical training) has become prohibitive, almost as much so as the unacceptable expedient in use too often today of pressing full-fledged engineers into service as repair technicians.

The only practicable solution at the moment is to either utilize technicians of lesser training or to train technicians in the basic technologies only and support them in some manner that does not require complete knowledge of the system to make them effective.

The JPA Approach

Research into methods for solving this problem has continued. For some years a great many experimental systems for training and supporting repair technicians have been developed experimentally, using a device known as Job Performance Aids, or JPAs. The basic approach in this system is to present some combination of brief text, checklists, and illustrations to guide the technician in troubleshooting and repair operations without the necessity for extensive training in theory of operation. (The well-known U.S. Navy SIMMS system was one early example of this.)

The Objective of This Project

We, Maintenance Corporation of America (MCA), believe that it is time to freeze these experimental designs and produce an operational model of a system that accomplishes the purposes stated here. It is the objective of the project described in this statement to produce such a system and put it to work operationally.

The Phases of Work

In general we foresee a three-phase program necessary to carry out a successful program and achieve the objective:

1.   Research into and study all known JPA, JPA-type, and similar or related designs of the past few years, and selection of those designs that appear most promising in achieving the results desired, as explained here.

2.   Actual tests and tryouts of the designs to produce a database of results sufficient to make a final choice of a design studied or the hybridization of design features into a new and final design.

3.   Validation of the final design chosen or evolved and preparation of a Validation Report.

The project must include monthly progress reports, to be reviewed by MCA's project manager, with a written Final Report on each phase submitted for MCA approval and end-of-phase presentations to MCA

---

continued

staff. The contractor must expect to meet with the MCA project manager for at least one in-process review of each phase of work. A Final Report on the entire project must be submitted for approval.

The Schedule

The schedule contemplated by MCA is as follows:

ITEM	DATE
Start of project	July 5, 1989
Phase I complete	October 10, 1989
Phase II complete	April 15, 1990
Phase III complete	June 30, 1990
Final Report submitted	July 30, 1990

Respondents are invited to offer an alternative schedule, if desired.

PROPOSAL INSTRUCTIONS

It is necessary, when requesting proposals, to tell respondents what you require that they include in their proposals, as well as what should be in the project plans, if you expect the proposals to be fully responsive and furnish all the information you need to accomplish your purposes. The proposal instructions are not properly part of the statement of work, however, but ought to be a separate document. Some who issue requests for proposals mandate a required format in great detail, often even to the extent of specifying a limitation in number of pages. This has the advantage of making it a bit easier to compare the proposals with each other, but like the overly detailed SOW it also tends to stifle the respondent's creativity and thus tends to deny the customer the benefits of that. Most often the requestor simply describes the information that must be furnished in the proposal.

A brief model of a set of proposal instructions is offered next to illustrate the type of information that belongs in such instructions.

PROPOSAL INSTRUCTIONS

In responding to this request please furnish the following information:

Your complete business name and address.

Your detailed plan to meet the needs described in the Statement of Work included herein

Identification and qualifications of your proposed project director and all key staff proposed to work on the project. Give their regular job titles in your company and the proposed titles or duties in the project.

> continued
>> An organization chart showing how the proposed project team will be organized and how/where the team fits into your organization overall.
>> Your overall organization, including all key personnel of your company.
>> Your company's qualifications for and experience in the work described.
>> The type of contract you propose, if other than the Time and Material contract described in the cover letter.
>> Your anticipated costs, with cost analysis showing how you arrive at and back up your estimates.
>> A matrix, to include a complete list of anticipated tasks and subtasks, with corresponding estimates of hours required of each proposed key staff member for each task and subtask.

PERSONNEL POLICY

Most organizations achieving a substantial number of personnel on the regular payroll find it necessary ultimately to develop a formal document describing personnel policy. In fact, it is when many organizations find it necessary for the first time to adopt a formal and official personnel policy that it becomes apparent that some kind of document of that policy is needed. (And in the case of cost-plus contracts with government agencies, the government may require that such a policy manual be included as part of the proposal.)

The extent and complexity of the documented personnel policy varies with the size and nature of the organization. Not surprisingly, the large organization is likely to have a more detailed set of policy statements and a thicker document than the small organization is. But even relatively small organizations often develop large personnel manuals when they are a technical- or professional-services enterprise where the majority of the staff are professionals and not union members. This is particularly the case in high-technology industries where qualified engineers and scientists are somewhat difficult to find and recruit. In fact, often the personnel manual is a necessary part of the literature used to interest prospects who are considering a number of potential employers and demand to know what kinds of working conditions and benefits they may expect as employees.

It is a common practice to introduce the content of the personnel policy manual with a signed statement from the organization's CEO (chief executive officer) greeting the new employee (it is assumed that the reader is a new employee), welcoming him or her to the organization with assurances that his or her contribution is valued and that a fine career awaits in the organization. Then the manual gets down to the specifics detailed here.

The minimal coverage of a personnel manual normally addresses the standard work week, paid time off (vacations, sick leave, and holidays) and how such time is earned, retirement benefits and when (or if) they are vested, and any other optional employees benefit plan, such as bonuses and stock options. Other matters that are often addressed in such manuals include these:

General hiring policies

Hospitalization and other group insurance plans.

A policy regarding rewards for employees who attract or recruit acceptable new employees (in some cases, when the company is in some line in which it is difficult to attract and hire new employees).

Promotion policies.

Annual reviews, how they are conducted, and what the outcomes are.

Employee organizations, such as a credit union or recreational group.

Policies regarding salary increases (often subdivided into merit increases and cost-of-living increases).

Suggestion program, describing procedures and rewards for worthy suggestions.

Procedures for making grievances known.

Along the lines of the purchasing manual discussed earlier, a personnel policy manual may be a simple sheaf of typed pages fastened with a corner staple, or it may be a more formal, typeset, and commercially bound document.

Chapter 9

Public Information

THE PR FUNCTION

PR is the commonly used acronym for the function known more formally as *public relations*. However, the slangy acronym *PR* is used far more often than the more formal term public relations and is consequently more easily and more swiftly recognized. Unfortunately, fiction writers, and especially Hollywood film makers, have created an impression of PR that is largely mythical or, at best, a gross exaggeration of PR and its practitioners. For years fiction writers, and especially Hollywood film makers, have portrayed and presented PR specialists as glib, flamboyant, ingeniously inventive and deceitful, fast talkers, con artists, and even as somewhat shifty and unscrupulous characters, as though PR was a less than respectable profession. They have been fond of presenting PR as the practice of thinking up and staging absolutely outrageous stunts that compel the press to publicize the event and the people involved in scare headlines and full front-page stories.

The truth is, of course, far less romantic than that. PR is a sober-sided, serious profession, depending far more on patient and lengthy, ongoing campaigns of continuous small publicity victories than on individual spectacular stunts. It is a serious business that supports a few large companies, a number of smaller ones, and a great many individual, often free-lance practitioners. It also supports many others on the staffs of companies large enough to need one or more full-time PR specialists of their own and/or maintain full-time public information offices within their regular establishments.

PR versus Advertising

In many cases advertising agencies offer PR services, as well as advertising assistance, although sometimes it's difficult to tell whether that or the reverse—PR companies offering advertising services—is the case. In any event the distinction between advertising and PR is not always a sharp one. In fact, sometimes they are virtually identical. For example, large organizations, such as supercorporations, often buy advertising of a type referred to as "institutional advertising," which is advertising in which they are not trying to sell a product or service per se, but only to build or enhance the organization's general image and prestige—to build public respect for the organization. Hughes Aircraft, for example, often runs major advertisements in news magazines to impress the readers with its work in the space programs. And many associations and corporations—Mobil Oil comes to mind as one—have often used paid advertising space to offer the public their political opinions and/or to champion one cause or another. This, although technically it is paid advertising—the media space or time has been purchased under standard commercial advertising agreements and terms—is a form of PR.

What Is PR?

For these and other reasons it is not easy to find a single, unequivocal definition of PR. PR is many things, conducted for many purposes, in many situations, and in many ways. Moreover, not all PR is the product of professional PR specialists, for many—perhaps most—of us find it necessary to practice a bit of PR at times, even when we do not realize that it is PR that we are practicing.

In the popular conception/misconception referred to earlier PR is commonly regarded as free advertising—free, at least, in the sense that there is no direct media cost. And that, truthfully, is probably the most common use of and purpose for PR. The reason is not that it is free, for arranging news coverage for PR purposes is often more costly in the end than buying space or air time. But PR is often far more effective than paid advertising for a variety of reasons, including primarily the fact that the average individual is far more likely to believe a news item than a paid advertisement. The average individual is probably also far more likely to notice and read or observe a news story than to read advertising copy or watch and listen to a commercial. It is a general truth, therefore, that the bulk of PR activity is aimed at attracting the interest and participation of the news media. But there are exceptions: PR activity also takes advantage of opportunities to get publicity in periodicals that are not truly news media in any sense. Too, it is directed at creating or shaping public opinion through mailing campaigns, some of those quite massive. And it is carried out in other more subtle ways, such as furnishing merchandise to TV game shows for the mention the contributors get, managing to have their products or uniforms easily recognizable in movies, and other such indirect means.

Still, creating a news story—gaining publicity directly for your product or service—is by far the most common objective of PR efforts. Entrepreneurs use PR to advertise the products and services they sell, candidates for office use PR to win votes, authors use PR to promote the sale of their books, and professional speakers use PR to win more speaking engagements and larger fees.

But even when PR is used to build a general image, rather to inspire sales directly, that is a form of selling via PR, even though it is indirect and perhaps is aimed at selling an idea, rather than some commercial product or service. And when an association, such as the Tobacco Institute, mounts a PR campaign to preserve its own interests or combat a threat (the growing sentiment and actions to restrict smoking in public places, in this case), it is engaging in a sales effort—the effort to sell its own point of view. Therefore it would be a rare occasion, indeed, when a PR campaign was undertaken for any purpose other than selling something, directly or indirectly.

PR Media

PR employs a number of methods and media for achieving its purposes, including the following ones:

News releases

Considering that the most common objective of PR is creating news, it is not surprising that the *news release* (known also as the press release, publicity release, and product release) is by far the most widely used tool of PR. (The fact that it is the most readily available, least expensive, and most easily created tool of PR—anyone can create releases easily—is also a major factor in the popularity and scope of its use.) An unending stream of releases is generated daily by individuals and organizations everywhere and on every conceivable subject.

Direct mail

The mail is a convenient vehicle for carrying out PR campaigns, and many organizations run advertisements inviting readers to send for information packages. When I was seeking a computer of my own, for example, I responded to a large number of such advertisements paid for by computer companies, and in many cases what I received was helpful material about computers in general with only indirect and quite subtle advertising of the sender's own product. Such direct-mail packages are far more closely related to PR than to normal advertising and direct marketing tactics. Of course, such packages utilize brochures and other materials, as well as letters.

Product releases

In more than one magazine there is a section describing new products, with a photo when a photo is appropriate, a brief description, and a price, usually. This is a service to readers who want news of new products. Getting a product into one of these sections is accomplished by using a news release, more appropriately called a **product release** in this case.

As to when to include photos, consider this: A photograph would not normally be necessary nor helpful in announcing a new computer software program but would be appropriate and probably required by an editor to describe a computer or a new kind of egg beater.

In most cases a black and white photograph is appropriate, although there are cases where a color photo ought to be supplied. Many editors prefer 8- × 10-inch glossies, but most will accept 4- × 5-inch glossies or even slightly smaller sizes. These can be bought in quantity at reasonable prices today, and cost should be no bar to using them.

Press kit

The press kit is often used as a major tool in PR, especially when you are preparing to conduct a press conference, setting up a booth in the exhibit hall of a convention or trade show (or maintaining a hospitality suite at such an event), or othewise wooing the press. Built around one or more releases, a typical press kit may include also brochures, photographs suitable for reproduction, writing materials for the convenience of the user, and other such items.

Public information office

The functions of a public information office and its staff are to answer specific queries from anyone who calls or writes and to mail out publicity/information materials in general. Usually these functions are combined with general PR functions, so that the public information staff is likely to also keep busy writing releases and other PR materials. Usually such an office is headed by a PR specialist (who is quite often a former journalist or even a practicing journalist).

Free speaker's bureau

Many organizations maintain a free speaker's bureau made up of the organization's executives and/or technical and professional specialists. For example, when I was employed as an editorial director by the Educational Science Division of U.S. Industries, I was a member of the organization's speaker's bureau and was sent out often to address groups and explain what we did and how we did it. And, as a variant on this, some companies will present a complete program to interested groups, often with movies or other audiovisual materials.

Miscellaneous

There are those other miscellaneous PR methods mentioned earlier, such as furnishing products to TV shows and movie makers. (Have you noticed in the credits following these shows such lines as "Miss Taylor's gowns by _____?" or "Rodney Ripple's wardrobe furnished by _____?") Or been able to see well-known products whose labels identifying them are quite plainly displayed? There are PR specialists whose principal duty is to see to it that their employers' products are prominently displayed as props in movies and TV shows with labels showing plainly. And sometimes they even manage to get their products' names worked into the dialogue used in these productions.

Another technique, especially when you are looking to publicize yourself, is to manage to be present at events where the press is busy photographing and identifying the individuals in the photographs.

Many entertainers and others in public life attend affairs that really bore them solely for this reason—the PR they can gain by being there.

One highly effective tactic that is used frequently by the experienced PR professionals is the news "leak" or "planted" story. This is especially the case with PR conducted in behalf of well-known public figures. The PR professional uses his or her many "contacts" to furnish a news item to or plant a story concerning the public figure with a columnist, talk-show host, reporter, free-lance magazine writer, or other individual who is in a position to get the item published. The ability to do this is one of the several advantages the true professional in PR has over those who are not full-time professional PR specialists.

CREATING RELEASES THAT GET PUBLISHED

By far the vast majority of releases written every day fall on their faces—fail to achieve publication. The reason is simple: They fail to be "newsworthy."

In the literal sense, newsworthiness means legitimacy as news. In the ancient cliché, if a dog bites a man it isn't news because it's too commonplace an event to be of interest to anyone; only when the reverse is true—when the unusual and unexpected event occurs—is news being made. Hoary example or not, it is a perfect illustration of what is and what is not newsworthy.

However, I use that term *newsworthy* here in a broader sense, for so-called news releases are more often than not the bearers of information (or alleged information) that is not truly news in any sense of that word. Still, to win the approval of an editor and find its way into print, the release must be worthy of being published for whatever reason, and so I use the term to refer to being what might be more properly called *publication*-worthy.

It is, of course, quite obvious to an editor that you want publicity, and that that is your motive in writing and mailing out your releases. In reading your release—and that is almost always the briefest of quick surveys, rather than true reading—the editor is mentally framing, "What's in it for me? Why should I publish this?" So it is the effectiveness with which your release answers that automatic query that determines whether the release does or does not win the prize of becoming published.

Editors do not publish news alone. They also publish articles, feature stories, sidebar stories, interviews, fillers, humorous squibs, and sundry other pieces for various reasons and purposes. They publish *whatever they believe will interest their readers*. And that is the key to it all. That is what makes a release newsworthy. That is what *sells* the release to the editor.

Perhaps some releases are automatically newsworthy by their nature. When Senator Quagmire decides to retire instead of running for another term, that is automatically newsworthy, as a rule, and the release is likely to find publication even if it is badly written and violates all the commonly accepted rules and standards for releases. On the other hand, the fact that Laundry Chemicals, Inc. has just introduced a greatly improved KoldWash Krystals product or invented a clever new dispenser package for it is not likely to interest any editor, no matter how cleverly the copy has been written.

Many releases are simply the text of a speech to be delivered, usually by someone of such prominence that, it is presumed, the media will wish to publish at least part of it. In this case the text is usually sent out as a release (although it might be sent out as a memorandum or special letter). But it is sent out well before the event so that the daily media (newspapers, radio, and TV) can "report" it immediately following the event. And to remind the editors of the timeliness factor the release is "embargoed" with a notice that gives the date (or the earliest date) on which it should be used.

The release in such a case carries a line that says "Embargoed until [date given] "or "Please release on [date]." But if the release is not embargoed it is always advisable to say "For immediate release." (In the absence of either statement the editor will assume that the item is for immediate release.)

By far the majority of topics used in and for releases fall between the extremes. Most are not automatically good stories, but most are not hopelessly impossible either. Most merely suffer from lack of imagination and creativity. That is, most could be *made* newsworthy with a bit of effort and cranial exercise.

Take that KoldWash Krystals story, for example. The fact of its being newly improved and introduced is not a newsworthy story; it's obvious advertising hype and only that. But perhaps it could be made newsworthy, with a bit of research and hard work.

How about a feature story, for example, tracing the history of laundering, from the struggles of women in early times, with the crudest of soaps and methods, to the modern soaps and machines and, finally, to modern detergents designed for modern machines and modern fabrics? Surely there must be some fascinating material there. (And surely prominent mention of KoldWash Krystals can be worked into the story from time to time.)

Or how about a story about methods and practices of laundering around the world today, especially in different kinds of societies, from the banks of the Nile to the towers of American high-rise apartments?

Or how about a science story about the development of modern laundry products, perhaps bringing in some prominent names of major chemical corporations?

Or how about a story of this modern scientific miracle that is being offered as the most effective laundry preparation yet?

Or a story about modern fabrics and the problems of finding suitable methods for laundering them?

It is finding such angles as these that makes the difference. But there are other considerations. For example, when I managed the Washington-area office of a multioffice corporation headquartered in New York City, the company sent me New York-datelined releases frequently, as they did all their many offices. We were to send them on to our local newspapers. But we did so with infrequent success because the releases were not of local interest. The solution was easy: I had someone on staff rewrite the releases, using our local dateline and stressing our local presence, although still citing the original material. We thus managed to get most of the releases published, at least in part.

Models of Releases

A general format for a release is shown in Figure 9–1. The elements and characteristics generally considered to be obligatory are these:

- Identification as a release by such words as RELEASE, NEWS, PRESS RELEASE, or other such term.
- Identification of issuing organization. May be and often is an ordinary letterhead of the organization.
- Dateline. City of origin and date.
- Double- or triple-spaced copy.
- Single-sided copy.
- Headline. Arbitrary; some advocate against it, some for it. I am for it, to capture the editor's interest and help him or her grasp the essence of the story immediately. The argument against is that editors prefer to write their own headlines, which is true enough, but is irrelevant because the editor is free to change the original headline and very likely will do so!
- Contact. Name and number to help the editor follow up, ask for photos, verify/validate, or otherwise pursue more information and perhaps to even get "the story behind the story."
- Guidance. "More" or "End" at bottom of page to help the editor know whether there is more copy and/or when the story ends.
- When to release. Should say "For immediate release" or "Embargoed until [some date]," as noted.

The Most Common Mistakes

There are several common mistakes that many people make in preparing releases. Those mistakes most likely to kill the chances for success of a release are these:

- The copy is not newsworthy in any sense of the word.
- The copy is single-spaced instead of double- or triple-spaced.
- The copy is typed on both sides of paper instead of on one side only.

FIGURE 9–1 Sample of a Release

HRH COMMUNICATIONS, INC.
P.O. Box 6067
Silver Spring, MD 20906

NEWS   6/28/88

    For immediate release   Contact:
                                                     Jane Eager
                                                    (301) 460-0000

        HOW TO SELL TO THE $200 BILLION GOVERNMENT MARKET

           Information Now Available in Audiocassettes

    For years business people have complained about the
difficulty of getting information and guidance in selling to the
U.S. Government, despite the literature on the subject, much of
it published by the government. Written literature,
unfortunately, has not proved very helpful to the newcomer to
this market.

    Now, for the first time, a complete information and
instruction package on selling to the huge federal government
market is offered to marketers in convenient audiocassette form.
The set includes four 1-hour cassettes and a 65-page directory of
government purchasing offices, with a summary of the Federal
Acquisition Regulations (FAR).

    The package was developed over the past year by a special
team of government-marketing experts, who interviewed dozens of
government purchasing officials and reviewed over 12,000 pages
of official documents to distill this 4-hour program.

    The program incorporates the latest information available,
as of October 1, 1987. It is available from HRH Communications,
Inc. at $98.50 (discounted for quantity purchases).

                       # # #

- There is no contact name given.
- The release fails to provide embargo date when release "reports" some event that has not taken place yet.

If you make a mistake that causes an editor to commit some faux pas and be embarrassed thereby you will seriously reduce your chances of ever having that editor consider your releases again. It is therefore especially important to be careful about accuracy in general and such other details as have been mentioned here; your relationships with editors are at stake, and that is an important factor in conducting PR successfully.

One of the common mistakes not mentioned yet because we have not yet raised the subject has to do with where to send releases. It is a mistake to address a release to a publication or other medium without specifying an individual destination. Remember that in large organizations mail simply addressed to the organization is usually opened in the mail room, where someone attempts to judge the proper destination within the organization. On a large newspaper your release is likely to wind up on a managing editor's or city editor's desk—but it could even wind up on the circulation manager's desk—if you have not specified otherwise. That individual may or may not spend the time reading your release and deciding that it ought to go to the business editor or food editor, or even the state desk. Or he or she may simply decide to be too busy to bother and drop it casually into the "circular file" without further thought. Or even if he or she decides to pass it on to someone else it is still likely to wind up in the wrong place and eventually find its way into that famous circular file just mentioned.

On the other hand, even if you do manage to get it to the individual editor, columnist, or other party you mean it for, it is still necessary that the release be "right" for that party—be of true interest. That is, you do not—should not—ordinarily write a release and then decide where to send it, but you should follow the reverse pattern, along the following line of procedure:

1. Define what kind of reader/listener/viewer you wish to reach and appeal to.
2. Decide what kinds of media—which periodicals, what columnists, what radio or TV programs, and so forth—are most suitable for reaching those prospects. (What do they read, watch, listen to?)
3. Decide what would interest the editor/columnist/producer, and so forth—how to slant your release.

If you proceed in any other way it is quite likely that you will wind up with the wrong release sent to the wrong destinations.

The only way to avoid this fate is to *know* where your release ought to go by following the logical routine described. You need not necessarily know the individual's name (although that often helps), but you must have the right functional title. And even that can vary from one publication to another. What one newspaper calls the "Financial Editor" another may title the "Business Editor," although the dullest mail room clerk may be able to make the translation. But it is best to know the publication and address editors by the correct functional titles.

This is even more critical when you want to send releases to columnists, in the hope that they will become interested in your announcements. These must normally be addressed by name, and since many are syndicated and are not on the staff of the individual periodical carrying the column, you must either determine what the columnist's mailing address is or send your release in care of the periodical.

And all of this is equally valid in sending releases to radio and TV station news rooms, show hosts, and producers.

Slanting copy is a simple concept. It means writing the release in such a way as to address the direct interests of a given audience in writing your presentation. Suppose, for example, that you are selling computer software—programs—and are preparing a release to help make your establishment more widely known. And suppose that you wish to offer a free demonstration and how-to-do-it seminar as a means for attracting prospects to your place of business.

There are several possibilities open to you. Your release will have to suggest some particular program or kind of program you will be demonstrating. Suppose you have a choice among a new inventory-control and -management program, a new word processor program, or the latest and most popular computer game. Which one is most likely to attract the prospects you want?

Obviously that depends on the kind of prospects you want. An inventory program is going to attract only businesspeople for whom inventory-control and management is important. It certainly is not likely to appeal to the owner of a small luncheonette or a high school youngster. But the game program will not appeal to the businessperson normally.

That's a rather obvious case. Not all are so obvious. But it points up something: You can create more than one version of release so that you can attract many people. But you must also think in terms of the periodicals and other media to which you will send your releases. The business or financial pages of a newspaper are not read by high school boys, and often not even by the proprietors of small, neighborhood businesses, as a rule. And, of course, editors know who their readers are and whether your release is appropriate for them, accordingly. Thus you need to slant your release so that it fits wherever you wish to send it—if slanting is possible, that is; it is not always a practicable idea.

Not everything can be slanted effectively. It would be difficult to slant a release for a male audience explaining how crocheting is making a strong comeback. Few men are likely to take up crocheting. On the other hand, relatively few women are enthusiastic about fly fishing. So an article or release on fly fishing might be slanted to fly fishermen with different interests—some like to tie their own flies while others prefer to buy them ready made and will try every new one they can find—but they have to have that common interest in fly fishing. (In fact, perhaps the most common factor among fly fishermen is their almost legendary zeal, which borders on fanaticism.) On the other hand, it is entirely possible that you might be able to slant material on fly fishing even to women who have no direct interest in fishing at all if you address the wives and sweethearts of fly fishermen with an appeal to buy fly-fishing gear or accessories as gifts for the zealots they love.

Many products lend themselves to multiple uses and users, and each potential use and user suggests the keys to a slant. In writing releases to publicize my own newsletters, books, and reports on marketing to government agencies, I found many ways to slant them to different audiences. The most obvious and most basic slanting opportunities were these:

1.   To companies already doing business with the government, the theme was how to do *more* business with the government.

2.   To companies who had done little or no business with the government, the theme here was how to break into the government market most effectively.

But there were many other possibilities. I could slant releases to small businesses, to minority-owned businesses,to very small businesses such as free-lancing individuals, to businesses by the nature of what they sold, to businesses by the nature of the kinds of customers they would be going after, and even more possibilities than these. With an active imagination and a bit of introspection on possible uses and users, slanting is usually not especially difficult.

This idea is not for releases only, however. It is equally useful in writing advertising copy, sales letters, brochures, magazine articles, and just about everything else that might be addressed to the public generally or to any specific class or group of people. The key is simply finding the link between the reader's interest and what you wish to publicize.

Chapter 10

Miscellaneous Data: A Reference File

THE MATTER OF PRESENTATION

In serving a meal, ambience has a great deal to do with the appreciation and enjoyment of the meal. In a private home or restaurant—and especially in a public restaurant—ambience refers to the general surroundings (atmosphere or aura) and graciousness of serving—the *presentation* of the meal. And in a letter, proposal, report, or other written item, ambience is equally important. Ambience is the sum of the atmosphere or aura and the correctness and good taste of the presentation overall, including such items as format, typestyles, paper, language, and several other elements that result, finally in adding to or detracting from your intended meaning and the impact of your message.

There are many protocols concerning the appearance and language of messages, especially formal exchanges concerning matters of state, and even in situations of far less formality there are many standards and practices considered to be proper and in good taste. A disregard for these, especially in the matter of salutations and forms of address—even one that is completely innocent—can give offense or convey a general impression that will weaken the message completely. (See, for example, the list of common mistakes many people make in writing publicity releases.)

Although some of these matters were discussed briefly in earlier chapters, and at the risk of being somewhat redundant in that regard, this chapter is offered as a convenient reference file to save you the trouble of searching through earlier chapters for the answers to questions of formats and special problems related to them. In this chapter you will find those suggested formats not covered in detail earlier for letters and other formal and informal messages including such details as proper methods of address for different addressees and different occasions.

LETTER FORMATS

Letters fall into numerous categories, but as far as style and formats are concerned most letters are either formal or informal, or business or personal, and even then their styles are not greatly different from each other.

Aside from that, much of format and style is a matter of personal preference and choice. For example, I personally prefer the block style, as in the following:

> Aside from that, much of format and style is a matter of personal preference and choice. For example, I personally prefer the block style.

while others prefer the indented style (5 or 10 spaces):

> Aside from that, much of format and style is a matter of personal preference and choice. For example, I personally prefer the block style.

The Forms of Address and Salutations

Salutations are equally a matter of personal choice (or of whatever you were taught when you attended public school!). My salutations are always

Dear Mr. McCarthy:

while others use

Dear Mr. McCarthy,

They are equally correct. Probably the use of a colon, rather than a comma, is a bit more formal, while the comma is more in keeping with the logic of conventional punctuation practices and principles.

The question of whether to use a comma or colon is a mechanical matter and is of no great importance. The matter of address and salutation, however, is quite another matter; it can be critically important.

Obviously, when you send personal letters to friends you use informal salutations, depending largely on your relationship—"Dear Joe" or "Hi, Stinky," for example. Addressing a stranger, however, even when your letter is a personal one and not truly formal, requires some thought and some knowledge of what is normally considered proper or, at least, acceptable practice. Technically, at least to the more conservative traditionalists, it is considered somewhat improper to address strangers as "Dear Mr. So-and-so," since that is presumed to infer a relatively intimate and friendly relationship. The convention espoused by those more conservatively inclined in matters of protocol is that that salutation is reserved to those to whom you are at least not a stranger. To strangers, when you must presumably be rather formal, this protocol says you must make your address to "*My* dear Mr. So-and-so:" This protocol is, however, not closely observed today, and you must exercise your own independent judgment as to whether this should become your own standard. But there are several other situations to consider in that respect, some of them more serious in my opinion than the foregoing one.

In these times of sensitivity to equal rights for all people, regardless of individual or even characteristic differences of any kind, it has become a bit of a problem to know how to address an organization when you have no idea of who is who in the organization. Until these times of greater consciousness of the right of equal consideration and treatment, it was a practice to address such organizations as "Gentlemen:" Today that is not only in bad taste, it is likely to be absolutely in error: Today it is by no means certain that the responsible leaders or executives of the organization are men; they may very well be and often are women.

In the same vein, whereas we have always addressed men formally as "Mr." without regard to their marital status or lack of it, we have always had the problem of whether to address a woman formally as "Miss" or "Mrs." when we were uncertain about her marital status. There never was a generic form of formal address to a woman that avoided this problem, so we have had to invent one recently, one that is a less-than-ideal solution but one that has become fairly popular. Today, when you are unsure about whether the woman you are addressing (a) is or has been married or (b) has a strong personal preference that the question not be considered at all, you may usually use the salutation "Ms." safely and would be well advised to do so.

I have found, too, very much to my discomfort and embarrassment, that many women today object strongly to being referred to by such terms as "ladies" or "girls," finding such terms condescending or otherwise derogatory. It is obviously more discreet and in better taste or at least far less likely to be offensive to use the generic term "women" today, although addressing an audience or general population as "Ladies and gentlemen" ought still to be acceptable.

There are several other cases that call for special attention. One of them is the case of addressing public officials, a case in which protocol is a definite consideration. Typical examples are offered in Figure 10–1, beginning with a proper salutation for the president of the United States, should you ever have occasion to correspond with the president!

FIGURE 10–1 Formal Salutations for Special Cases

Individual	Address	Salutation
President of the United States	The Honorable John Doe	My dear Mr. President
Vice President of the United States	The Honorable John Doe	My dear Mr. Vice President
Senators and other such officials	The Honorable John Doe	My dear Mr. Doe
Ambassador	The Honorable John Doe	My dear Mr. Ambassador
Governor	The Honorable John Doe	My dear Governor Doe
The Pope	His Holiness Pope John Paul II	Most Holy Father Your Holiness
Priest	The Reverend John Doe	Dear Reverend Father
Nun	Sister Jane Doe	Reverend Sister
		Dear Sister Jane Doe
Rabbi	Rabbi John Doe	My dear Rabbi Doe
Professor	Professor John Doe	My dear Professor Doe
Any Ph.D.	Dr. John Doe	My dear Dr. Doe

The table is constructed on the premise that all the individuals will be men, which is not necessarily the case today when we have many women serving in Congress and in other important jobs in government and elsewhere. In most cases the salutation would change to "My dear Madam _____" in such situations.

The salutations given in the table are considered somewhat informal, although proper, for such cases. For more formal usage you may use the salutation "Sir" or "Madam," rather than the ones given in the table.

Special Titles

Although we pride ourselves in being a classless society—one in which we are all equal, at least in freedoms and rights—we do confer many special titles on individuals, recognizing special achievements and/or the attainment of special status of some kind. In the figure you may have noticed the address to "Dr." and "Professor." Anyone with a doctoral degree of any kind is entitled to be addressed as "Doctor," and those who become professors are entitled to have that term used in addressing and saluting them too.

Military people are entitled to be addressed by titles of rank. There is one kind of special case here: When the rank is one of those with two terms, such as Lieutenant Colonel or Major General, the address is always to the second and higher designation. A lieutenant colonel is therefore addressed verbally as "Colonel," although addressed as "Lieutenant Colonel John Doe" in writing his or her address. The salutation would normally be, like the verbal address, "My dear Colonel."

Complimentary Closes

Complimentary closes may likewise be formal or informal. "Respectfully" is considered to be rather formal and stiff today, with "Sincerely" and "Very truly" in more popular usage. "Cordially" is relatively informal used in a letter to a stranger and, of course, "Regards" or "Best wishes" are quite informal and generally used only in letters to friends.

Notice of Enclosure(s)

You may have noticed the term *Encl.* or *Enclosure* below the signature in some business letters where there was something else in the envelope. This is designed to be a notice to clerks or anyone else, other than the addressee, who may open the letter that there is something else enclosed with the letter. (The addressee would normally know that as a result of reading the letter and would not need the notice.) Some writers use only the abbreviation Encl. to remind anyone opening the letter that there is something else enclosed, while others identify the other material specifically.

The usual practice is to type that notice several lines below the signature on the left-hand side of the letter. (This is illustrated in models that appear later.)

Distribution Notices

In many cases, especially in routine business correspondence, carbon copies of the original letter are sent to others for filing and information purposes. Although today we rarely use carbon paper for making copies—office copiers are far more convenient and less messy—the custom of marking the letter "cc:" (for "carbon copy(ies)" has persisted. The term is followed by the names or other identification of the destinations of the copies. This notice appears, like the enclosure notice, beneath the signature, on the left-hand side. (This, too, is illustrated later.)

Signature

Sales letters and other letters mailed in bulk may have a rubber stamp or lithographed signature, but that is a discourtesy when used in individual letters. Other than the case of letters mailed in bulk or copies sent to others for file and information purposes (those are generally not signed at all), all original letters ought to bear the actual signature (not a facsimile) of the sender.

A FEW MISCELLANEOUS FORMAT MATTERS

Less serious but not less important if you wish your letters to appear truly professional and as if you really *cared* about how they look, are some mechanical details of layout and format. Some of these details are optional, as in the case of block style versus indented paragraph styles, but others are not optional at all. There are a few important rules or, at least, principles.

Readability, Real and Apparent

The physical appearance of the letter is important for more than one reason. Aside from the general impression of professionalism and caring—or the lack of it—there is the matter of readability and *apparent* readability. There are a great many myths and mistaken notions about this, so that actual readability and apparent readability are sometimes in conflict. For example, many people believe that double-spaced copy is easier to read than single-spaced copy, and in the same vein many believe that copy set in all capitals is easier to read than copy set in both upper- and lower-case letters.

Both of these notions are wrong, and the reason they are wrong is quite understandable: They are wrong because we have been trained to read text as upper and lower case letters in single-spaced format, just as we have been trained to read from left to right. While variations from this may *appear* to be easier to read, actual tests have demonstrated the opposite. And if you doubt the effect of our early training in reading, try reading English in the style of oriental ideographs—in vertical columns—or in the style of Hebrew—from right to left. Or try reading a lengthy text—at least several pages—in all capitals.

Making Your Letters *Appear* More Readable

If appearance belies reality in some cases, there are others in which appearances reflect reality. One of these is the matter of physical balance of text in a letter.

The type should be balanced on the page. This is especially important for short letters, letters of about one half a page or less, so that the type is not bunched near the top of the page, with most of the bottom portion of the page blank. (See Figures 10–2 and 10–3, which illustrate this.)

Text that is "set solid"—large, unbroken blocks of text—appears formidable and is intimidating to readers. It *appears* to be difficult to read, whether it is or not. Here again appearance does not reflect reality. We have ample evidence that the actual readability of text depends most of all on how interesting it is to the reader, although the choice of language and sentence structure has some effect. The Job Corps experience was only one of many that demonstrated the effect of motivation on reading ability: If sufficiently motivated—interested, that is—readers will infer the correct meanings of many words that are unfamiliar to them and will manage to get the main meanings out of even "purple prose" passages. On the other hand, the most enlightened use of simple sentence structure and commonly known words cannot overcome the stultifying effect of deadly dull writing. Ideally, the text ought to be interesting, clearly expressed, and attractively presented if it is to do its job at all.

Part of the appearance depends on leaving adequate margins. Margins ought to be at least one inch, but margins slightly larger—1½ inches—are even better.

To avoid that psychological effect of text that is set solid it is desirable to break up the large passages of text by keeping paragraphs as short as possible—by starting new paragraphs as often as possible, that is.

That is not an entirely arbitrary matter, for the accepted principles of composition dictate that each paragraph be about some topic which is introduced by the first sentence of the paragraph, and that a new paragraph must thus be about another topic. That, however, can be arranged by using a little ingenuity in organizing your letters and making each paragraph highly specialized in the topics it addresses.

FIGURE 10–2 Unbalanced Letter

```
                        HRH COMMUNICATIONS, INC.
                P.O. Box 6067    Silver Spring, MD 20906


                                                    January 3, 1994


    Jerry Harper
    2154 River Road
    Haleysville, MD 20111

    Dear Mr. Harper:

    It is our pleasure to respond to your invitation to quote prices
    for furnishing your new offices, per your request for quotation
    RFQ-78-6-94.  Our quotation is enclosed here.

    Please feel free to call on us for further information if needed.


                                            Sincerely,



                                            Peter Macklewaite
                                            VP Marketing


    Encl. Quotation

    cc: J. Hepplewhite, Comptroller
        Marian Morgan, Executive Sec'y
        Bid Files
```

Still another matter is that of whether to place the date and complimentary close on the left- or right-hand side of the page. (Some few people prefer to center the dateline on the page, especially when the letterhead is centered.) Traditionally, these went at the right-hand side, as in Figures 10–2 and 10–3, but in modern times more and more letter writers are placing these at the left-hand side, beginning flush with the left-hand margin, as in Figure 10–4. This is so well accepted today that it may be considered to be purely a matter of your personal choice.

FIGURE 10-3 Balanced Letter

```
                        HRH COMMUNICATIONS, INC.
                P.O. Box 6067    Silver Spring, MD 20906




                                                   January 3, 1994




        Jerry Harper
        2154 River Road
        Haleysville, MD 20111

        Dear Mr. Harper:

        It is our pleasure to respond to your invitation to quote prices
        for furnishing your new offices, per your request for quotation
        RFQ-78-6-94.  Our quotation is enclosed here.

        Please feel free to call on us for further information if needed.


                                              Sincerely,



                                              Peter Macklewaite
                                              VP Marketing



        Encl. Quotation

        cc: J. Hepplewhite, Comptroller
            Marian Morgan, Executive Sec'y
            Bid Files
```

GRAMMAR, PUNCTUATION, AND RELATED MATTERS

There will be no course in grammar here, not even a minicourse, for that is well beyond the scope of this book, and excellent texts on grammar are readily available. (A few will be cited in the bibliography here.) Consult one of these if you feel the need for a brushup. However, there are a few related, individual matters worthy of mention in passing, and those will be covered briefly here.

FIGURE 10–4 An Alternative Style

```
                         HRH COMMUNICATIONS, INC.
                  P.O. Box 6067    Silver Spring, MD 20906




        January 3, 1994




        Jerry Harper
        2154 River Road
        Haleysville, MD 20111

        Dear Mr. Harper:

        It is our pleasure to respond to your invitation to quote prices
        for furnishing your new offices, per your request for quotation
        RFQ-78-6-94.  Our quotation is enclosed here.

        Please feel free to call on us for further information if needed.


        Sincerely,



        Peter Macklewaite
        VP Marketing



        Encl. Quotation

        cc: J. Hepplewhite, Comptroller
            Marian Morgan, Executive Sec'y
            Bid Files
```

First it ought to be understood that while spellings are usually absolute (although there are many cases where alternate spellings are acceptable), grammar and punctuation "rules" are not really rules for how to express language, but are guidelines reflecting the opinions of certain people deemed to be authorities in the use of the language. So we have the purists who denounce as unspeakably coarse and unacceptable the splitting of an infinitive or the ending of a sentence with a preposition, while we have had such eminent masters of English usage as Winston

Churchill who denounced such standards as being unimaginative and divorced from reality. Winston Churchill's famous remark that he used to illustrate the fallacy of unbending rules such as these was "This is an impertinence, up with which I shall not put," in referring to the dictum against ending a sentence with a preposition. He thus illustrated rather dramatically a sensible principle: Do try to observe these principles, such as avoiding the splitting of an infinitive, but not if the alternative to a split infinitive or ending a sentence with a preposition is an ungainly and ungracious expression.

Another mistaken notion is that there is something wrong in using the personal pronoun "I" in writing. Samuel Clemens snorted that "Only editors, royalty, and people with tapeworm have the right to say 'we' when they mean 'I'," but the one-time restriction against using "I" is commonly considered to have been put to rest with the writings of Montaigne (Michel) some time ago. In any case, there is little reason to say "we" unless you truly mean "we."

Rhetoric

Rhetoric is one subject where rules become nearly impossible, for rhetoric has to do primarily with the choice of the right words and their gracious use. It is far more an art than a science, and assaults on the language in this area are quite painful to many.

In my own case I am especially saddened by the growing and expanding misuse of the word "convinced." To be convinced means to be induced to believe something, never to be led to take an action. That is, to say something such as "Joe convinced Betty to meet him" is a horrible assault on the language in my opinion. Here the sentence ought to read either "Joe *persuaded* Betty to meet him" or "Joe convinced Betty that it would be a good idea to meet him." You *never* convince anyone *to* (do something), but only *of* (something).

This is an extreme case, and one that I and others find exceptionally distasteful, but there are many others. "Like" and "as" reflect another case. That tiresome advertising phrase about the cigarettes that "taste good like a cigarette should" was grammatically all wrong, for "like" modifies nouns, not verbs; it is an adjective, not an adverb. Those cigarettes should have tasted "good *as* a cigarette should," "as" being the adverb necessary to make the sentence grammatically proper.

These two examples point up a common problem. There are many words in English so like other words in sound or spelling that it is difficult to remember exactly what their differences are in meaning and so to remember how to use them properly. And to further complicate the picture some of these words can be used as more than one part of speech—*effect* can be both a noun and a verb, for example. Some of the common and most troublesome such pairs of words are the following. (Respective meanings follow the words to enhance the illustration.)

affect, effect: influence; bring about or result
principal, principle: chief, school official, or investment capital; basic
    truth
accept, except: receive, agree; leave out
allusion, illusion: reference; false image
appraise, apprise: evaluate; advise or inform
biannual, biennial: twice a year; every two years
calendar, calender: chart of days/months; smoothing device
compliment, complement: praise or commend; complete
continually, continuously: repeatedly, without stopping
council, counsel: board of people; advice
its, it's: possessive of it; contraction of it is
lead, led: a heavy metal; showed the way
reign, rein: to rule; check or control
stationary, stationery: fixed in one position; writing supplies
your, you're: possessive of you; contraction of you are

Punctuation

Punctuation falls into the same class of "rules" that are really not hard
and fast rules at all. There are at least three schools of punctuation:
closed, open, and mixed. Again, it is Samuel Clemens who left us a
memorable remark on the subject. He protested violently when editors
tampered with his punctuation. He insisted that no editor—no one—
knew as well as he just what he was trying to say and therefore no one
had the right or the competence to alter his punctuation.

That may be a bit extreme, given that many writers are not professional writers nor especially well qualified to punctuate their own work,
but it does point up the arbitrary nature of so-called rules for punctuation. In my own case I went to school before there was such a vogue as
open punctuation (or perhaps it was before I had the opportunity to
learn that there was such an idea), and I have consequently had to adjust my thinking to this idea of relatively little punctuation, especially
with regard to the sparse use of commas. (The adjustment did not come
easily, after years of believing that there was only one set of rules for
punctuation!)

In any case, the whole idea of grammar and punctuation is to try to
help the reader perceive your whole meaning, with all its nuances and
accents, and you should try to achieve that.

Spelling

If there is any overwhelmingly common weakness among writers who
are not professional writers (although professional writers are not ex-
cepted from this, either) it is a sharply pronounced weakness in spelling.
We are, too many of us, poor spellers.

One reason for this problem is the nature of English and the fact that we really speak American here, because English as spoken in England is somewhat different in both pronunciation and spelling of a great many words. However, a large part of the problem is due to the fact that we have imported many thousands of words into English from many other languages—Latin, French, Spanish, German, and others—so that we have extremely few hard and fast rules for spelling. Therefore almost all spelling rules have many exceptions. We are taught as children, for example, that when we spell words with *e* and *i* together in them we should remember that the rule is "i before e, except after c, or when sounded as a, as in neighbor and weigh." If you can remember that little verse, you are well along the way to mastering the ei/ie spelling problem. Otherwise it can be difficult to always be sure how to spell such words.

We also often have trouble remembering the plurals of words, especially those words that have come into English from another language and which therefore do not normally take an *s* or *es* to make the plural. And, oddly enough, we are usually more familiar with the plural form, so it is often the singular form that we do not know, nor do we even know that we are using the plural form. One of the most common examples of this is a word that has come into widespread use in this computer age: *data*, which is the plural of *datum*.

The trouble comes about when we use these terms in sentences with the wrong verbs. One of the most common problems, for example, is that of saying or writing such things as, "The data is being collected," when the correct form would be, "The data are being collected." Try using *are* and *is* on the following terms, for example, among which are some of the most troublesome of these pairs:

PLURAL FORM	SINGULAR FORM
agenda	agendum
alumnae	alumna
alumni	alumnus
analyses	analysis
antennas, antennae	antenna
appendixes, appendices	appendix
axes	axis
bacteria	bacterium
bases	basis
crises	crisis
curricula	curriculum
data	datum
diagnoses	diagnosis
errata	erratum
indexes, indices	index
matrices	matrix
media	medium
minutiae	minutia

continued	
PLURAL FORM	**SINGULAR FORM**
parentheses	parenthesis
radii	radius
strata	stratum
theses	thesis

Unfortunately, the incorrect use of words can lead to bizarre results, often to the detriment of your image as the writer or, even worse, to the detriment of your organization's image. Here are a couple of examples of what can happen when a writer is not careful to be sure that he or she is using the right words or, conversely, knows the precise meaning of the words:

In some types of equipment where the failure of a circuit would be catastrophic the engineers often "back up" all the critical circuits with duplicate circuits that will be switched on automatically if the original circuit fails. A technical writer preparing a user manual for such a piece of equipment confidently assured his readers of the complete "duplicity" of the circuits in the computer he was writing about, which was not exactly the quality customers wished their computers to have.

In another case of technical writing the engineer-writer wished to explain how all the connections (of which there were a great many in the system) were assigned to the rows upon rows of numbered terminals. He headed this discussion, "The Assignation of the Terminals," thereby raising a few eyebrows.

Words and Expressions to Shun

One of the hallmarks of the inexperienced writer is the use of trite and hackneyed cliches, such as "the bottom line," "a breakdown in communications," "sweet as sugar," and "slow as molasses." But another writing sin is the repeated use and overuse of some favored word or term, until it becomes trite and hackneyed in the context of whatever you are writing. (One individual in my experience, for example, was so enamored of "adept" and "expertise" that he worked overtime at dragging these into every possible paragraph, until readers begged for mercy! And a third symptom is the use of redundant expressions, such as "past experience" and "past history." What else can those things be but "past?" And the term "wealthy millionaire" is not an unheard-of redundancy either.

Occasionally we run into oxymorons, too, which are expressions consisting of words or ideas that are incompatible with each other because they negate each other. "Honest thief" and "little giant," for example, are oxymorons. If you wish to make a specific point by using such a term for its special effect, be sure that you do so in such a way that the reader knows that you are doing so deliberately for special effect and not in ignorance.

HOW TO MAKE WRITING (AND READING) AN EASIER TASK

"Writing" is not concerned with words alone. In fact, words are actually rather poor tools for communication, for they are only symbols, and each writer and reader must undertake the chores of translating images and ideas into those word symbols and retranslating those word symbols into the images and ideas they are supposed to represent. The original images and ideas almost always lose a great deal in those processes, unfortunately. But writing is an act of communication and should utilize all devices that aid communication, including photographs, drawings, and charts, a few examples of which have been shown in earlier pages. Among the more common types of graphs and charts that can be constructed rather easily are bar charts, pie charts, flow charts, and plots (see Figure 10-5).

The use of illustrations makes life easier for both the writer and the reader. Every good illustration relieves you of struggling with words alone to get a message or image across to a reader, and in many cases it is far easier to convey what is in your mind with a graphic illustration of

FIGURE 10-5 A Flow Chart and an Organization Chart

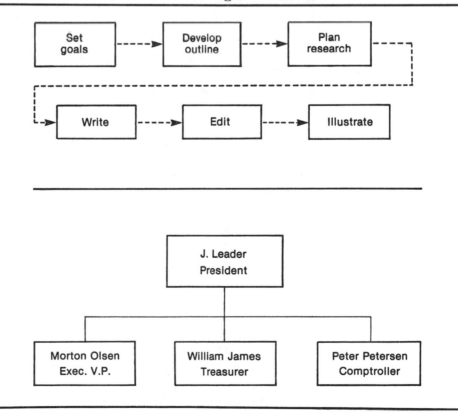

some kind. But the reader benefits equally, for understanding also becomes easier with good illustrations: Using good illustrations is a win-win situation for both writer and reader. And while writing and illustrating are more art than science, there are some guidelines to consider when using such illustrations.

How to Judge the Quality of an Illustration

A good illustration requires little explanation. That is the way to test the quality of any illustration: Does it require explanation, and if so, how much? Is the illustration clear or is it "clever"? Forget about clever devices and artistic considerations; the purpose of an illustration is to communicate information accurately and efficiently. If the reader has to puzzle over the meaning or study the illustration at great length to understand it, the reader will probably sigh and go on. The basic rule is to always make it as easy as possible on the reader. Cleverness is all too often the death of meaning and understanding, and therefore the death of the writer's effort.

RESEARCH

Inadequate research—which means not having enough information and/or not knowing the subject well enough—is far more often the root cause of bad writing than is any inability to use the language skillfully enough. An important key to writing well is, then, knowing how to research properly.

Logically enough—and unfortunately this is not nearly as obvious as it ought to be—the first and most important step in research is one that must be taken before the research effort begins. It is knowing what you want to know—setting a clear and specific objective of the research.

That can be a simple or a complex task. If you are answering a customer complaint it is important to research your own files and be sure that you know exactly what the *facts* are before you attempt to evaluate the customer's claims and allegations. On the other hand, if you are writing a report or a manual, you must be absolutely clear in your mind what objective that report or manual is supposed to achieve and what information you need to achieve it. In fact, even before you set out on your research you should have worked up some sort of preliminary outline and a written objective.

That presumes that you know enough about the subject to do that—to prepare an outline. But sometimes you may have to undertake to write about something you do not know well enough to draft even a rough or preliminary outline. In that case you may have to do some preliminary research so that you can develop a working outline. But even then—and even when you know your subject rather well—always assume that your outline is preliminary and subject to change as you broaden your knowledge and deepen your well of raw material resulting from your research. (There would be little point in the research other-wise!) In that special case your first research objective would be to gather enough information to develop a working outline and design your main research plan.

The Research Plan

The research plan is generally a rather informal plan. It consists primar-ily of setting down your main objective (sometimes with subordinate objectives where the task is a relatively large and complex one) and the main sources of information.

Typical sources are people (interviews) and documents (files, re-ports, books, and other such material). And as in the case of research and preliminary outlines, early research often uncovers sources you hadn't thought of or known about, so these should be added to your re-search plan. Here are a few suggested sources:

Libraries, public and otherwise. These include the extensive spe-cialized libraries many major corporations, government agencies, and others keep and sometimes make available to the public.

Company records (your own company, that is). Often the informa-tion you need is in your own files!

Associations. There are thousands of associations of all kinds, from trade associations to professional societies, and many of these can and will help.

Public information offices. Large corporations, government agen-cies, and many other organizations maintain those public information offices mentioned earlier. They are usually quite eager to help.

Government publications. The federal government publishes a great many books, reports, pamphlets, and sundry other documents through the Government Printing Office and other federal agencies. There are few subjects that have not been written about in one or more of these publications.

Public databases. A great sea of information has been opened by the advent of the personal (desktop) computer and the evolution of online databases that have been inspired by that development. This will be covered in this chapter.

Other special sources. Quite often the early stages of your research will guide you to other sources. Moreover, there are several publications designed especially to guide you to information sources. These publica-tions will be listed later.

When Is Research Complete?

There is no pat answer to when research is complete, because each situa-tion is different. However, there are some clues—indicators to suggest that it is time to end the research:

- You find that you are getting almost entirely redundant information—information you already have.
- You find that the information you are developing is too trivial or too irrelevant to your objectives to be useful.
- You are convinced, for whatever reason, that you now have all or nearly all the information you need to achieve your objectives.

This does not necessarily mean that your research is truly over and done with, however. It is possible that even after you begin writing you will come across a gap in the information that you had not detected before, and that you therefore must return to your research effort to search out some special area.

REPORT FORMATS

There are a number of report formats possible, depending primarily on the objectives of the report you are writing. Financial reports, such as profit and loss statements and balance sheets, are usually little more than tabulated figures. Reports of special projects, such as studies or research and development programs, usually fall into two broad categories, as witness the following two:

Progress report

The major goal of a progress report, which is normally one of a series produced at regular periods such as monthly, is made clear by its generic title. The objective is to explain where things stand in terms of progress. To do this a typical report organization includes the following sections or chapters:

1. Introduction, often a brief recap of the previous report.
2. Current status, usually as compared with earlier (original) estimates of where things should be at this point, as a measure of progress or the lack of it. Discussion of special items, such as problems mentioned in previous report and/or predictions of previous report and what has happened vis-à-vis those in this reporting period.
3. Rationale explaining why/how current status is whatever it is.
4. Noteworthy events during reporting period—problems or unanticipated events, for example, and projections of actions planned concerning these.
5. Specific plans, schedules, predictions for next reporting period—what will be done to solve problems, overcome difficulties, recover lost time, adjust schedule, or other.

Final report

A final report, whether or not there were periodic reports, generally pursues a somewhat different course than do periodic reports, often along these general lines:

1. General orientation in entire matter being reported, with objectives and brief history.
2. Narrative account (history) of matter being reported on.
3. Review and analysis of data gathered, experiences, or other significant events/products of the matter, with explanation of and rationale for analytical method(s) used.
4. Conclusions drawn from review and analysis.
5. Recommendations, based on analysis and review, and rationale for the recommendations. (May include alternatives.)

WORD PROCESSING: IMPORTANT WRITING AID

The microprocessor, a revolutionary breakthrough in electronic high technology, has had an appropriately revolutionary effect in many fields, not the least of which is in business offices generally. The new device led directly to the rapid development of personal—desktop—computers, for which the most popular application proved to be word processing.

A word processor is not a machine; it is a software program installed in a machine—in a computer. (And it can be almost any computer.) That is true even in the case of "dedicated" word processors, computers designed to do word processing only, which were never particularly prominent or dominant in word processing and have steadily grown even less so. It is a rare office today that does not have at least one desktop computer, and in most it is (they are) used for word processing far more than for anything else—often for nothing else. The typewriter industry has been dealt a serious blow by word processing, and typewriter manufacturers have been busily converting to the manufacture of computer printers, high-tech typewriters without keyboards.

One serious problem with word processing has been the abysmal lack of understanding about its most effective application. Unfortunately, too many offices have treated the computer and word processor as a super-typewriter. That is, instead of hiring "typists," they now advertise for and hire "word processor operators." And instead of handing typists sheafs of lined yellow paper covered with handwriting with instructions to type them up as rough drafts, they now hand those sheafs of lined yellow paper over to word processor operators with instructions to word process them up as rough drafts. Thus little has changed, except that "typing" is now being done on much more expensive systems by much more highly paid operators at much higher final costs.

This lack of understanding is costly in many ways. Word processing is a much better way of typing and revising copy. But that is the lesser part of the revolution and almost insignificant, compared to what word processing really is. The real significance of word processing is not that it is a better way but that it is a different way. That means that it is not better because it is more efficient as a production tool, but it is better because it is light years more effective as a *writing* tool and—even more than that—as a *thinking* tool. That latter is, in fact, the key, along with other enhancements which will be discussed.

The key to proper—most effective and most appropriate—use of word processing lies in recognizing it as the writing tool it is. That means that the writers—those who are doing the writing, whether they are or are not professional writers—must work at the keyboard, rather than with pencils and ruled yellow pads. My own case illustrates this:

I resisted turning to word processing for some time after it became a viable option for me simply because it had been represented (or, more accurately, *mis*represented) for so long as more efficient and speedier in the *mechanics* of turning out copy ready for the editor. As a professional writer, highly proficient in the mechanics of turning out copy and even somewhat innovative in developing my own more efficient cut-and-paste methods, I was sure that word processing would not greatly increase my rate of production.

I was not entirely wrong in that: Word processing has increased my *rate* of manuscript production somewhat, but that is not the truly significant change. The significant change is in the *quality* of my manuscript. That has grown by some inestimable amount. That is because today I do many times more rewriting, revision, and polishing of copy than I ever did before, producing far better copy (or so I fondly believe!) and still a little more rapidly than before. That is because revision has become so *easy* it is almost fun to do.

Revision/Rewriting Methodology

In my own working method I do not ordinarily print out copy until I have done much revision—self-editing, rewriting, and polishing of copy. It is rather easy to do this on-screen, as compared with doing it on paper, once you develop an easy familiarity with the system. But this is only part of the benefit and the reason the writer ought to work at the keyboard. There are numerous other benefits and advantages that the writer will never experience without doing the actual inputting (working at the keyboard).

Swipe Files

"Swipe files" are files of standard or boilerplate material that you can use over and over, with or without some adaptation. The term takes on new meaning when it is applied to computer files stored on a floppy disk. It is easy to call them up—and you are making copies when you do so, the original still intact—and incorporate them into whatever you are currently writing, with or without modification. These can be text, resumes, drawings, or any other material that can be stored. As you proceed these files tend to grow steadily, so that you have an ever richer resource stored in your bank of swipe files. (Many of the files you modify and adapt prove useful for later applications, and so are added to your bank.) Among the most useful swipe files are those of computer-generated drawings—charts, plots, graphs, and the like. They are a bit laborious to generate the first time, but relatively easy to modify and use again once they are established in your bank of swipe files. Therefore, they can save you a great deal of time in subsequent uses.

Online Research

With the addition of a modem to your computer you can use your telephone line to communicate with any other computer equipped with a modem. Today there are hundreds of on-line databases—information banks—you can subscribe to and get information from by "downloading" files to your own computer. For instance, when a client wanted some information about certain government markets I got the bulk of the information from such a database over the telephone by requesting a search of the database files in a computer-to-computer link and printed the data out on my own system. This printout alone constituted the bulk of my report, and the whole project therefore consumed extremely little of my time.

General Communication

The modem-telephone link offers other benefits. For one, it can put you in touch with others via electronic bulletin boards, where you send and receive electronic mail. I often post an appeal for information on such boards and get help from others, just as I respond to their appeals and supply information when I am able to. But you can also communicate directly with another individual's computer if the other computer is also equipped properly with a modem and communications software, and I have found that a useful convenience, too. I have communicated and collaborated with other writers through this link, for example, but you can communicate with anyone for any purpose in this manner.

PD Software

There is an abundance of free software—computer programs—to be had by downloading them from bulletin boards. These are programs written by hobbyists and enthusiasts who are willing to donate these to public use by placing them in the public domain (hence the term PD). Among those I have found useful in writing are programs that count the words in a manuscript, help with indexing and footnoting, check spellings, do simple outlining, make "fog counts," and measure reading levels.

There are many novel programs you can pick up, too, and some of these can be useful in writing. For example, one program enables me to instantly project on-screen any month in any year since the mid-19th century or in any future century. Another enables me to make up a master file of all my files and prepare a directory. Another recovers any file I have accidentally erased—a true life saver! And another condenses files I wish to store in archives into "libraries" that take up about one half the disk space they would otherwise require.

Helpful Commercial Software

Although many of the free—public domain—software programs are quite excellent, you must generally buy regular commercial software when you need the more sophisticated programs. One class of software that has gained a great deal of recognition and steadily growing popularity lately is something referred to and described variously as "idea processors" and "outliners." Most prominent among these are KAMAS™ and Out-Think™, the latter also by the makers of KAMAS.

These programs are a great aid to many writers, even to experienced, professional writers, but especially to those for whom writing is an occasional chore and one for which they have neither trained themselves nor which they particularly relish. Basically, these are programs that have the following general characteristics:

1. They assist you in developing a general outline of your subject.
2. You can expand any item in your outline with either additional subordinate items or with a text passage.
3. You can collapse or expand your outline to get a macroscopic or microscopic view of the outline/subject.
4. You can readily shift items around.
5. You can copy items that tend to repeat themselves.

Depending on which program you are using, you can do many other things along these same lines. The idea is to help you develop ideas, and these programs include manuals of instruction intended to help you learn how to get the most out of these programs.

There are other useful programs too, of course. One class of these is the key-redefinition program, which enables you to store items that you can call up at will with a single key. (Two that I have used are SmartKey™ and XtraKey™, the latter probably more sophisticated than the former.) You can prepare an entire line, title, paragraph, or even a full page of some boilerplated or standard material and have the computer insert it by pressing a single key. I have my name, address, and telephone number in one such key, for example, and the names and addresses of others with whom I correspond on other keys so I can address letters and envelopes with a single key ("h" for my own name, for example).

Most word processors can do searching to help you find things quickly in a file and to make changes when you have erred somehow—for example, to change (automatically) every "Hetty Green" to "Hetty

Greene." But that works only within a given file, and you must do it over and over for each file if you have many files to be so treated. However, I purchased a little program, Electra-Find™, that will search all the files on a disk, or as many disks as I wish to stipulate, upon a single command! That is an order-of-magnitude improvement over the internal "global search" feature of the typical word processor. It's especially useful when you can't remember whether you did or did not mention something earlier in a manuscript; you can send that little program in quest of the information and you will know within a few minutes.

There is no doubt that the writing chore is infinitely easier when supported with an effective word processor.

Chapter 11

An Administrative Guide

TODAY'S BUSINESS OFFICE

It is no coincidence that the most popular use of today's desktop computers in offices—the chief reason for buying such computers, in fact—is word processing. It simply reflects recognition of the steadily increasing need in all modern business organizations—in *all* organizations of all kinds, for that matter—of generating "paper" of all kinds. Word processing is the modern breakthrough, even more revolutionary in automating correspondence and other, related aspects of office work than was the electric typewriter. (But of course the word processor is far more than an automation device, and we will discuss this presently.)

In the theoretical office scenario the executive has a highly competent and efficient secretary who opens the morning mail, screens out the obvious unwanted junk, pulls files relevant to letters the executive will obviously have to see and respond to, and attends to many tasks without troubling the executive—tasks that call for mailing a brochure, redirecting the mail to some other desk, and writing routine responses. The executive in this scenario routinely signs letters his or her efficient secretary has prepared and scrawls notes on some of the other incoming correspondence as instructions to the secretary, drafts answers to a few letters on lined yellow pads, puts some aside for more serious consideration, and responds to some with telephone calls.

Unfortunately that scenario is mostly fiction today, if it was ever fact, with only rare exception. It is questionable whether many executives are fortunate enough to have secretaries that well trained or whether many executives are secure enough to trust secretaries to take over much of the writing responsibility. It is simply not happening often.

Much more commonly today the executive instructs the secretary to open the mail and bring it all in for the executive to spend hours on, scrawling on the inevitable yellow paper, having responses typed as drafts to be marked up and retyped before they can be signed and sent out.

Moreover, aside from that daily routine of dealing with the correspondence alone, which is itself a time-consuming chore that absorbs far too much of the costly time of the average executive, there are the many special writing chores that come along—preparing bids and quotations and requests for bids and proposals; writing reports, proposals, brochures, releases, sales letters; and all the other items described and discussed earlier. They are not all daily needs, although in many offices one or more of these needs arises daily, but they consume a great deal of time in any event. And while many of these are important chores directly affecting the important business of sales and marketing—business that is worthy of the executive's time and attention—much of the work involved is routine and should be handled by staff workers.

The overall goal of this book is to reduce the amount of time and effort required to attend to correspondence and other writing chores in the typical business office and to reduce that time and effort for not only the executive but for the secretary and any other staff workers who spend far too much time in such work, often at "reinventing the wheel" (designing everything from scratch each time).

The specific objectives through which this is to be achieved is to (1) organize a complete system for this kind of work and (2) create that system in such a way that secretaries and clerical staffs can take over more of the routine writing chores.

It is that latter benefit that is the major advantage of standardizing as much of the typical business writing as possible. But this also saves the time that many executives and others often devote to searching out models, such as old proposals and other documents stored away in dusty files. Once the system is established, good models are readily at hand for almost all applications. But the system must be designed and in place first.

This book has furnished the bricks and mortar, and even some of the interior furnishings, but it is not itself a complete plan, for the plan must be tailored to your own needs—customized by you. That is the next step, and it is what this chapter is all about.

THE NEED FOR A UTILIZATION PLAN

If you are an individual or small organization with occasional need for just about every kind of writing described in this book, you will probably do well to simply use the book itself as your standard reference and guide, using the index provided as the chief means for searching out the most appropriate examples and instructions. There would be little point in doing otherwise.

For most people—individuals and organizations, large and small—the situation is different. You (your organization) may write proposals frequently, rarely, or never. And the same may be said for reports, collection letters, news releases, and any of the many other items discussed, exemplified, and presented in these pages. Therefore, while you may find it useful to use or even institutionalize this book as an instruction manual, reference guide, or standardization document within your organization, the application will almost always be different for different organizations. In consideration of this and the need for efficient use of this material, this final chapter is offered to help you adapt this book to your own needs and make it maximally useful for you.

Establishing the Priorities of Your Needs

The first step, logically, is to decide which kinds of items are most relevant to your needs. It would probably be helpful to actually write these out in a list, assigning them priorities. To assist you in this a worksheet form is offered (Figure 11-1).

Selecting Most Appropriate Models

Once you have done this you should go to the relevant chapters of the book and select those models, with accompanying general instructions and observations, which are most appropriate to your own applications. It is not likely that any of these models will be exactly what you want, and it would be highly impractical to try to design a model to fit every situation and every need, so those you choose will almost surely have to be modified to suit your own situation. (Of course, your idealized models will each have their own share of blanks to be filled in for each individual use.)

To make this a practical chore, rather than a major and special undertaking, you can simply make an extra copy of the letter or report you

FIGURE 11-1 A Worksheet to Establish Priorities

INSTRUCTIONS: Assign a priority (1 the highest) to each type of writing listed and do the same (writing in specific types) for those items where there are subdivisions, such as correspondence and reports.

[ ] PROPOSALS   [ ] RELEASES
[ ] BROCHURES   [ ] DIRECT-MAIL PACKAGES
[ ] LETTERS OF AGREEMENT   [ ] GENERAL ADMINISTRATIVE
[ ] SALES LETTERS   [ ] COLLECTION LETTERS
[ ] GENERAL CORRESPONDENCE
    [ ] _____
    [ ] _____
[ ] REPORTS
    [ ] _____
    [ ] _____
[ ] OTHER: _____
[ ] _____

write, based on this book, and accumulate these samples, building a collection adapted to your own special needs. You can then index your models as this book is indexed to help users find things readily.

In time you will build up a complete set of such models *of your own special applications* of the models in this book. These are the basis of your own system manual and guide, which you can, of course, supplement with your own instructions, policy statements, or whatever is appropriate.

Alternatives

It is possible that you may have some difficulty in doing some of the things suggested here. For example, maybe the issues you are asked to make decisions about in filling out the worksheet of Figure 11–1 are simply not that clear-cut. Maybe it is simply not that easy to determine which items should be of highest priority or judged to be most frequently needed. The alternatives for such cases are plain. There are three logical ones:

1. Simply make arbitrary decisions. Perhaps the difficulty is that frequencies of needs do not vary enough among several items to make priority rankings very meaningful. In that case it is of little consequence to make the distinctions between 1, 2, 3, and so forth; an arbitrary set of choices is more appropriate.

2. Suppose you simply have not paid a great deal of attention to the writing chores in your organization and can't even make a good guess at frequency of uses. In that case you may wish to make the decisions arbitrarily, but as preliminary or draft decisions to be adjusted later as you study actual uses and get a better idea of what they are.

3. You don't have to make the priority judgments immediately. You can simply postpone the decision until you have observed and recorded actual usage accumulated over some period, as in item 2.

4. But suppose that you are a large, multiunit organization in which usages vary widely from one unit to another. (A marketing department, for example, is likely to have much more need for sales letters or direct-mail packages than for responses to complaints, while an order department may have to write many direct letters to customers, and a special-projects team would be writing progress reports.) You may thus do best to have each operating unit do its own study and submit results to you, or even develop its own, internal style guide and reference manual.

5. Finally, as an alternative to item 4, you may ask each operating unit to submit its own estimate of most-needed writing assistance and types of writing most often called for and assemble all of this data for the entire organization.

Of course, you may also choose to hybridize two or more of the suggested alternatives, and so combine whatever you think are the best features of each.

THE TROUBLE WITH FORM LETTERS

Despite the instructions, the models, and the suggested standardization offered in this book, I do not advocate building a complete file of form letters as the answer to your writing problems. Many organizations use form letters freely, often with good effect. It is relatively easy to design a set of standard form letters and use these to respond to letters from customers or the public generally. It is too easy, in fact, which leads many individuals with bureaucratic mental sets to overuse form letters. That is, they send form letters in almost every case, whether appropriate or not. For example, I had occasion not long ago to write a letter to the postmaster of a local post office complaining that they were failing to forward my mail, despite my having filled out the correct forms. Instead of replying to my complaint or complying with my request, this postmaster sent me a totally irrelevant and preprinted form letter telling me how sincerely the U.S. Postal Service appreciated my patronage and how eagerly they were trying to serve me well! (It was only after I sent this form letter on to the Postmaster General with my query as to why it was sent me that matters were finally straightened out.)

Automated form letters—form letters which are ground out like sausages by mindless computers carrying out mechanical instructions—can be even worse. Having once done business (more than a few years ago) as Herman Holtz Publications, I am still getting mail addressed to "Mr. Publications" and even "Mr. and Mrs. Publications." Worse yet, because some computer systems limit the number of characters permitted in an address, I get letters addressed to "Herman Holtz Publicatio." (I wonder whether General Motors gets letters addressed to "Mr. Moto" or the U.S. Treasury Department gets letters addressed to "Mr. Depart?")

It is efficient to use form letters whenever and wherever they can be used. But, aside from such hazards as the horror stories here told—and such incidents can be costly to good will and sales in business—form letters do not solve all correspondence problems, nor is it possible to design form letters to solve all problems; the need for direct or personal responses in many cases is inescapable, despite the problems—the high cost of the labor required to draft individual, personal responses—that accompany the need. But the situation is not hopeless; there is a practical and workable compromise between the form letter and the personal letter, one that borrows the best elements from each and is readily adaptable to the needs of most organizations.

To explain this idea, I must refer to an actual example, a case history of an actual project in which I developed such a system on a custom basis for what was then the Wind Energy Branch of the Energy Research Development Administration, an organization that later became a part of today's Energy Department. The basic idea of the system I developed for them is readily adaptable to the needs of the business world.

The head of that branch insisted that all letters of inquiry and comment merited an individual, personal answer; he would not permit form letters to be used. But the volume of mail had begun to overwhelm the organization: There was a backlog of some 200 yet-unanswered letters, some of them dating back two years, all of which the branch manager insisted must be answered!

The branch had tried to respond with a computerized system using standard paragraphs stored in the system. (It was a mainframe computer; the desktop computer was just beginning to appear on the scene.) Problem number one: There were not nearly enough suitable standard paragraphs in the system, and it would probably have been impractical to have developed enough standard paragraphs to cope with all needs; such a system is too open-ended for practical application. Problem number two: The operators—typists and secretaries, in fact—could not make the decisions as to which paragraphs to use because most of the letters concerned technical matters. Problem number three: There was not enough technical/professional staff to make those decisions and still have time to do the scientific studies and development work of the agency.

Study of the 200 unanswered letters, based on the knowledge gained by answering them—*all* of them—resulted in classifying them into about six broad classifications. And that led to the development of the system for handling them with minimal demands on the time of the engineering and scientific professionals on the staff.

The compromise that solved the problem was this:

1. The development of about six technical papers or reports that were responsive and relevant to well over 90 percent of the letters.
2. The development of about six brief form letters that could be easily printed out as individual, personal letters.
3. A form for rapid analysis (by a professional) of each incoming letter to place it in one of the several classifications.
4. Provision on the form to instruct a typist/secretary which of the several brief individualized form letters to use and which papers/reports/brochures to cite and enclose with the letter.

Thus the system that finally evolved was not excessively demanding of technical/professional time, did furnish a responsive and individually typed (personal) letter, and provided all the technical information the original writer had asked for. (Most asked for information or reactions to ideas suggested in their letters and what the head of the branch referred to, with some irony, as "one-page inventions.")

It met all the requirements, and is completely adaptable to be used in business. (In fact, some elements of it are used in business as individual elements, but not as complete systems.)

Adapting and (Adopting) the System

Some of the letters suggested and many presented in these pages were/are themselves brief enough to be installed in a word processor as form letters that can be printed out individually via a suitable "mailmerge" type of program. Collection letters and letters apologizing for a delayed shipment, for example, usually lend themselves readily to that kind of application. However, there are many letters in which much more detail is needed, and yet the letters do fall into a single classification. For example, there are those letters in which a customer is demanding a refund or an exchange of allegedly defective merchandise, or is complaining that a sale item was out of stock by the time he or she arrived at the store seeking the item. These are among the many types of letters that may be answered "personally" with a brief but individually typed response, along with a preprinted paper or brochure of some kind offering some standardized information.

Following are just a few (starters) of the many possible ideas for enclosures—policy statements, prescribed procedures, standard forms, brochures, and other such boilerplate—that can be used with brief letters, individually typed or printed out by a word processing system so that they are, indeed, personal letters, and yet can be automated as form letters, with enclosures such as these:

Explanation of why all shipments on some item or in some period were delayed, with usual apology, and so forth.
Apology for being unable to meet the demand for some special sale item, with explanation of policy (e.g., a rain check enclosed).
Policy and instructions on applying for exchange or refund.
Explanation of standard charges.
Explanation of standard contract terms.
Standard Letter of Agreement.
Form used for request for quotation, bid, or proposal.
Application forms for credit card, employment, other.
Policy on "as is" sales items or closeouts.

PAPER SYSTEM OR COMPUTER SYSTEM?

In today's world there is little excuse for even the smallest business office to lack the basic automation of a desktop computer and word processor. The system described in this chapter can be assembled as a "manual" or "paper" system—a set of forms and instructions on paper in a binder—but it is a far more efficient system when it is assembled as a computerized system, with the elements on floppy disks, supported by a small instruction manual.

The advantages of automating the system by installing it on floppy disks for use in a word processing system are numerous:

1. "Typing," even addressing each letter and envelope individually, becomes automatic, carried out by the printer that is part of the computer system.
2. All files, including form letters and form enclosures, and related correspondence, are on disk from which they:
   a. Can be copied at will in seconds.
   b. Can be modified or customized quickly for each usage.
   c. Can be modified to use as new forms.

    d. Can be continually edited and polished to improve it, as experience dictates.

    e. Can be combined or used in part.

    f. Can be summoned up quickly on-screen for reference.

    g. Can be compared with each other to select the most appropriate one for any given need.

    h. Can be incorporated, in part or wholly, directly into a personal letter, if desired.

All of these capabilities lend the system enormous flexibility which could only be matched in a manual or "paper" system with a great expenditure of labor at a correspondingly low level of relative efficiency. Even then there are certain other advantages in having the system "in the computer" (or, more accurately, on disks and readily loaded into the computer). One of these is the ready availability of the system. Where manuals and other printed systems are often mislaid, borrowed by someone and not to be found immediately, or otherwise unavailable when needed, it's simplicity itself to make duplicate copies of disks and keep them readily at hand. Another is the relatively small degree of dependence on a word processor operator: Once established as a disk-based system, anyone who can operate the computer at all can order the printouts with a few simple commands; the system does the rest.

This does not apply to correspondence alone, but to many other writing chores in addition to attending to correspondence as a routine morning chore. It applies to any kind of writing, although especially to those writing chores that are required often enough that they consume an appreciable amount of time. It applies to such things as bids, sales letters, proposals, reports, and quotations. Computer files can and should include such other boilerplate as:

1. Standard prices/price lists.
2. Forms for requesting and/or supplying bids and quotations.
3. Forms for requesting proposals.
4. Materials to be included in proposals.
5. Item descriptions.
6. Reference files of bids, quotations, proposals, releases, other materials prepared earlier.

THE SYSTEM LIBRARY

Such a system is built around its library, which is built up, as described, of standard forms, models, and boilerplate enclosures. But there is more needed to make the library complete so that it supports all the activities of the organization, especially those concerned with sales and marketing. The library ought to include reference materials, too, information to be available, not necessarily to be reproduced. This would include, as one outstanding example, files of information by and about competitors—competitors' brochures, proposals, sales letters, and other such items.

But that is only one aspect of the system library you should maintain. There is also the matter of software that will increase your capabilities for turning out written end-items. Your system library ought to include a section of software programs relevant to writing. Word processors are, of course, very well known today by just about everyone in the business world. But there are many other closely related and equally useful programs that are not nearly so well known.

WORD PROCESSING

Basic word processing is made up of two separate and distinct functions: editing and formatting. The editing function has to do with composing the text, the formatting with organizing and structuring it. Originally each of these functions was carried out by an individual program, but as computer memories grew larger with the advancing technology the two were combined to form word processors.

Many other programs relevant to writing and word processing have grown up in the meantime, such as dictionaries on disk and programs that check spelling, count the number of words in a manuscript, generate and place footnotes, create indexes, and organize bibliographies, to name just a few. And, as larger and larger computer memories and storage capabilities are offered in ordinary desktop computers—which translates into the capacity to handle larger and more sophisticated programs—some of these types of programs have been included in word processors, although the tendency overall has been to offer them as separate programs. In any case, the capabilities offered by a desktop computer and a good word processor are not truly complete today without at least some of these other programs. As a minimum your system ought to include as many as possible of the following types of software support of your word processing to make the entire writing job easier.

Spelling checker. There are many such programs in existence. Typically, a spelling checker incorporates a dictionary on the disk (my own has about 45,000 words, but larger ones are available) and automatically reviews the files you ask it to review, checking the spelling of your words. When it finds one that does not agree with its own dictionary or is a strange word it asks you to decide what you want to do about it. (You can look up spellings in the disk-based dictionary, of course.) Most such programs allow you to add words to your dictionary or to build up separate dictionaries of special terms. (You can make up and use several dictionaries, if that suits your operations best.)

Grammar checker. These are less popular and of limited helpfulness because so many questions of grammar are based on human judgment—more art than science—and so are difficult to automate. Still, some users like to have their manuscripts checked by such a program as this.

Search and find. Most word processors include both search-and-find and search-and-replace functions, in which the program will find any term or word you specify and/or change terms you want changed. That function, however, can be executed only within the file in which it is ordered. If you want to search many files—for example, each chapter of a lengthy proposal or manual—you must load each file and carry out the search separately in each file. There is, however, at least one program that will search all files on a disk or on as many disks as you care to have searched with only one command. It is a program called Electra-Find™, by O'Neill Software.

Key redefiners.   There are a number of programs available today that redefine your keys and permit you to set up "macros" (common abbreviation for macroinstructions). These are especially useful in writing when you use certain terms, expressions, and other items repeatedly. For example, although I have one key set to print out my name and address, I have many others. When I must use some lengthy name or expression, such as The Amalgamated Fruit Canners of America, repeatedly, I save myself a great deal of time and energy by setting a key to print it out each time. But you can also use such programs to have a single keystroke print a lengthy series of commands. (I use such a macro to order a spooler loaded and return to the original program.)

I use both SmartKey, a pioneering program that is still probably the most popular one, and XtraKey, a more recent development and a somewhat more sophisticated one, offering a number of special features that SmartKey does not offer. Such programs are quite popular, however, so there are many others available.

Idea processors.   Programs variously identified as idea processors and thought processors have been gaining a great deal of popularity. These are programs that in their simplest configurations make it easy to create outlines. However, they offer features that facilitate shifting items around, expanding the outline, inserting blocks of text, collapsing the outline temporarily to study only key points, and otherwise manipulating your ideas and your words to help you think out matters and organize your thoughts. Probably best known is the pioneer program of this type, KAMAS, which later produced the simpler Out-Think, and a more recent arrival, Thoughtline™, which is considerably simpler and easier to use, but far less sophisticated than the others.

Squeeze and library programs.   There are programs that will "squeeze" the files you want to store away in dead files or transmit via telephone lines. This reduces the amount of disk space the files require and reduces the time (and therefore the tolls) for transmitting the files. There are also programs that combine related files, squeezed or unsqueezed, into "libraries," which further reduces the disk space required and greatly simplifies the cataloging and directory listings required.

Model letters.   There are some floppy-disk versions of letter models. These are not really programs at all, although they are computer software. They are simply collections of letters—computer files—usually organized by category (e.g., real estate letters, collection letters, complaint letters, etc). They are, of course, intended as approximate models, each to be customized to your own special needs.

Miscellaneous.   There are programs for all those miscellaneous tasks of compiling bibliographies, indexes, and footnotes, for measuring the reading level of text (e.g., "fog count" or "fog index"), and for helping with sundry other writing chores.

Free and Nearly-Free Software

There is today an abundance of free software programs written by enthusiasts and given freely to any who wish to use them. Although generally termed "public domain" software because it is given freely for public use, technically most of it is not truly in the public domain. In most cases the author has copyrighted the software and published it with a notice stating that anyone may use the software but cannot resell it or incorporate it in programs to be sold commercially. (Programs for squeezing files and assembling them into libraries are abundantly available in the public domain area.)

There is also a growing amount of "shareware," which is distributed in the same manner as the PD (public domain) software, but with the notice that if the user likes the program and uses it regularly, a donation would be appreciated (some reasonable sum is often suggested as being appropriate), and in return for the donation the author will send documentation (instructions) and updates (later revisions and improvements to the program).

These programs are found on public electronic bulletin boards and distributed through computer clubs and people who sell disks loaded with such programs, usually at modest prices of from about $8 to $12 per disk. (The charge is for the disk and service, as it must be under the terms of the copyright owner, not for the programs.)

Not all of these programs are great. Some, in fact, are pretty bad. But there are a great many excellent programs available, some of them as good as or better than anything available commercially. The "Modem 7" series of communication (computer to computer via telephone) programs, for example are probably as good as anything produced commercially, and quite possibly the best available, other than perhaps the "MEX" programs, which are also PD. In general, however (at least according to my personal experience), it is the smaller free programs that are excellent. Free word processors and idea processors, for example, tend to be rather simple and quite limited in capabilities, as compared with the commercial versions of such programs. Still, I am using many such programs in preference to commercial programs I also have in my own library because I find them superior to the commercial programs. In many cases there is a simple explanation for that: The hobbyist-enthusiast has no vested interest in doing anything but making the program as simple and as functional as possible, since he or she is not trying to sell it. The commercial software publisher, on the other hand, often appears to believe that simple and direct methods are not good business and that the more complex the program can be made the higher a selling price it will fetch. For example, many of us use the public domain "sweep" programs for file manipulations—copying, erasing, renaming, and so forth—in preference to commerical programs for doing the same things because the PD programs are far simpler, faster, and easier to use. (For one thing, they require far fewer keystrokes to operate and far less learning to use.)

Desktop Publishing

Desktop publishing has become a popular concept, steadily gaining prominence in computer publications. It has been sparked, at least in part, by Apple Computers' Macintosh® computer, a computer that is especially strong in creating graphics. Not long after the Macintosh appeared, the new laser printers became available, although they were still rather expensive (approximately $2,000 and up at this time). These offer good quality printing with great flexibility to produce graphic illustrations. (Laser printing is a marriage of lasers, xerographics, and computer technologies to produce a revolutionary new kind of printing.) With other computer makers rushing to enhance their computers with good graphics capabilities, we have seen the rise of "desktop publishing," which consists of the three elements: a versatile computer with a large memory, a high-quality printer and/or plotter, and appropriate graphics-generating software.

As a new technology, desktop publishing is still young, but it is growing up rapidly and is worth considering for any organization that turns out a large quantity of written work on a regular basis. It represents a completely in-house capability, and the promised freedom from unreliable vendor support is itself a powerful argument for the new idea.

A few typical programs and the names of their manufacturers will be listed in the appendix as examples of what is available.

TELECOMMUNICATIONS RESEARCH AND ONLINE DATABASES

For the telecommunications research mentioned earlier you need the capability to dial up other computers to make a variety of databases available to you. Most of these are subscription systems: You pay a fee for using them plus the toll charges for the telephone line if the computer you are calling is not in your own vicinity. (Many of these are connected to communication links so that the toll charges are less than they would be for ordinary long-lines connections, however.)

These databases are quite numerous and many are highly specialized, designed to serve specific professions and individuals, such as lawyers, doctors, real estate brokers, stock brokers, investors, writers, and others. (A sampling is offered in the appendix.)

To take advantage of this resource you need both hardware and software to complement your computer. You need a device called a *modem* (an acronym for *modulator-demodulator*) and suitable software—a communications program. Some computers have modems built into them—*internal* modems—or can offer them as options, but most use external modems mounted in their own cases. I use the Hayes 1200 modem, considered by many to be *the* model modem, so much so that many modem manufacturers have emulated the Hayes and advertise their units as "Hayes compatible" to point to the resemblance in the hope that the prospect will see little difference between the two but price.

Many modems are sold with suitable software for using them, and all modem sellers will be able to recommend suitable software if it is not included in the sale. However, PD software comes to the rescue: It is unlikely that you will ever run into a situation where any of the PD Modem 7 communications programs will not do the job for you. The earlier versions are titled MDM712MD.COM and MDM730MD.COM, but the latest version is MDM740MD.COM (which is the version I use), and it is eminently satisfactory. It is easy to learn and easy to use and highly resistant to "crashing"—getting confused and abandoning you. (Some programs will crash quite easily, even on a single incorrect keystroke, but the Modem 7 programs have proved to be quite rugged in keeping their minds on business in all circumstances.)

A FEW FINAL WORDS

No one can can design or deliver a complete master plan for your writing needs. Writing is far more an art than a science, and it depends for its success on the wit and energy of its practitioners. The whole idea underlying this book has been to encourage you and to save your time by giving you models and directing your attention to other sources so that you would not have to spend your time discovering these for yourself. In the next and final element, an appendix, you will find a few references and a few listings. These are merely exemplary, and investigating them will open many more doors to help in building your own in-house writing capabilities.

References and Ancillary Sources

WHAT YOU WILL FIND IN THIS APPENDIX

There are many excellent sources of additional information on subjects related to the various chapters of this book. Recommendations made here are based on my own prejudices as sources that have helped shape my own views, are in my own library, proved helpful to me in some way, impressed me as excellent work, are the work of individuals whom I respect and admire, and/or will, in my opinion, be helpful to you. I also unblushingly list my own works when I believe the recommendation to be appropriate.

I have tried to make this list as helpful as possible by organizing it into groups under generic subject titles, rather than in alphabetical order, and by title first, rather than by the more conventional method of listing the author first. Despite this effort to group these publications by subjects, some cover more than one subject. Barnes & Noble's *Business Writing,* for example, has some excellent coverage of grammar and punctuation, and my own *Word Processing for Business Publications* discusses both business writing and the use of word processing in the business office.

Other than the general grouping of the publication there is no significance to the order in which they appear.

ON BUSINESS WRITING

Janis, J. Harold, and Howard R. Dressner. *Business Writing.* New York: Barnes & Noble Books, 1956.

Cresci, Martha W. *Complete Book of Model Business Letters.* Portland, Ore.: Parker Publishing, 1976.

Blumenthal, Lassor A. *Successful Business Writing.* New York: Perigee Books, 1976.

Fielden, John S., Ronald E. Dulek, and Jean D. Fielden. *Elements of Business Writing.* New York: Prentice-Hall, 1983.

Holtz, Herman. *Word Processing for Business Publications*. New York: McGraw-Hill, 1984.

DIRECTORIES AND GUIDES TO INFORMATION SOURCES

Brohaugh, William, ed. *The Writer's Resource Guide*. Cincinnati, Ohio: Writer's Digest Books, 1979.

Lesko, Matthew. *Information USA*. New York: Viking, 1983.

Nordland, Rod. *Names and Numbers*. New York: John Wiley & Sons, 1978.

The National Directory of Addresses and Telephone Numbers. New York: Concord Reference Books, annual.

SALES AND ADVERTISING

Lewis, Herschell Gordon. *Direct Mail Copy That Sells*. New York: Prentice-Hall, 1984.

Holtz, Herman. *Mail Order Magic*. New York: McGraw-Hill, 1983.

ON WRITING

Bernstein, Theodore. *The Careful Writer*. New York: Atheneum Publishers, 1965.

Weisman, Herman. *Technical Report Writing*. Indianapolis, Ind.: Bobbs-Merrill, 1966.

Holtz, Herman. *The Consultant's Guide to Proposal Writing*. New York: John Wiley & Sons, 1986.

Newman, Edwin. *On Language*. New York: Warner Books, 1980.

Strunk, William, Jr., and E. B. White. *The Elements of Style*. New York: Macmillan, 1972.

A FEW SOFTWARE PROGRAMS AND SUPPLIERS

There is a superabundance of software offered commercially. The following lists are therefore the briefest of samplings, offered here primarily to exemplify the resources available, and certainly not intended to represent a true cross-section of the software market.

Grammar

Grammatik is a product of Digital Marketing/Pro Tem.

Punctuation and Style is a product of Oasis Systems.

Graphics

SCS-Draw is a product of Softaids.

Stats Graph is a product of Supersoft3.

Sci-Graf, FontEdit, and Graf 3.0 are products of Microcomputer Systems Consultants.

Formation is a product PBT Software.

Idea Processors

KAMAS and Out-Think are products of Kamasoft.

Thoughtline is a product of Spite Software.

Key Redefiners

XtraKey is a product of Xpert Software.

SmartKey is a product of Software Research Technologies.

Desktop Publishing

The Newsroom™ is a product of Springboard Software.

Miscellaneous

Bibliography, Footnote and Pair, Index, Bibliography and Footnote are all products of Digital Marketing/Pro Tem.

Electra-Find is a product of O'Neill Software.

Footnotes Unlimited and The Indexer are products of Franklin Legal Software.

A FEW ONLINE DATABASES

Following is a small sampling of the many on-line databases available. In many cases a given database is available through more than one on-line service because the on-line service does not always own the database which they make available or to which they provide access. It is wise, therefore, to research thoroughly before deciding which service to use.

BRS, 1200 Route 7, Latham, NY 12110: Databases in medicine, education, engineering, science, and medicine.

Compuserve, 5000 Arlington Centre Boulevard, Columbus, OH 43220: a well-known public database and service for lay people.

Dialog Information Services, Inc., 3460 Hillview Avenue, Palo Alto, CA 94304: Access to more than 180 databases on many, many subjects.

ITT Dialcom, 1109 Spring Street, Silver Spring, MD 20910: An electronic mail system with access to airlines flight information, news, and many other databases.

National Library of Medicine, 8600 Rockville Pike, Bethesda, MD 20209: MEDLINE and MEDLARS databases, medical information provided to physicians and hospitals, including diagnostic assistance.

West Publishing Co., Box 43526, St. Paul, MN 55164: Legal information, including research into case law, precedents, and so forth.

Index